The Hollywood West

The Hollywood West

Lives of Film Legends Who Shaped It

Edited by

Richard W. Etulain & Glenda Riley

Fulcrum Publishing
GOLDEN, COLORADO

Copyright © 2001 Richard W. Etulain and Glenda Riley

All rights reserved. No part of this book may be
reproduced, stored in a retrieval system, or transmitted in
any form or by any means, electronic, mechanical,
photocopying, recording, or otherwise, without written
permission from the publisher.

Library of Congress Cataloging-in-Publication Data

The Hollywood West: lives of film legends who shaped it /
edited by Richard W. Etulain & Glenda Riley.
    p. cm. — (Notable westerners)
Includes bibliographical references and index.
    ISBN 1-55591-434-9
    1. Western films—United States—Historic and criticism.
2. Motion picture actors and actresses—United States—
Biography. I. Etulain, Richard W. II. Riley, Glenda, 1938–
III. Series.
    PN1995.9.W4 H65 2001
    791.43'6278—dc21   00-009659

Printed in Canada
0 9 8 7 6 5 4 3 2 1

Editorial: Daniel Forrest-Bank, Amy Timms
Design: Rudy Ramos
Cover design: Bill Spahr
Cover art: Painting copyright © Thom Ross. John Wayne as
Ethan Edwards, from the film *The Searchers,* directed by
John Ford. Painting courtesy of Rusty and Trish York,
Chandler, Arizona.

Fulcrum Publishing
16100 Table Mountain Parkway, Suite 300
Golden, Colorado 80403
(800) 992-2908 • (303) 277-1623
www.fulcrum-books.com

Contents

Series Foreword

Along with the editors of *The Hollywood West*, Fulcrum Publishing is proud to be the publisher of the Notable Westerners series. The books in this series explore the real stories behind the personalities and events that continue to forge our national character. Other books in the series include *By Grit & Grace: Eleven Women Who Shaped the American West* and *With Badges & Bullets: Lawmen & Outlaws in the Old West*.

The American West—land of myth, epitome of the independent American spirit. When we think of the men and women who influenced the West, we tend to think in terms of caricatures, of larger-than-life heros and heroines. Notable men and women have always loomed large on the open and wide landscapes of the American West. From the earliest Native American leaders to more recent westerners, these influential people have attracted the attention of travelers, historians, and writers. Often, such visitors focus on how these heros and heroines of the region were important in shaping and reshaping images of the West.

Editors Richard W. Etulain and Glenda Riley draw on their long experience in western history and their wide associations with western historians of varied racial, ethnic, gender, and social backgrounds. To these books, contributors bring expertise in their fields, knowledge of significant individuals, and lucid writing styles. The result is a variety of essays providing insight into the movers and shakers of a unique region of the United States. The American West not only helped form the American national character, but continues to provide an endless source of fascination for Americans and non-Americans alike.

Acknowledgments

The editors would like to thank several people and organizations for their help and support in preparing this book. First of all, we are much indebted to the contributors for taking the time from their full schedules to prepare essays for this collection. Their professionalism and insightful analyses are particularly appreciated.

Richard W. Etulain would like to thank the Center for the American West and the Research Allocations Fund at the University of New Mexico for supporting his research. He is also indebted to Cindy Tyson, David Key, and Suzanne Sermon for their fine work assisting him on this book.

Glenda Riley would like to express gratitude to Ball State University, especially to the Alexander M. Bracken Fund, to the Department of History at Ball State, and to research assistant Deborah L. Rogers.

Finally, the editors wish to indicate their appreciation to Bob Baron, Sam Scinta, and Daniel Forrest-Bank of Fulcrum Publishing for their encouragement and aid.

RICHARD W. ETULAIN
University of New Mexico

GLENDA RILEY
Ball State University

Introduction

RICHARD W. ETULAIN

The first Western films appeared early in the twentieth century, two decades after the initial Buffalo Bill Wild West shows and ten years after the earliest western fiction of Owen Wister. These new motion pictures built upon a large and growing interest in the frontier and Old West in the United States. Indeed, Hollywood Westerns became successful, less from innovations in content and format and more because they closely paralleled cultural trends in American society. In the first generation of their existence—and well into the 1930s—cinematic Westerns reinforced, rather than transformed, popular ideas about the American West.

By the early 1920s, most of the film-going public was familiar with the conventional ingredients of the Hollywood Western. Movie companies relocated in southern California after a brief stay on the East Coast and elsewhere, clustered around the new Hollywood suburb of Los Angeles. Taking advantage of the sunny days and the open spaces near the West Coast, moviemakers capitalized on the rising popularity of the cowboy figure. Playing heroic men on horseback, capturing thieves and other bad men, silent stars, such as Broncho Billy Anderson, William S. Hart, and Tom Mix, provided the first, tradition-setting roles for cinematic cowboys.

During the 1920s, other types of Hollywood Westerns appeared. Directors James Cruze and John Ford helped produce the first epic Westerns in *The Covered Wagon* (1923) and *The Iron Horse* (1924). Celebrating the Oregon Trail and the building of the transcontinental railroad, these films illustrated Hollywood's interest in pageantry, patriotism, and the reputed glories of the Old West. Few cowboy Westerns featured Indians as opponents, although in such films as D. W. Griffith's *The Battle at Elderbush Gulch* (1913) and *The Covered Wagon* Native Americans were depicted as barbaric villains. In *The Vanishing American* (1925), however, the human side of Indians was emphasized. Meanwhile, Lillian Gish, Mae Marsh, and other women starred in several films, but not until World War II was the Western anything but a masculine genre.

The arrival of sound films at the end of the 1920s saw the emergence of a fresh set of heros and signaled new directions for the Western in the 1930s. Over the next ten years Gene Autry and the husband-and-wife team Roy Rogers and Dale Evans gained large reputations for their singing Westerns. At the same time, John Wayne and Gary Cooper proved themselves as worthy heirs to the well-established tradition of larger-than-life Western heros.

The period from the late 1930s through the 1940s and 1950s witnessed solidifications of existing patterns and a few small changes in the Western genre. During this time, Wayne and Cooper became two of Hollywood's leading stars. Wayne was lionized for his roles in such films as *Stagecoach* (1939), *Red River* (1948), and *Fort Apache* (1948). Cooper was forever immortalized in *The Plainsman* (1936), *The Westerner* (1940), and *High Noon* (1952). Concurrently, John Ford emerged as the country's most successful director of Westerns. When he and Wayne teamed up in such films as *Stagecoach*, *Fort Apache*, *The Searchers* (1956), and *The Man Who Shot Liberty Valance* (1962), the Western reached peaks of achievement.

Two women stars, Barbara Stanwyck and Katy Jurado, launched notable careers in Westerns during this golden era. Although Stanwyck often played in roles opposite well-known heroes, she also made a name for herself in such films as *Union Pacific* (1939), *The Cattle Queen of Montana* (1954), and *Maverick Queen* (1956). Meanwhile, had Katy Jurado starred only in *High Noon*, she would be well remembered as a talented Mexican actress. Her passion, sensuousness, and outspokenness in this film alone make her an especially important figure in the development of the Western.

In the 1940s and 1950s, Native Americans also played their first leading roles in Westerns. Between 1949 and 1957, Jay Silverheels starred as Tonto, the sidekick to the white masked-man hero in the popular television series *The Lone Ranger*. After these rather passive renditions of Native American roles, Silverheels became an activist in Indian actor organizations. Iron Eyes Cody, who may have been an Italian rather than an Indian, played dozens of parts as a Native American and eventually went on to become a celebrated promoter for environmental awareness. Both Silverheels and Cody won their cinematic spurs playing alongside white heroes, but it was not until Chief Dan George burst into the limelight with his powerful personal performance as Old Lodge Skins in *Little Big Man* (1970) that Native Americans were finally beginning to command larger and more significant roles in Hollywood. More recent Indian stars have played increasingly nontraditional roles in Westerns, such as Wes Studi's assertive performances in *Dances with Wolves* (1990), *The Last of the Mohicans* (1992), and *Geronimo* (1993).

The 1960s dramatically reshaped the content and mood of Hollywood Westerns. If *High Noon* and *Shane* (1953) represented the classic Western before the mid-1960s, the Spaghetti Westerns of Clint Eastwood and director Sergio Leone and such films as *The Wild Bunch* (1969) and *Little Big Man* pointedly reminded viewers how much the Western was changing. Intense violence, explicit sexuality, and more significant roles for minority groups marked this new form of the genre. Although John Wayne continued to make Westerns in the 1960s and 1970s, and won an Oscar for his role in *True Grit* (1969), the Hollywood Western had virtually reshaped itself into a different genre by the late 1960s. Still, in many ways it reflected societal trends in the United States, particularly the social and cultural turmoil of the 1960s and 1970s.

As the emotional intensity of the 1960s gradually subsided by the 1980s, directors, producers, and actors seemed uncertain about the state of the Hollywood Western. Should it become a vehicle for humor and satire, as it was in *Blazing Saddles* (1974)? Should it showcase non-Western stars as *Barbarosa* (1982) did for singer Willie Nelson? Or should the Western become a conduit for social and cultural criticism as Robert Redford's environmental messages in *Jeremiah Johnson* (1972) or the heavy-handed statements in Michael Cimino's four-hour *Heaven's Gate* (1980)? Could the genre move in new directions with a modern feminist film like *Thelma and Louise* (1991)?

In the midst of these uncertainties, many film critics in the 1980s prematurely predicted the demise of the Western. The 1990s proved these naysayers wrong as the Western swept to new heights of popularity. *Dances with Wolves*, a revisionist-style Western sympathetic to Native Americans and depicting non-Indian opponents as a remuda of farting, suicidal, and savage whites, won several Oscars, including best film of the year. It was the first Oscar for a Western in nearly sixty years. Two years later, Clint Eastwood directed and starred in *Unforgiven* (1992), which also landed several Oscars, including one for best picture. These two award-winning films signaled a resurgence of the Hollywood Western that continued throughout the 1990s, proving the genre far from moribund.

The essays gathered in this collection provide a brief history of the Hollywood Western during the twentieth century. The chapters serve two other purposes: as they focus on one or more leading actors or actresses, they also examine shifting sociocultural trends in America that influenced the shape and content of many Westerns. Taken as a whole, these essays furnish scholars and general readers alike with an overview of one of America's most significant film genres.

In the opening essay, Richard W. Etulain discusses the important contributions of Broncho Billy Anderson, William S. Hart, and Tom Mix in shaping the first cinematic depictions of movie cowboys. All three actors starred in adventuresome silent films featuring scene after scene of action and conflict. Anderson and Hart, especially, played good, bad men, whose transformations to white-hatted heroes powered the plots of dozens of Westerns. By 1930, as Etulain shows, this triumvirate had experienced their halcyon days, with Anderson and Hart already retired and Mix stumbling along as an outdated movie hero and circus rider.

Next, Raymond E. White, a noted specialist on B (or low-budget) Westerns, furnishes a valuable overview of Roy Rogers and Dale Evans. Deftly introducing the early lives of Rogers and Evans, including the traumas of their previously flawed marriages and emotional disappointments, White moves on to the couple's first starring roles and the flowering of their important careers. In addition, the author discusses the duo's contributions to other facets of popular culture outside Hollywood. Discussing the activities of Rogers and Evans from the 1930s into the 1990s, White provides a helpful summary of more than a half-century of shifting popular images and attitudes toward the American West.

Film scholars Ray Merlock and Jack Nachbar furnish a helpful introduction to another notable "singing cowboy" of the Western, Gene Autry. Bit by bit, as these two authors plainly show, Autry made his way up a career ladder from music programs in New York City and Chicago in the 1920s and 1930s to go on to Hollywood where he became a contributing force of many Western films. Autry played hundreds of romantic cowboys, first in the *Phantom Empire* series (1935) and *Tumbling Tumbleweeds* (1938) and later in *The Last Roundup* (1947). He starred in dozens of other low-budget Westerns, as well as on his radio show *Melody Ranch* and on television with his *Gene Autry Show*. Toward the end of Autry's life, as Merlock and Nachbar note in their revealing profile, he took interest in other mediums of popular entertainment, purchasing a major league baseball team and establishing the Autry Museum of Western Heritage in Los Angeles.

In his superb chapter on John Ford, Ronald L. Davis clearly delineates the director's huge impact on the Hollywood Western. Drawing on his extensive studies of Ford, John Wayne, and several other actors, Davis expertly shows how Ford "lifted the Western film to epic proportions." Davis is particularly evenhanded in his profile, noting the many strengths of Ford's memorable Westerns even as he describes the director's numerous character flaws. A quarter century after John Ford's death, he remains our premier director of Westerns.

John Lenihan's balanced profile of John Wayne skillfully depicts the career of Hollywood's leading Western hero. Moving chronologically through Wayne's life, Lenihan traces his early years in poverty-row (inexpensively made) Westerns, his enormous successes in *Stagecoach* and *Red River*, and the cavalry Westerns of the 1940s and 1950s. He also provides capsule discussions of Wayne's later successes: *The Searchers*, *Rio Bravo* (1959), *The Man Who Shot Liberty Valance*, *True Grit*, and *The Shootist* (1976). Lenihan correctly concludes that Wayne is remembered for his personification of "frontier individualism" but that he also "endured in large part because . . . [his] films . . . kept pace with the times."

Of John Wayne's contemporaries, Gary Cooper provided the most competition as Hollywood's leading star of the Western. As Louis Tanner explains in his fair-minded essay, Cooper's long career "ran from the innocence of silent movies to the disillusionment of the Cold War cinema." In the opening pages of his essay, Tanner elucidates Cooper's western backgrounds and his emergence as a Hollywood hero. From *The Virginian* (1929) to *The Plainsman* (1936), and on to his best-known role in *High Noon*, Cooper won repeated accolades for his superb acting. He was, Tanner convincingly shows, a man of manifold talents who put his unforgettable and personal brand on the Hollywood Western.

A contemporary of John Wayne and Gary Cooper, Barbara Stanwyck proved that a talented, hard-working actress could break into the Western. As Glenda Riley makes clear in her tightly argued essay, Stanwyck deserves credit for "feminizing" the Western. In such films as *Annie Oakley* (1935), *Union Pacific*, *The Maverick Queen*, and later as Victoria Barkley in the popular television series *The Big Valley* (1965–1969), Stanwyck portrayed strong and courageous women. As Riley persuasively concludes, Barbara Stanwyck contributed much to the Western because, as in her private life, she "was dedicated to testing and breaking America's social and cultural boundaries."

Katy Jurado also played important if underrecognized roles in the development of the Western, as Cheryl Foote argues in her well-written biography of the Mexican actress. In her memorable part as Helen Ramírez in *High Noon*, Jurado displayed, Foote writes, "her great abilities" as an actress. No actress before or since has surpassed her achievements in a similar role; it was "the high point for Mexicanas in American film." Jurado's nuanced depiction of an Indian wife in *Broken Lance* (1954) also won her an Oscar nomination that year for best supporting actress. Among the few men and women of color starring in Westerns, Katy Jurado occupies a leading position.

Meanwhile, Gretchen Bataille, drawing from her extensive research on Native Americans, summarizes Indian roles in the Western. Using the careers of Jay Silverheels, Iron Eyes Cody, and Chief Dan George as illustrations, she argues that "Hollywood's image of Native Americans . . . may be more rooted in the imagined West than we want to believe." Still, as Bataille duly notes, the recent sterling roles of Cherokee actor Wes Studi and the outspoken screenplays of Indian writers Gerald Vizenor and Sherman Alexie suggest that future Native American images in the Hollywood Western will finally break from the stereotypes of the past.

In the concluding essay, James Hoy encapsulates the central importance of Clint Eastwood to the Hollywood Western over the past four decades. First, as Rowdy Yates in the popular television series *Rawhide* from 1959 to the mid-1960s and then in the so-called "spaghetti" or "dollar" Westerns of the late 1960s, Eastwood emerged as a well-known star of the Western. Playing amoral, hard-bitten, sell-your-soul-to-the-highest-bidder roles during the Vietnam and Watergate years, Eastwood personified antiheroic protagonists much at odds with earlier Cooper and Wayne heroes. In his best-known role as the tortured, ambivalent hero in the Oscar-winning *Unforgiven*, Eastwood perfectly illustrates the new gray hero who dominates many fictional Westerns at the end of the twentieth century.

Taken together, these ten essays dramatize a full century of Hollywood Westerns. Most important, they trace the memorable contributions of leading heros and heroines from Broncho Billy Anderson and William S. Hart to John Wayne and Gary Cooper and on to Barbara Stanwyck, Katy Jurado, and Native American actors. We learn of the widespread popularity of Roy Rogers, Dale Evans, and Gene Autry. The monumental achievements of director John Ford and actor Clint Eastwood are also examined. In addition, the essays deal with shifting American attitudes that have shaped the Western since its inception in the early part of the century. In short, the biographies and histories of these notable westerners bring into sharp focus the most important characters and themes of the Hollywood Western, thereby helping us to understand the magic American West that continues to enthrall audiences around the globe.

◆ one ◆

Broncho Billy,
William S. Hart, and Tom Mix

The Rise of the Hollywood Western

RICHARD W. ETULAIN

The huge success of the film *The Great Train Robbery* (1903) helped to launch the Western. Regarded by many as the first Western, this immensely popular film built on earlier images of the American West and initiated novel ways of treating the region in an entirely new medium. Thus, early in the twentieth century the Hollywood West was born.

The Great Train Robbery attracted so much enthusiastic response, in part, because it drew on the sensational reputations of outlaws Jesse and Frank James and Butch Cassidy and the Sundance Kid. During the previous generation, the notorious activities of these frontier characters had flashed across hundreds of headlines as the country's most wanted railroad and bank robbers. Although the smashing new film did not deal directly with these outlaws, it evoked a romantic tradition that stretched as far back as to adventuresome European highwaymen and bandits such as Robin Hood, Dick Turpin, and Claude Duval.

In addition to building on these Old West and outlaw traditions, *The Great Train Robbery* featured a new, major ingredient to the Western. Even if movie marquees failed to disclose the fact, the film included the actor who became the first Western star, Broncho Billy Anderson. In the next decade Broncho Billy emerged as the most widely recognized hero of the film Western. Then, just as Anderson's star began to fade in the mid-1910s, two other heroes of the cinematic sagebrush, William S. Hart and Tom Mix, galloped onto the scene. During the next few years, perhaps until Hart's final film, *Tumbleweeds* (1925), he dominated Western roles. Meanwhile, Mix steadily gained a durable reputation as a devil-may-care cowboy star and probably was the best-known hero when talkies invaded Hollywood toward the end of the 1920s.

Broncho Billy Anderson, William S. Hart, and Tom Mix were not the whole story of the film Western before 1930, but they did become the most lionized stars of the cinematic West during these three decades. Within these years, this cowboy triumvirate illustrated many of the themes and ideas that Hollywood featured in its Westerns. As a result, the careers of these stars illuminate the formative years of the film Western.

The early years of Gilbert Max Aronson (Broncho Billy Anderson) remain an enigma. Born in Little Rock, Arkansas, in 1882, he roamed a good deal in his early years, working at several jobs as a young man. While still a teenager he relocated to St. Louis, Missouri, where he was employed briefly as a salesman before trying his hand at acting. Of stocky build, Aronson did not seem much like an actor. For a short time he attempted to break into vaudeville. Then, thinking that the best opportunities for actors lay in the East, he moved to New York City in 1901. Working for a few months as an artist's model, he soon returned to another vaudeville troupe. Sometime during his first two years in New York, Aronson gained a new name, (G. M.) Max Anderson. His big break came in 1903 with *The Great Train Robbery*.

Early in the twentieth century, New York City bubbled with activity in the novel area of filmmaking. Infant film companies such as Edison, Biograph, and Vitagraph began turning out one-reel (less than ten minutes) "movies." Working with poverty-level budgets, unskilled actors, and plot-less action scenes, these early filmmakers scrambled to find locations, funding, and appealing stories for their new medium. An aspiring actor who made himself attractive to one of these companies could make a living wage.

One of the most significant producer–directors during this time was Edwin S. Porter of the Edison Company. In 1903, Porter helped produce *The Life of an American Fireman,* which featured many of the staples of the early movies. With heroic firemen, action sequences, and a just-in-time rescue—all in a few minutes—the short film left viewers entertained, perhaps thrilled, and certainly satisfied. Those same elements were featured in Porter's dynamic *The Great Train Robbery*.

The Great Train Robbery launched Max Anderson's career as a film actor, even though he was not featured as a star. When director Porter asked Anderson if he could ride a horse in the action film he was planning, Anderson replied that he "was born on a horse." Perhaps thinking he could cinch the job, he told Porter "I was raised in Missouri and can ride like a Texas Ranger." Anderson's residence in Missouri was the only truth; the rest were just southwestern stretchers.

Broncho Billy Anderson (Max Aronson), the first of the cowboy movie stars.

Porter took Anderson at his word and cast him for several parts in the film. He was to be one of the train robbers, a passenger on the train, and a dancer in another scene. Obviously Porter intended to make as inexpensive a film as possible, so the director expected Anderson to earn his wages in the one-reeler. But Anderson's exaggerations about his horse-riding skills got him in trouble early in the filming. When he attempted to mount his horse from the wrong side, Anderson was thrown, and his horse galloped away, thereby forcing him to walk part of the way back to the studio. A hard-riding Texas Ranger he was not.

But *The Great Train Robbery* had a large impact on Anderson's career in other more important ways. Many years later, Anderson told an interviewer about the key importance of the 1903 movie: "This thriller took motion pictures out of diapers, put them in rompers, and fathered an unending line of American horse-operas." Excited by the film's popularity as well as by its positive reviews, Anderson jumped into the film business as an actor and director for Vitagraph. Although Porter and the Edison Company seemed uninterested in building on the sensational successes of *The Great Train Robbery*, Vitagraph encouraged Anderson's ambitions to make new movies about a Wild West.

Moving to Chicago in 1907, Anderson tried to interest other owners and producers in making Westerns to capitalize on the popularity of *The Great Train Robbery*. When his first negotiations with Colonel William Nicholas Selig failed to spawn any projects, Anderson turned to his old friend George K. Spoor. Together they organized Essanay Company (S and A = Spoor and Anderson). Within a short time, the new company enjoyed dramatic successes, especially later with such actors and actresses as Wallace Beery, Charlie Chaplin, and Gloria Swanson. As part of his duties, Anderson took a small crew to Colorado to make films in the shadow of the Rockies. Then, learning that other companies had discovered the lures of southern California for making films, Anderson hurried to Los Angeles. Later in 1908, Anderson and his Essanay crew moved north to Niles, California, in the Bay Area.

One of the first films Anderson produced at the Niles location was *Broncho Billy and the Baby* (1908). Without permission to do so, Anderson used a recent story in the *Saturday Evening Post* by Peter B. Kyne as the story line for the film. Anderson also cast himself as the hero of the movie when he was unable to locate a satisfactory male lead. *Broncho Billy and the Baby* included several ingredients that became Broncho Billy trademarks. It is the sentimental story of an outlaw redeemed through his efforts to help an injured child. The parents of the saved child adopt Broncho Billy, introduce him to religion and the Bible, and finally send him on his way reformed. This one reeler introduced Broncho Billy the good, badman, the shy hero around women, and the fearless gunman, who, without violence, helps society before riding off. By this time, Anderson had learned to ride a horse and thus displayed the horsemanship skills that audiences came to expect of Western heroes.

Now with the new name "Broncho Billy" and a model for short Westerns, Anderson proceeded to turn out movies by the hundreds. Indeed, between 1908 and 1915, he may have put together as many as four hundred Westerns. Anderson later described the process of producing his brief, action-filled films at his Niles location: "I made them like popcorn. I'd write 'em in the morning and make 'em in the afternoon. Sometimes I had the scenario written on my cuff."

The year 1915 proved to be another turning point in Broncho Billy's career. The federal government, threatening to break up moviemaking monopolies, moved against the early, entrenched companies, including Vitagraph, Selig, and Essanay. Tiring of the assembly-line productions of his one- and two-reel Westerns, Anderson sold his holdings in Essanay. As part of the negotiations, he agreed to stay out of films for two years and to cease using the name Broncho Billy when he returned to the screen. In the early 1910s, Anderson had been remarkably successful, making as much as $125,000 annually as actor, director, and producer.

Late in the decade, Broncho Billy launched a comeback. At first, he tried to make five-reel feature Westerns starring himself as the hero. But in his absence William S. Hart and Tom Mix had dashed onto the scene as Western heroes. Anderson soon found that these new stars had already captured the Western genre, barring his re-entry. In the early 1920s, Anderson tried his hand at comedies, but he ran afoul of movie mogul Louis B. Mayer and decided to retire rather than continue acting.

For more than twenty years Broncho Billy seemed to disappear from the Hollywood scene. But he was not entirely forgotten. In the 1940s, he was awarded a special Academy Award for his central role in establishing the Western. A decade later he took part in an NBC special, along with John Wayne, Gary Cooper, John Ford, and a host of other actors and directors, chronicling the rise of the Western. Then, in 1965, a half-century after he filmed his last Broncho Billy film, Anderson played a cameo role in *The Bounty Hunter*. Broncho Billy died in 1971 virtually unnoticed in a retirement home in the Hollywood area.

Those final obscure years were far removed from the decade or so following (G. M.) Max Anderson's initial appearance in *The Great Train Robbery*. In fact, nearly every Hollywood authority credits Broncho Billy with a central role in the development of the Western. One noted film historian puts the matter baldly: to Broncho Billy "belongs the credit for creating the screen image of the western hero." Another scholar states the case for Anderson's importance in nearly identical words: "He was literally creating the Western star, and laying the groundwork for cowboy heroes yet unborn."

At first glance, Broncho Billy Anderson seemed an unlikely hero for the Western. He lacked the tall, lean physique of John Wayne or Gary Cooper; he never became an accomplished rider; and he was not a polished actor. Later viewers also criticized his plotless movies and the obscure quality of his numerous roles. These critics wonder how could he have been a central figure in the history of the Horse Opera when he seemed so unlike many later heroes of the Western?

These pundits overlook important facets of Broncho Billy's large contributions to the Western. Anderson pioneered the Western. Since there were no film models to follow, he established many of the familiar elements that gradually hardened into a new genre. His one and two reelers overflowed with action and adventure. Broncho Billy also introduced the "good, badman" character who later became a standard figure in 1920s, especially in the films of Anderson's best-known successor, William S. Hart. In these roles, Broncho Billy seemed a rascal but proved to be a man of true grit with a heart of gold. In *Broncho Billy's Redemption* (1910), for example, Billy helps a

William S. Hart, known for his dramatic and moralistic cowboy roles.

girl and her father even though he may be arrested for his efforts. At the same time, Anderson introduced the "reformed by love" theme to the Western, in which the love of a virginal heroine sets the hero on the new path of righteousness. This idea became a central emphasis in William Hart's best-known Westerns.

Even though other naysayers have condemned Broncho Billy's Westerns as stereotypical and mawkish, Jon Tuska, nonpareil specialist in the Western, salutes Anderson's films as realistic and humor-filled. Tuska adds that the Broncho Billy hero continued to influence Westerns produced before 1930. Equally significant, Broncho Billy made the cowboy the most popular hero of Western films just as novelist Owen Wister did for fictional Westerns, particularly in *The Virginian* (1902), which appeared one year before the release of *The Great Train Robbery*.

By the outbreak of World War I, Broncho Billy Anderson had done more than any other person to introduce and popularize what became known as the Hollywood Western. An energetic actor, a man of action, and an improving director, he helped make stories about the cowboy West a popular movie type. For these large contributions, he deserves recognition as one of the forefathers of the Hollywood Western.

Even before Broncho Billy's star status began to falter in the mid-1910s, a new cowboy hero had emerged. Soon after his first appearance in a Western in 1914, William S. Hart quickly became the best-known protagonist of Westerns and remained so into the late 1920s. Even though his movie career lasted scarcely a decade, his impact on the movie industry was enormous.

Although William S. Hart was born in Newburgh, New York, in 1865 and spent most of his adult years in the East before 1914, he always stressed his boyhood years in the upper Midwest in his autobiographical writings. During those years in the late 1860s and early 1870s, he traveled with his father (a flour miller), became aquainted with Native Americans, and began a life-long love affair with the frontier and American West. When Hart's father lost his job and his mother suffered severe health problems, the family was forced to return to New York. During these financial crises, the teenage Hart helped support his family even during his apprenticeship as an actor. After a short period of training, Hart launched his acting career. Over the course of the next thirty years he gradually built a strong reputation as a stage actor. In addition to numerous Shakespearean roles, he starred in dramatic productions of *The Squaw Man, The Virginian,* and other western dramas. These roles allowed Hart to indulge his fascination for things western.

Hart's love of the West and his growing interest in films soon intersected.

A stubborn man who often thought his views of the American West were the only correct perspectives, he was angered with what he considered the "burlesque manner" in which some films treated the West. Convinced that films should always be realistic and factually accurate, Hart set out to remedy what he believed were fallacious cinematic views of the West. He was certain he could show directors and producers, as well as audiences, the truth about the region of the country he loved.

While in California in 1914 with a traveling troupe, Hart spoke to his friend Thomas H. Ince, an actor turned producer, about taking part in Western films. Ince was not too interested in Westerns and thought of them as a dying breed. Still, when Ince took Hart to a movie lot, the stage actor was even more convinced he should change careers. Fifteen years later in his autobiography, *My Life East and West* (1929), Hart recalled the epiphanic moment: "I was enraptured and told him [Ince] so. The very primitiveness of the whole life out there, the cowboys and Indians, staggered me. I loved it. They had everything to make Western pictures. The West was right there!"

Finally giving in to Hart's persistence, Ince allowed Hart to make several Westerns at a weekly salary of $75. At first, Hart worked with other directors but then pressured Ince to direct his own Westerns. Ince relented again, and together they completed *The Bargain* (1914), Hart's first feature film. Before the movie's release, Hart had returned east to take up other acting duties. When previews of *The Bargain* impressed viewers, the parsimonious Ince wired Hart an offer of $125 per week to star in and direct Westerns. Not knowing that *The Bargain* was gaining rave notices and that Ince was under-paying him, Hart quickly accepted the offer and moved west to California with his beloved sister, Mary.

With youthful enthusiasm, Hart jumped into making more than twenty one- and two-reeler Westerns during 1914–1915. They were immensely successful, and Hart immediately gained notoriety as a rising star. When other Hollywood stars like Douglas Fairbanks were rumored to have negotiated incredible contracts, Ince reluctantly sweetened Hart's salary to $1,000 per week in 1915. In these quickly made Westerns, Hart often played, as he did in *The Disciple* (1915), the hero who struggles with difficult moral choices. Throughout his career, Hart seemed to enjoy roles that called for moral drama, etched in clear, black-and-white dimensions. In these earlier films Hart also introduced the close relationship between the cowboy and his horse. Next to his sister, Mary, his pinto pony Fritz was the love of Hart's life.

The release of *Hell's Hinges* in 1916 was an early high point in Hart's movie career. A five-reel, feature film made for $32,000 and codirected by Hart, this movie quickly gathered superb reviews and probably established Hart as Hollywood's leading Western star. One of Hart's best films, *Hell's Hinges* deserves recognition as a classic early Western. The movie encapsulates many of Hart's favorite themes and his characteristic traits. On one level it is a moralistic parable about character reformation. Hart plays the leading role of Blaze Tracey, a good, badman who, like so many of Hart's protagonists, is transformed through the love of a virtuous woman. In a setting reminiscent of an Old Testament Sodom, Tracey, reflecting the "badness" of this frontier town and serving as a tool of the community's villain, Slick Miller, sets out to destroy a church congregation. When Blaze discovers the transparent weaknesses of the newly arrived pastor from the East, the Reverend Robert Henley, the badman eagerly undertakes a mission to demolish the shepherd and his flock.

Then enters the familiar catalyst of the good woman, who appears in so many of Hart's Westerns. Faith, the sister of the ineffectual minister, is the strong character her brother can never be. When Blaze Tracey meets Faith, he immediately hesitates in his evil errand to destroy the church. Seeing that Blaze is now undependable, Slick Miller uses a saloon girl to seduce the minister after a drinking spree. Afterward, Miller and his dance hall henchmen attack and set fire to the church. Conveniently out of town as Slick Miller carries out his malignant design, Blaze returns just in time to drag the dying pastor Henley from the burning church. Then, like the wrath of God, Tracey descends on Miller and his gang in the saloon, shoots out its lights, and torches their haven. After Hell's Hinges is destroyed by fire, Blaze and Faith bury her brother and leave town together.

The moral reformation of Blaze Tracey, through his finding Faith, takes place in the kind of gritty frontier West that was so appealing to Hart. Whenever he directed a film, or could control its making, Hart called for dusty, bleak, and even harsh settings for his stories. He refused to polish and glamorize his frontier, to romanticize it as Tom Mix's Westerns often did. As one scholar has written: "Hart chose to portray the West as raw, violent, and somber just as he portrayed the man who tamed it." In this demanding landscape, a man's rejuvenation was possible—if he could find his faith.

Hart's role in *The Return of Draw Egan*, (1916) follows a similar formula. A former outlaw leader, "Draw" Egan, surfaces in Yellow Dog, a frontier hamlet dominated by an evil crowd. Reformed from his desperado past, Egan (Hart) sets out as the town's newly appointed sheriff to drive out the villains.

Draw's resurrection, motivated in part through his attraction to a pure, young woman, follows the familiar pattern of transformation in Hart's good, badman characters. Once Draw's goodness becomes apparent, the community-minded element of Yellow Dog embraces him as their savior.

In the late 1910s, Hart played several kinds of roles, including some as a Native American, but his moralistic fervor and his commitment to a realistic West continued as his most notable trademarks. Once Hart had decided how Westerns ought to portray frontier life, he stoutly resisted changes, even though directors and critics urged him to be less sentimental, less preachy, and more willing to play roles other than the romantic lead. Hart seemed impervious to their suggestions.

Hart's part in *The Toll Gate* (1920), another of his major Westerns, reveals how similar his roles had become. Codirected by Hart and based on his own story entitled "By Their Fruits Ye Shall Know Him," this six-reel Western tells the story of an outlaw with a heart of gold. In this movie— Hart's most financially successful film—he stars as Black Deering, another outlaw who a virtuous woman reforms.

Early in the story, the bandit leader Deering is betrayed to the law by his second in command, Tom Jordan. Escaping from his captors, Deering destroys the cantina Jordan has purchased with his betrayal rewards and flees. Nearby, Deering befriends a woman whose husband has abandoned her and rescues her son from a threatening disaster. When Deering discovers that the woman is Jordan's wife, he thinks of gaining further revenge at her expense. But in this mother and son, Black Deering confronts true goodness and is transformed. Although he destroys Jordan, the hero looks after the widow before riding off across the border. These abundant action scenes, combined with the intense conflict between good and bad forces so typical of Hart's Westerns, were the major attractions of *The Toll Gate.*

Unfortunately, and yet understandably, by the early 1920s audiences tired of Hart's predictable plots and ideas. The mood of the United States was changing in the aftermath of World War I. Hart's excessive emphasis on virtue seemed to remind Americans of the increasingly discredited moralism of President Woodrow Wilson. They were bent on moving in different directions, as the election in 1920 of Warren G. Harding on a platform of "normalcy" indicated. Because Hart was unwilling—or perhaps incapable— of changing his roles and adapting to a climate of opinion, his popularity declined. Disappointed and disillusioned, Hart considered permanent retirement. But he could not immediately bring himself to do so and continued to star in several Westerns before the mid-1920s.

One of the most revealing of these films was *Wild Bill Hickok* (1923). In playing Wild Bill, Hart portrayed one of his heroes. Hart's Hickok, not unexpectedly, exudes courage, bravery, and masculinity. Early, he stands off a gang bent on destroying him, and later, in an even more spectacular scene, he fends off a group of cutthroats while standing alone on the streets of Dodge City. Adapted from one of Hart's own stories, the film seriously bruised fact by dragging in President Abraham Lincoln and General George Custer, and by placing other characters like Calamity Jane and Bat Masterson in roles that were historically inaccurate. Evidently Hart did not see these readjustments of historical fact as betrayals to his usual addiction to realism.

Hart hoped that *Wild Bill Hickok* and his other films of the early 1920s would revive his earlier reputation as the leading star of Westerns. But he balked at making any major changes in his films, despite the urgings to do so from several directors. To compete with Tom Mix and other rising stars, they encouraged him to lighten up, to downplay his moralism, and to include more adventure in his plots. Rather than heed these suggestions, Hart stubbornly followed his own predilections.

Hoping to prove himself right and his critics wrong, Hart planned a breakthrough, epic Western. Working with his own production company and a budget of more than $300,000 (his largest ever for a film), Hart filmed *Tumbleweeds*, the dramatic story of a land rush into late nineteenth-century Oklahoma Territory. Although it did not have the large draws of *The Toll Gate, Tumbleweeds* may have been Hart's finest cinematic effort. It was also his final film.

Hart plays the role of Don Carver, the range boss of the Box K Ranch who loses his job when the Cherokee Strip opens for settlement. In something of a Romeo and Juliet twist, the cowboy falls in love with a girl accompanying the sodbusters. Despite nearing sixty, Hart still had to have the romantic lead. Unfortunately, most of the film's love scenes seemed unrealistic to viewers who had seen Hart too often in these roles. The most memorable sections of *Tumbleweeds*, however, depicted the giant land rush into the strip. Hart disallowed any "staged" action sequences, but even his demand for accuracy did not detract from the convincingly portrayed sections of this engrossing story. Viewers at the end of the twentieth century still find these portions of the film believable and entertaining.

Built around the now familiar "end-of-the-West" theme, *Tumbleweeds* opened to an enthusiastic reception. But United Artists, the film's distributor, sabotaged Hart's efforts by cutting the movie's length to peddle it to smaller theaters. Hart sued United Artists and won, but he probably lost nearly $500,000 as a result of the unaccountable actions of United Artists. With both his wallet and confidence bruised, the actor seemed to lose heart and retired from films to his Newhall Ranch. Although he made a few public appearances over the next two decades, including a remarkable nine-minute sound prologue for a remake of *Tumbleweeds* (1939), Hart essentially disappeared from the Hollywood West until his death in 1946.

Of these three cowboy stars, William S. Hart was the most complex. Although Hart tried to project the image of the simple straightforward man in his personal as well as professional life, he was far more complex than that. Sincere, dependable, and ambitious, Hart was so convinced of his rightness that he ultimately found many human relationships difficult. He frequently quarreled with directors, disagreed with critics, and over-reacted to others' opinions. Moreover, his incurable romanticism often led to repeated infatuations with his leading ladies. Only one, Winifred Westover, accepted his proposal of marriage, but that relationship, even though it produced a son, lasted only a few months. Later, his son broke from his father when Hart demanded that he live up to his expectations or suffer disinheritance. In fact, Hart seemed much closer to his sister, Mary, than to anyone else.

On the other hand, William S. Hart committed himself wholeheartedly to his occupation. "I love acting," he wrote in his autobiography. "I love the art of making motion pictures. It is the breath of life to me!" This fervor, sometimes tinctured with his sentimentality and patriotism, characterized all of Hart's films. Even when he played outlaws or other bad men, reviewers often saluted the transparent "goodness" of Hart's characters.

Hart's strong convictions clearly colored the tone and content of his Westerns. Above all, he aimed at verisimilitude and depicted the West, at least physically, as he thought it had been. Dusty, gritty scenes, informal dress, jerrybuilt architecture—all these components characterized his movies. He also employed Native Americans and working cowboys to heighten the "reality effect" he desired. As actor, as director, and often as storywriter, Hart participated much more actively in these facets of moviemaking than Broncho Billy and Tom Mix, and he attempted to superimpose his "austere style" on all his films. For William S. Hart, making movies was no mere play-acting; it was the projection of his deeply held beliefs to his viewers.

Not surprisingly, the reactions of interpreters, past and present, to Hart are as varied as his own complexities. Noted film scholars George Fenin and William Everson perhaps overstate their case in asserting that Hart's films "represent the very heart and core of that which is so casually referred to as Hollywood's Western tradition." Conversely, the equally well-versed film historian Jon Tuska allows Hart too little impact in arguing that "in terms of long-range influence, Hart's effect was negligible." Even less to be considered is the snobbish, arrogant conclusion of film critic Robert Warshow, who, in writing about Hart and Tom Mix, asserted that in the "wooden absoluteness of their virtue" these two heroes "represented little that an adult could take seriously."

On the contrary, despite Hart's excessive moralism — as well as his bent toward self-righteousness and the melodramatic, which often limited his achievements as an actor — his influence was multifaceted. Hart's commitment to realism coupled with his love for the Old West aided in the development of the film and a fictional type that some consider America's unique contribution to storytelling. If Hart's dramatic sins often shone through, his large contributions are even more memorable and enduring. Perhaps literary scholar Michael Schoenecke says it best in one sentence: "Vigorous plots tinged with a Victorian streak of purity that drew on the dramatic conflicts of frontier life catapulted Hart to the forefront of the American motion picture industry." Even while noting Hart's limitations, one must accord him first place among the most influential stars of the silent Western.

Well before Broncho Billy retired early and William S. Hart made his last Western, Tom Mix burst onto the scene. As early as 1909–1910, Mix worked for the Selig Company as a supporting actor and bronco buster, and until the mid-1930s he continued making series Westerns. In the first quarter of the twentieth century, Mix starred in hundreds of films about the West. Mix was so popular and his films were so successful that in the early 1920s he surpassed Hart as Hollywood's best-known Western hero and was dubbed "America's Champion Cowboy."

Mix's origins remain obscure because he or his publicity agent manu-factured yarns about his beginnings well beyond the facts. These puffed accounts spoke of western backgrounds, of Indian ancestry, of distinguished and gallant service in several wars, and of several stints as a valiant law offi-cer on the southwestern frontier. Although none of these claims were true, all became part of Mix's legend, which surrounded him well into the middle part of the century.

The truth seemed much less extravagant. He was born in Mix Run, Pennsylvania, in 1880. At age 10, after attending the Buffalo Bill's Wild West traveling arena show, Mix became fascinated with horses and guns. Later he joined the Navy during the Spanish–American War, but saw no action and spent his time guarding an eastern powder works company against sabotage. Although in the service during conflicts in the Philippines and in South Africa in the Boer War, Mix stayed stateside. Tiring of these mundane inactivities, he went AWOL, with the "deserter" designation remaining on his service record throughout his lifetime.

In the next decade, Mix lived a "vagabond existence." He worked briefly at several occupations, including bartending. By 1910, he had gone through two marriages and begun a third. Meanwhile, Mix had become a skilled cowboy. First as a part-time ranch hand and then as a rider for Colonel Joe Miller's famed 101 Ranch, he became a bronco buster, able to handle the most active mounts. On a few occasions Mix displayed his mastery of horses as well as his riding and roping skills in local and regional rodeos and Wild West shows.

Mix's first contact with the film industry came in 1909–1910. Hired as a stockhandler for the Selig Polyscope Company, he soon went before the cameras, especially to display his skills as a rider and showman. He was immediately successful and began to star in Westerns. Before 1917, Mix made more than sixty films, mostly Westerns, for Selig. These quickly made and financially remunerative movies were the exact opposite of the Westerns Hart starred in after 1914. Mix was a stunt man who took neither himself nor his West nearly as seriously as Hart. Instead, Mix's Westerns were full of *joi de vivre,* of Mix's boyishness, of action and adventure. As American studies' scholar William Tydeman has written, the plots of the Selig Westerns "were usually an excuse for showcasing Mix's riding and stunting."

Gradually, Mix became known for Westerns in which, literally, "horsing around" was the main attraction. Some reviewers thought of his Westerns for Selig as the Keystone Cops on horseback. On occasion, Mix wrote and directed some of these shorter movies, but he had the good sense to limit most of his efforts to entertaining acting in the longer, five-reel features. Emphasizing action and adventure even more than Broncho Billy, Mix also showed little interest in the good, badman characters associated with Broncho Billy and Hart. Nor did Mix star in the end-of-the-West or closing frontier Westerns that often featured Hart. In addition, the Selig films included little romance, again differentiating them from those standard ingredients in Hart's Westerns and to a lesser degree in Broncho Billy's films.

Mix's jump to Fox studios in 1917 signaled a major career change for him. Indeed, some film historians wonder why Mix stayed with Selig so

Tom Mix, the nattily dressed and trick-riding cowboy star.

long, or why he didn't join Universal where he might have worked with director John Ford or actor Harry Carey. At Fox, Mix made even clearer the differences between himself and Hart, his main competitor for the leading cowboy star. More and more Mix aimed his Westerns at preadolescents. As a result, love scenes nearly disappeared and were replaced with even more action and adventure. In the eleven years Mix worked at Fox he became known as a physically daring entertainer, a star who avoided doubles whenever possible and who relished the dangerous stunts of his roles.

In addition to the heightened action and adventure in his films at Fox, Mix adopted the flamboyant dress that typified the remainder of his career. Attired in white suits, large hats, and flashy accessories, Mix paraded his buoyant and dashing masculinity. As one authority on Mix notes, "customed elegance, daredevil adventure, and physical prowess" characterized nearly all of his films at Fox. Mix even incorporated the New West into his plots, using cars and sometimes planes as part of his daring action scenes.

The Fox Westerns were amazingly successful. By the early 1920s, Mix moved well beyond Hart as Hollywood's leading Western star. By the mid-1920s, he was making (and lavishly spending) more than $15,000 per week. Fox happily complied with Mix's desire to make Westerns that were "short, action-packed, and good to look at." They also encouraged his showy dress and lifestyle. After all, he was pulling in millions of dollars for the company.

No one should point to these early Mix Westerns as notable aesthetic achievements. None rivaled, for example, Hart's *Hell's Hinges*, *The Toll Gate*, or *Tumbleweeds* in this regard. Nonetheless, critics of that time often praised the Fox Westerns of Tom Mix for their superb popular entertainment. For example, *Just Tony* (1922), starring Mix's horse and building on Hart's similar film *Pinto Ben* (1915), featured Tony in a series of stunts illustrating humanlike emotions. *The Great K and A Train Robbery* (1926) also won accolades as "pure action." In addition, Mix drew on the popularity of fictional Westerns by Zane Grey and Max Brand (Frederick Faust) in such films as *The Lone Star Ranger* (1923), *Riders of the Purple Sage* (1925), *The Rainbow Trail* (1925), and *The Last Trail* (1927), and later in *Destry Rides Again* and *The Fourth Horseman* (both in 1932).

Tom Mix made important contributions to the sensational popularity of the Western in the 1920s. More than twice as many Westerns were made in the decade between World War I and the Depression as those of any other film type, and Mix probably was the best-known star of the Western. His Westerns seemed to reflect the times, a movement away from the moral fervor of Woodrow Wilson and toward the more relaxed, less reformist impulses of Warren G. Harding and Calvin Coolidge. Rather than the gritty, gray, and closely plotted films of William S. Hart, Mix's Westerns "moved," featuring more and more action, trick riding, comic devices, and the virility of its star.

Mix's career took another sharp turn in 1928. In quick succession he quit Fox, made a series of silents that flopped, and perhaps lost nearly $1 million. Forfeiting his mansion and ranch, Mix joined the Sells-Floto Circus, where he could in all ways be the center of attention. Those ingredients of Mix's Hollywood career that attracted audiences—his horsemanship, his roping skills, his garish dress, and his boyish personality—greatly added to his career as a circus performer. He sometimes earned $20,000 a week under the big top.

But Mix still yearned for Hollywood and returned to the movies in 1932–1933 to make a series of talkies for Universal. Here was a new challenge for him. Where the silents were perfect vehicles for action-packed plots, the talkies demanded other skills. True, Mix had some difficulty adjusting to the new demands of sound, but that awkwardness has been exaggerated. As the first of the new series, *Destry Rides Again* (1932) reclaimed many Mix fans. Universal paid him $10,000 a week and devoted a $100,000 budget to these well-produced films. But Mix seemed unable to stick with a demanding routine. Retiring again from filmmaking on Christmas Day of 1932, he returned to the circus arena. Three years later Mix reappeared for his last hurrah as a film star, making his only serial of fifteen films, *The Miracle Rider* (1935). Although the series did well, new Westerns such as the classic *Stagecoach* (1939) had clearly passed him by. Mix took up with the circus one last time and never returned to films before an automobile accident in Arizona claimed his life in 1940.

The legend of Tom Mix lived on after his death. A Tom Mix radio program, begun in 1933 and later sponsored by Ralston foods, thrilled American youngsters until 1950. Although Mix never appeared on the program—it did not pay well—his reputation for action and adventure powered the radio series. Toys and trademark clothing also played on the Tom Mix name well after his demise.

Before his death, a myth-made Tom Mix was well established in the minds and hearts of American moviegoers. For film audiences Mix represented less the good, badman that made Broncho Billy and William S. Hart so popular and more the hero who accidentally becomes involved in helping others. Violence and killing were absent from his films, replaced by daredevil action and a "slim folksiness" that became recognizable characteristics of the legendary Mix Western. As one film critic noted, Mix epitomized the "sexless, flirt and run Western" that continued into the 1930s and 1940s with the singing cowboy films of Gene Autry and Roy Rogers. Mix felt no urge to put the "real West" on screen, nor did he particularly enjoy his melodramatic Westerns. Still, Mix knew entertainment was the key, so, good businessman that he was, he continued to star in frenetic films that featured nonstop action.

On the other hand, Mix seemed to relish, on the surface, the showy lifestyle his huge income allowed him. He drove large, expensive cars with steer horns mounted on the front and, it is rumored, lived in a Hollywood mansion on which an electric sign flashed his name day and night for curious sightseers. Mix enjoyed his popularity—quite possibly earning twice as much as Hart during his career—and consciously lived up to his image. Viewed in larger context, in his rhinestone roles, Tom Mix provided a link between the cowboy figure Buck Taylor of Buffalo Bill's Wild West show and the nattily dressed cowboys of later times.

But there was another side of Mix. He often was a deeply troubled and unhappy man. Married often but not for long, he seemed unable to establish and keep lasting relationships. Nor did his acting bring him much happiness. He did not care much for his showy Westerns, but they funded his extravagant lifestyle, so he stayed in the saddle. Toward the end of his life, in the late 1930s, he realized that films had changed so dramatically that he had been pushed aside. If the mythic Mix could live on, the living Mix no longer rode point in popular Westerns.

It would be misleading to imply that Broncho Billy, William S. Hart, and Tom Mix monopolized the silent Western era. That was not the case. In the 1920s, for example, such actors as Buck Jones, Harry Carey, Ken Maynard, and Hoot Gibson were major attractions. Each became known for different trademark roles. Gibson was a prankster, Maynard and Jones were showmen like Mix, and Carey was a throwback to earlier, less action-driven Westerns. Together, these and other stars helped make the cowboy figure the most popular hero in silent Westerns.

Alongside these heroes, a few directors also played major roles in the development of the early Western. As early as 1913 in his *Battle at Elderbush Gulch*, famed director D. W. Griffith had depicted Indians as "savage" opponents of white settlers. Even before the end of World War I, but especially in *The Iron Horse* (1924), John Ford displayed his superb abilities in humanizing history. Directors Edwin S. Porter, Thomas Ince, and James Cruze also put their brands on Westerns made before 1930. Although these directors were major cogs in the film machines that engineered the Western, audiences were attracted primarily to the cowboy stars. As the most popular stars of Westerns, Broncho Billy, Hart, and Mix—not the directors—grabbed the attention of mushrooming numbers of moviegoers.

In less than three decades, the Western had become Hollywood's most popular genre. From *The Great Train Robbery* in 1903 to the first talkies in the late 1920s, the Western, especially in its focus on the Old West and its stress on the cowboy hero, was immensely successful. Yet by 1930, despite all its success, the Western seemed at a new juncture. Although a few stars such as Tom Mix, Buck Jones, and Hoot Gibson continued to star in sound Westerns, new faces of immense future importance began to appear. In 1929, Gary Cooper played the lead figure in Paramount's remake of *The Virginian*, and one year later *The Big Trail* starred an ex-University of Southern California football player who had recently changed his name form Marion Michael Morrison to John ("Duke") Wayne. And by the mid-1930s, the two best-known singing cowboys, Gene Autry and Roy Rogers, had become guitar-strumming heroes. The winds of change were blowing the Western in new directions.

Most significantly, during their first decades, Hollywood Westerns established several notable traditions. At the same time that filmmakers were discovering the large appetites of Western fans, writers about the American West catered to similar interests among hundreds of thousands of readers. In churning out these Westerns, Hollywood and dozens of novelists followed the now-familiar western story line, established in the nineteenth century in the novels of James Fenimore Cooper, in the Wild West show of Buffalo Bill Cody, and in the works of numerous dime novelists. That story line featured a white, male hero competing with challenging new environments and a variety of human opponents. Usually these heroes were cowboys, but in the first decades of the twentieth century they often became generic frontier riders, more recognizable as lawbringers and gunmen than as working cowboys. In addition, filmmakers, like their cousins working the fictional frontier, worried little about complexity. White-hatted heroes did battle with black-hatted (and usually black-hearted) villains. Nor did directors or producers make much room for women or minority stars during the silent era of the Western. By the early 1930s, the most recognizable figure in the Hollywood Western was the cowboy hero, blood brother to fictional and Wild West heroes like General Custer, Wild Bill Hickok, Billy the Kid, and Wyatt Earp who also rode gallantly in the minds and hearts of millions of Americans. In helping to formulate and to popularize this new cinematic hero, Broncho Billy Anderson, William S. Hart, and Tom Mix played major roles.

two

Roy Rogers and Dale Evans

King and Queen of the West

RAYMOND E. WHITE

For almost three-quarters of the twentieth century, Roy Rogers and Dale Evans entertained millions of Americans and in so doing created personal and professional personas that rested in the nostalgia of the American West. Born in the 1910s, both performers rode to fame on the back of the media technology that matured over the course of their lifetimes. Their careers in radio, film, recording, and television, as well as the shrewd efforts in merchandising their names and images, made them modern-day symbols of the mythic American West. Indeed, their western identity with twentieth-century Americans is so strong that mention of their names evokes immediate recognition and mental images of the romantic and imaginary West.

In that mythical West, Roy Rogers on horseback, toting a gun and a guitar, rode through exotic Western movie locales singing romantic cowboy ballads and making a nostalgic appeal to millions of Americans from the 1930s to the 1950s. Dale Evans portrayed an independent woman in the same magical locales, prompting audiences to believe that Western heroines were more than passive, dependent females. Together in their performances, Rogers and Evans possessed a special chemistry that permitted them to show an American West that was optimistic, lighthearted, and musical.

Roy Rogers and Dale Evans combined not only their professional careers but their personal lives as well. Married for more than fifty years, they successfully meshed the raising of a large family with exceedingly busy, professional lives. Occasionally, the Rogers children performed with their parents at state fairs, sang with the couple on recordings, or acted in their television adventure series. Currently, the Rogers's children and grandchildren continue to perpetuate the Rogers–Evans legacy. Roy Rogers, Jr., and Cheryl Rogers–Barnett run the Roy Rogers–Dale Evans Museum in

Victorville, California, and oversee the development of RogersDale, a western-theme entertainment and retail project in Temecula, California. Three of the Rogers' granddaughters recently organized a vocal trio called The Rogers Legacy. Rogers and Evans's determined effort to incorporate their children into their professional activities resulted from a strong sense of family that fit the couple's conception of their roles as fictive American frontier personalities.

A vital part of Rogers and Evans's family life was their deeply held Christian beliefs. So important were these convictions that the couple chose to incorporate them into their public performances. In their radio and television dramas, their rodeo performances, and in some aspects of their music, Rogers and Evans meshed Christian beliefs with their interpretation of the historical and mythical American West. Combining family and Christian values with western adventure struck a responsive cord among American parents during the 1950s and may partially explain why Rogers and Evans's partnership worked so well. Indeed, the combination of their personal and professional lives brought the couple a success that they probably would never have achieved as individual performers.

Rogers and Evans's dual professional life began in 1944 when they first starred together in the Republic Western *The Cowboy and the Senorita.* Prior to that film, they had individual professional careers in which they worked hard to perfect the talents and skills that made their relationship so successful. Indeed, the development of these skills began when Roy Rogers was a boy growing up in southern Ohio, and Dale Evans was a child in her native state of Texas and growing up in Arkansas. A look at their early lives and individual personalities and successes adds to the understanding of their combined careers as western performers.

Roy Rogers was born Leonard Franklin Slye on November 5, 1911, in Cincinnati, Ohio. The third of four children born to Andrew and Matte Slye, he grew up with three sisters on a houseboat docked at Portsmouth, Ohio, and on a farm in the nearby area of Duck Run. His parents and his childhood experiences shaped and molded the musical talents that he used professionally in his later public life. Music was especially important to the Slye family, and young Leonard began playing stringed instruments at an early age. His father, Andrew, was a self-taught guitarist and mandolin player who had performed on a showboat and, with his four brothers, at square dances throughout Ohio. Matte Slye also played string instruments and loved to sing. The family regularly entertained itself and neighbors at weekly square dances, where Leonard became an accomplished caller by his tenth birthday.

21

He also, at an early age, used his voice for yodeling, a skill that he perfected as he responded to his mother when she called him and his sisters in from play. The parental instruction, practice, and family performances provided Leonard Slye with important musical skills that helped him when he began to perform professionally.

Dale Evans's formative years likewise influenced her professional life. Indeed, she had western roots, being born in Uvalde, Texas, on October 31, 1912, almost exactly one year after Leonard Slye's birth in Ohio. Her parents, Walter and Betty Sue Wood Smith, named their daughter Frances Octavia Smith. She spent the first seven years of her life on a farm in Ellis County, Texas, before the family, in 1919, moved to Oceola, Arkansas, a farming community near the Mississippi River. Here, Frances grew up and developed her interest in music and performance. Her mother was musical and played the piano at the local Baptist church. Frances was a bright, precocious, and energetic child who never missed an opportunity to sing, whether at church or at a family gathering. She felt that "music was always in my soul, and performing came naturally." Frances performed publicly for the first time in church when she sang the hymn "In the Garden." She took piano lessons for a short time when she was eight but found the scales boring and quit. Playing by ear, improvising, and composing proved more satisfying to her. In high school, she played piano with a ukulele band. Her early passion for music and performance prompted fantasies of a professional career and undoubtedly gave her the confidence to take advantages of later opportunities.

Frances's other childhood dreams related to Western movie star Tom Mix, whom she fantasized about marrying when she grew up. She eagerly watched his movies and in later life said that she "had always loved cow-pokes and horses." Spending her early years in Texas and riding horses on her grandfather's west Texas ranch may have prompted her childhood attraction to Mix and cowboys. Certainly, her western roots were strong and authentic. In reality, however, she never thought she would one day marry a movie cowboy.

In addition to Mix and music, Frances's other passion as an adolescent was Thomas Frederick Fox, a young man several years her senior. Their ardor for each other was serious, and at the age of fourteen, she and Thomas eloped. The marriage failed within a year, but a son, Tom, was born, a circumstance that gave Frances a responsibility greater than most young women her age. By this time Frances and her mother resided in Memphis, Tennessee. With her mother's help to raise Tom, Frances began to reconstruct her life, first by attending business school and then by finding work as a secretary in an insurance office.

Although Frances found work to support herself and Tom, her mind remained on music. In fact, she often sang at the typewriter as she worked. Her boss, aware of her musical talents, asked Frances if she wanted to perform on a radio program that his company sponsored. She sprang at the chance and soon had a spot singing once a week on a small Memphis radio station. That opportunity led to other engagements and ultimately to an unpaid position as a vocalist at WMC, Memphis's largest commercial radio outlet. Here she performed for several months as Frances Fox, singing blues and popular songs, and in part, fulfilling her childhood fantasy. At age seventeen, two years before Leonard Slye made his first radio appearance in southern California, Frances was performing professionally and beginning to develop the talents that would prove to be so important in later years.

In 1930, about the same time that Frances Fox began her professional career on Memphis radio, the Slye family, in search of better economic opportunities, migrated to California. Driving west with his parents, young Leonard must have felt a tinge of excitement as he viewed, for the first time, the rolling prairies, towering mountains, and exotic deserts of the far West. Like thousands of other Americans who had made the trek, he undoubtedly experienced feelings of optimism and hope as he and his family began a new life in the Golden State. Indeed, Leonard Slye's eventual success as a western movie star and entertainer must have confirmed for him the reality of the mythic West and the rewards that it supposedly offered. This initial experience with the West forever tied young Slye to the region and positively influenced his interpretation of western music and the fictional portrayal of the American cowboy. The mythical West made Leonard Slye (Roy Rogers) a rich and famous man, and in his every professional act, for the rest of his life, he promoted the idea of a legendary and imaginary West.

Leonard Slye arrived in California with an optimism that he never lost. He maintained that positive attitude as he sought work to support himself and his family in the tough times of the Depression. Initially, Leonard and his father found jobs driving gravel trucks and working as migrant fruit pickers, but Leonard soon realized how important music was to him and that he wanted to pursue it professionally. At this point he capitalized on the musical skills he had developed as a child in Ohio. Initially, he and his cousin, Stanley Slye, performed together at beach parties and lodge gatherings for volunteer contributions. In 1931, an appearance on an amateur talent radio contest landed Leonard a job with the Rocky Mountaineers, a western musical group that performed on radio and for local parties in the Long Beach area. It was with the Mountaineers that Slye first assumed a western persona and began to lay the foundation for the great cowboy symbol that he would become. Also, while working with the Mountaineers, he met Bob Nolan and Tim Spencer, two musicians who later joined him to form the Sons of the Pioneers.

When the Rocky Mountaineers broke up, Slye and Spencer performed briefly with the International Cowboys and eventually with the O-Bar-O Cowboys, whom they even toured with through Arizona, New Mexico, and Texas in the summer of 1933. Returning to California, broke and somewhat discouraged, the group dispersed, with Slye joining a radio hillbilly group, Jack and His Texas Outlaws, and Tim Spencer finding work with the Safeway grocery chain. Bob Nolan, who had not been on the southwestern tour, worked as a caddy at a Los Angeles area golf course.

Despite discouragement and the odds against success, Leonard Slye remained optimistic and determined to form a successful western musical group. He wanted a professional music career, and his experience with the Rocky Mountaineers and other country bands convinced him of the possibilities of success. Moreover, Americans in the 1930s responded enthusiastically to cowboy singers and the nostalgia their music engendered. Aware of this trend in southern California, Slye persuaded his two friends, Bob Nolan and Tim Spencer, to quit their jobs and try to put together a western trio based on guitars and vocals. Within a year and a half, the talented Farr brothers, Hugh and Karl, who played fiddle and guitar, joined the fledgling Sons of the Pioneers, making the original group complete. Through hard work and hours of practice, the Sons of the Pioneers became the most famous western musical group in the country, with numerous imitators copying its style and repertoire of cowboy music. The superb songs of Bob Nolan and Tim Spencer enhanced the group's originality and western orientation. Leonard Slye's foresight and determination in organizing and promoting the Sons of the Pioneers stands as one of his most significant contributions to the perpetuation of the romantic and imaginary West.

Shortly after their start, the Pioneers landed a job on the Los Angeles radio station KFWB, performing with Jack and His Texas Outlaws. The group became an immediate success and soon got its own radio show and individual jobs as staff musicians on other programs. The exposure of their distinctive style and sound on radio led to recording opportunities for the Pioneers. In 1934, they began a year-long project, recording more than

280 songs for Standard Radio Transcriptions. These tunes, which ranged from spirituals to western cowboy ballads, were put together in syndicated programs and broadcasted on stations in various parts of the country, giving Leonard Slye and the Pioneers their first national exposure. They also provided Leonard Slye's first recordings and revealed his voice when he was twenty-three years old. Although his voice had yet to reach its full richness, Slye possessed a sophisticated technical and phrasing quality that would increase with age and experience.

In the same year that the Sons of the Pioneers began recording the transcriptions, they also gained a contract with Decca Records. By 1936, they had recorded thirty songs for the company with two-thirds of the tunes having a western or cowboy orientation. The Decca recordings gave the band additional exposure and increased their professional opportunities as an established western musical group. That same year the Pioneers were invited to the Texas Centennial celebration in Dallas, where they performed in cowboy garb. Leonard Slye was beginning, more self-consciously, to develop the cowboy and western image that would distinguish his entire career.

When the Pioneers appeared in Dallas, Frances and her son, Tom, attended the Centennial celebration and heard the group perform. Although Frances, at this point, did not meet the Pioneers personally, she appreciated their music and their skill as musicians, something she was able to judge because of her own professional experience. Frances had achieved considerable success in her career since 1930, but it had not come without a struggle.

Moving from Memphis to Chicago in the early 1930s, she overextended herself trying to find work as a singer while supporting herself as a file clerk and taking care of her young son. A second unhappy marriage and divorce adversely affected her emotional life. Things changed for the better in 1935 when she obtained her first paying job as a professional vocalist on radio station WHAS in Louisville, Kentucky. Moreover, it was at this station that Frances got her professional name—Dale Evans. The program manager insisted on the name, believing that radio announcers would find it easy to pronounce.

The Louisville experience helped her secure a similar position on the staff of Dallas station WFAA. Here, she married again. This time, it was to Robert Dale Butts, a pianist and arranger, whom she met while working in Louisville. Evans's performances at WFAA focused on popular music and jazz, a style that she continued to perform when she and Robert moved to Chicago to expand their professional music careers. Evans first got a job singing at the Edgewater Beach Hotel before going on the road for a year with the Anson Weeks Orchestra. Desiring a more settled professional life, Evans returned to Chicago to sing at nightclubs and ultimately to perform as a vocalist on radio station WBBM, a CBS affiliate. One program, *That Gal from Texas,* had a distinct western flavor and revealed Evans to be something more than a pop and jazz performer. On the program, she publicly made a connection with her Texas and western roots, but she still had a distance to go before changing her image.

While Dale Evans's domestic and professional life changed, so did that of Leonard Slye. In 1933, he had married Lucile Ascolese, but pressure on the couple resulting from Slye's constant practicing and performing eventually led to their divorce within a year and a half. Immediately following the divorce, Slye married again to Arlene Wilkins, a match that proved more successful than the first and produced three children.

Before Slye's second marriage, the Sons of the Pioneers gained small roles in movie shorts and feature films. They made appearances in the Bing Crosby picture, *Rhythm on the Range* (1936), as well as singing roles in the low-budget Westerns of Gene Autry, Dick Foran, and Charles Starrett. Like the recordings, these film appearances established Leonard Slye as a western performer and undoubtedly set him thinking about a career starring in Western films. The singing movie cowboy was just beginning to gain popularity, and Slye wanted to be more than a member of a western singing group with secondary roles in cowboy movies. He wanted to be a Western movie star, and with music altering the role of the traditional action hero, he thought he had an opportunity to do so. Gene Autry, at the newly formed Republic Pictures, had already established the persona of the singing cowboy that other Hollywood film factories quickly copied. Autry's model was the one that Slye also chose to emulate, and in 1936 he auditioned with Universal Pictures for the role of a singing cowboy. Another actor got the job, but a second opportunity came the following year when Autry had contract problems with Republic and threatened to strike. Republic's officials looked around for a replacement and decided on Slye, whom they hired and first used in supporting roles billed as Dick Weston. Within a year, Gene Autry refused to work, and Republic quickly changed Dick Weston's name to Roy Rogers and gave him top billing in *Under Western Stars* (1938), a film originally scheduled for Autry. The hard work, determination, and persistence paid off for Leonard Slye as he realized his dream. Within eight short years, he rose from an unknown migrant worker to a singing star in a Hollywood Western.

From the outset of his film career, Roy Rogers projected the romanticized image of the West and the American cowboy, often dressed up with Republic's modernized plots. In *Under Western Stars*, Rogers portrays a successful congressional candidate who tries to help local ranchers deal with water problems in the Dust Bowl. At one point in the film, the young congressman, in an attempt to influence members of the congressional appropriations committee to support a federal water relief act, sings the song "Dust" while standing next to a movie screen showing Dust Bowl scenes. A dust storm and a staged holdup finally convince the congressmen of the ranchers' need for federal help. Interestingly, the plot in Rogers's first starring film mirrored the problems facing western farmers and ranchers in the Depression and the role that the federal government played in solving them. Although the plot mixed heroic cowboy individualism and nostalgia with twentieth-century reality, the combination provided traditional western fantasy and set Roy Rogers on the trail to Hollywood stardom.

From his first year in films, Rogers became one of the top box-office Western stars. His rich singing voice, boyish good looks, and romantic projection of the American cowboy all contributed to his instant success. Within a year of the release of his first starring feature, Rogers ranked third behind Gene Autry and William Boyd (Hopalong Cassidy) in the *Motion Picture Herald*'s poll of top money-making Western stars. Within five years, and Gene Autry's departure for the armed forces in World War II, Roy Rogers rose to the top of that poll and remained there until 1955.

Between the release of Rogers's first starring feature at Republic Pictures in 1938 and his last in 1951, the studio produced eighty-three Roy Rogers Westerns, establishing the young star as a prominent and successful Western film personality. In all of his movies, Rogers portrayed the traditional fictional cowboy who individually and effectively dealt with a variety of western problems and scoundrels. Rogers's films, as well as other B Westerns of the period, possessed a strong nostalgic appeal to audiences. They were successors of earlier silent Westerns, which in turn were outgrowths of dime and western adventure novels and Wild West shows. In the uncertain times of the Depression-era 1930s and the war years of the 1940s, these films reassured Americans of their ability to face and survive crises. Rogers and other B Western heroes presented a spirit of optimism and hope, a feeling deeply ingrained in Americans. Perhaps one could not change his or her immediate economic or employment status or do much about the horrors of World War II, but in the darkness of the local theater, Roy Rogers could solve society's problems in about one hour. In that instance, Rogers's B Westerns provided

Dale Evans and Roy Rogers in the 1950s. Used by permission of The Roy Rogers–Dale Evans Museum.

fantasy and escapist entertainment that reaffirmed the role of the mythic West in twentieth-century America.

As Roy Rogers's persona evolved and his career expanded in the early 1940s, his family also changed. In 1942, Roy and Arlene adopted a child, their first daughter, Cheryl Darlene. Within a year, Arlene became pregnant, and in April 1943, she gave birth to their second daughter, Linda Lou. The expansion of the family delighted the couple and, combined with Rogers's professional success, gave them a sense of fulfillment and accomplishment.

About the time that Roy Rogers had his initial success as a Western star, Hollywood began to show interest in Dale Evans. While she was working at WBBM in Chicago, a Hollywood talent agent contacted her requesting a resume and photographs. At first, Evans resisted the inquiries, but ultimately she responded and made the decision to investigate show business in Hollywood. In 1941, she moved to Los Angeles and signed a contract with Twentieth Century Fox studios. Evans's husband and her son, Tom, followed shortly thereafter. Pressure from her agent, who believed the starlet should be twenty-one and single, prompted Evans to deny her son's existence and pass him off as her brother. The decision troubled Evans, but she went along with her agent's request in favor of promoting her own professional career. Her contract with Fox resulted in bit parts in three feature films, which proved disappointing, so much so that she sought a new agent and returned to radio. Her new manager, Art Rush, who happened also to represent Roy Rogers, got her an audition as a vocalist on the *Chase and Sanborn Hour*, a comedy variety show starring Edgar Bergen and Charlie McCarthy. She performed on the show for one year from September 1942 to September 1943 and was subsequently fired because she refused to date the program's advertising executive.

During the year that Evans performed on the *Chase and Sanborn Hour*, she became irritated with Art Rush because he seemed to pay more attention to Roy Rogers's career than to her own. This irritation eventually prompted her to hire a new agent, Danny Winkler, who landed her a contract with Republic Pictures. She made a few rustic musicals before studio officials decided to pair her with Roy Rogers. When she signed with Republic, Evans had no expectation of appearing in Westerns or working with Roy Rogers, but studio president, Herbert J. Yates, saw in Evans's talents an opportunity to enhance the musical Westerns of his top cowboy star. The decision to pair Evans with Rogers worked, and during the next two and a half years, the couple made twenty-one features together. The remarkable ensemble cast, which also included George Gabby Hayes and the Sons of the Pioneers, set a standard for Rogers's Republic Westerns.

In these films, as well as in the seven additional features that Evans made with Rogers in the late 1940s and early 1950s, the couple created a matchless screen combination that captured the public's imagination. Republic's scriptwriters gave Evans substantive roles in which she portrayed smart, independent, and resourceful western heroines, who maintained conventional feminine qualities but reflected roles that fit those of American women in the 1940s. These Republic Westerns established Dale Evans's image as a western performer. It was a role that she assumed easily, and although she wanted nonwestern roles, the elaborate production numbers in these films provided an outlet for her musical talents. In addition to her work at Republic, Evans continued her pop vocal career on the Jack Carson and the Jimmy Durante radio shows and traveled extensively to entertain wartime GIs at bases around the country.

Before Evans joined Rogers at Republic, the cowboy star's Westerns varied widely in content. Initially, some of Rogers's films were period pieces set in the historical West and dealt with the Pony Express, the Civil War, Reconstruction, cattle rustling, and the railroad. In two films, Rogers played dual roles portraying such characters as Billy the Kid in *Billy the Kid Returns* (1938) and Jesse James in *Jesse James at Bay* (1941). By the early 1940s, Republic scriptwriters placed the stories in the twentieth century with more contemporary scenarios. Like *Under Western Stars*, some of the films reflected the times in which they were made. The use of contemporary themes permitted the expansion of musical content in Rogers's features, which prompted an appeal to adult audiences. Moreover, the change occurred in the early days of World War II, about the time when the Sons of the Pioneers joined Rogers in the films. Republic officials may have thought that an emphasis on music and light romantic comedy in Rogers's Westerns provided audiences with escapism and fantasy in troubled wartime. But even with fantasy as a major ingredient, the films mirrored events of the period. For instance, *King of the Cowboys* (1943) contained a World War II theme, and *Hands Across the Border* (1944) emphasized the necessity of positive international relations with Latin American countries during wartime. In the postwar period, *Bells of Coronado* (1950) and *Spoilers of the Plains* (1951) featured Cold War themes, whereas other films focused on contemporary issues. *Heldorado* (1946) dealt with organized crime, and *Springtime in the Rockies* (1947) and *Down Dakota Way* (1949) highlighted the conservation of natural resources.

In addition to these contemporary themes, Rogers's films sought to educate and to entertain juvenile audiences. Within the plot of a film, Rogers sometimes spoke directly to the audience about public issues, morality, patriotism, or the impact of modern technology. Dale Evans, playing a scientist in *Susanna Pass* (1949), provided information on the procedures that hatcheries use in breeding fish, and *In Old Amarillo* (1951) shows Rogers revealing the methods for seeding clouds to produce rain. In his feature Westerns, Rogers felt a responsibility to remind or instruct his young audiences about these issues. Even though residents of the American frontier were often wasteful and thoughtless in the exploitation of natural resources, Roy Rogers in the mid-twentieth century preached the need for a different approach, one that emphasized good citizenship and responsibility. Indeed, he used the images of the American West and the plots of traditional Westerns as subtle learning agents for American youth. In using his heroic or cowboy status to teach others, Rogers effectively connected, in the minds of his young fans, a relationship between contemporary public issues and the mythic American West.

Although Rogers's films were action features about that mythic frontier, music comprised an important component of the productions as well. Obviously, music had been a part of historical ranch life and cowboy work, and in the early twentieth century performers, such as Carl Sprague and Jules Verne Allen in their stage, radio, and recording performances, gave western music a wide audience. It was natural that Hollywood producers would incorporate such music into their Westerns when sound pictures developed in the late 1920s and early 1930s. As previously mentioned, Rogers and the Sons of the Pioneers capitalized on this development when they first appeared in Westerns in the mid-1930s. Moreover, when Republic Pictures signed Rogers as a cowboy actor, they did so because he possessed skills as a singer. Rogers's features usually included five or more traditional western songs, tunes such as "Blue Shadows on the Trail," "Stars Over the Prairie," or "When Payday Rolls Around." The Sons of the Pioneers added a special musical quality to the Rogers films when they joined him at Republic in 1941.

In the mid-1940s, however, the music became more elaborate when producers and directors concluded the features with seven- or eight-minute production numbers that spotlighted Rogers, Dale Evans, the Sons of the Pioneers, and a cast of elaborately dressed singers and dancers performing on lavish sets. The concluding performance of *Man from Oklahoma* (1945), with costumed Indians, dancing Oklahoma pioneers, and the Sons of the Pioneers in Indian garb singing "Cherro, Cherro, Cherokee," provides an interesting example of these ornate musical features. Rogers's musical Westerns, like those of Gene Autry and Tex Ritter, helped to popularize country-western music in a way that few other media forms did. Moreover, they fastened in the American mind Roy Rogers's image as a stereotypical singing cowboy.

Although western music was an important factor in shaping Rogers's persona, he also worked hard in other ways to perfect a heroic cowboy image. He refused movie parts that might tarnish that image and avoided such things as smoking and drinking in public. His youthful fans were important to him, so he sought to portray a spotless cowboy hero. Moreover, his handsome features, quiet unassuming manner, and considerable equestrian skills made him a believable film hero. In the 1940s, Rogers complemented these physical qualities with a stylish western wardrobe of formfitting trousers, colorful shirts, ornate boots, and a tall white hat. Truly, Rogers enjoyed his work and liked the western character that he and Republic molded for his pictures and the public.

Adding substantially to Roy Rogers's western image was his beautiful golden palomino, Trigger, a horse that Rogers used in all of his feature films and the one hundred television shows produced in the 1950s. The cowboy star established a personal connection with the animal from the moment he first mounted the horse and determined early that he wanted to buy him from Hudkins Stables. Rogers initially leased Trigger and then purchased the horse in 1943 for $2,500, paying $500 down and the remaining amount in a lump sum a short time later. Trigger was well worth the price. He was a smart horse, always camera ready, and eager to perform. Rogers carefully avoided overworking the animal and used doubles for Trigger in portions of his films, television productions, and public appearances. Trigger's importance to Rogers's career was confirmed when the horse received billing above all the actors except the star, a fact about which Dale Evans sometimes complained. Further, the studio labeled Trigger as the "Smartest Horse in the Movies." Indeed, Roy Rogers and Trigger, in the minds of most Western movie fans, were inseparable, which added to the star's image of a symbolic American cowboy.

If Trigger helped to shape Roy Rogers's cowboy image, so did Art Rush, who became the star's manager in 1940. Initially based on a handshake, the business and personal relationship between Rogers and Rush lasted nearly fifty years, until 1989, when Rush died. The agreement proved fortuitous for Rogers and provided the star with a measure of financial security. Especially significant was Rush's role in helping Rogers develop financial opportunities outside his work at Republic Pictures. Herbert J. Yates, president of Republic, paid Rogers a miserly salary that placed the star in a state of financial uncertainty. With Rush's help, Rogers became better organized, capitalized on his personal appearances, established his own rodeo, began to endorse products, signed a contract for a comic book series, and in 1944, starred in *The Roy Rogers Show*, a Mutual network radio program. Moreover, Rush's official connection with the RCA Victor Record Company may have prompted Rogers's change from Decca to RCA in the mid-1940s.

Art Rush not only assisted the star financially, but also molded and promoted Roy Rogers's image as a performer symbolizing the mythic American West. Starting in the 1940s and continuing into the 1950s, Rush took Rogers's persona and developed a multimillion dollar merchandising bonanza that enriched the star and stamped his western image on the minds of a new generation of Americans. Rogers possessed a precise image of himself as a western performer, and in conjunction with Rush, he perfected a romanticized likeness of a traditional American cowboy. His flashy western garb, his horse Trigger, his endorsed products, as well as films, radio shows, TV programs, comic books, and personal appearances, all tied Rogers to the West and presented a carefully tailored image to the American public.

Just as Roy Rogers began to expand his marketing activity and gained Dale Evans as a leading lady, the domestic lives of the two stars changed significantly, which directly affected their professional and private lives. Evans and her third husband, Robert Dale Butts, decided to divorce as a result of their active and diverging careers. The parting was an amicable one, and Butts, who also worked at Republic Pictures, later supervised the music on some of Rogers and Evans's Westerns. Meanwhile, death tragically affected Rogers's life in 1946 when his wife, Arlene, died from a brain embolism shortly after the birth of their son, Roy Rogers, Jr. (Dusty). Her death shook Rogers, who depended on Arlene to maintain domestic tranquility in their busy lives. Rogers and Evans were already friends, but with Arlene's unexpected death, their relationship deepened. As Roy confided in Dale about his grief and his worry about his three small children, their friendship grew into love. Sitting astride Trigger, Rogers proposed marriage to Evans as they awaited their cue to enter the arena for one of their rodeo performances. Although startled, Evans said, "Yes." On New Year's Eve in 1947, more than a year after Arlene's death, Roy Rogers and Dale Evans became husband and wife. The marriage initiated a strong personal and professional relationship that lasted until Rogers's death in 1998.

Combining hectic professional and domestic lives presented a challenge to Rogers and Evans, especially with three small children in the family. Evans's son, Tom, was now a student at the University of Southern California. Evans was particularly concerned and worried about making her fourth marriage work. Ultimately, she found peace of mind in her Christian faith, a force that became so important to the couple that they began to incorporate it into their public appearances in the late 1940s. Capping off their rodeo performances with patriotic–religious numbers caused some of their advisors to hesitate, but the determined couple prevailed. In the 1950s, Rogers and Evans introduced Christian themes into the scripts of both their radio and television series. Moreover, they recorded religious music, and in 1953, Evans's book *Angel Unaware* was published, the first of more than two dozen inspirational books she wrote. Even though Rogers and Evans introduced a spiritual element into their public performances, it never overshadowed the western images that they had so carefully developed.

Angel Unaware became a best-seller and was based on the Rogers's experience with their only natural born child, Robin Elizabeth, who suffered from Down's syndrome. Born in 1950, Robin lived for two years. Her death proved painful for the family, but their religious faith, the writing of the book, and the adoption of two additional children, Sandy and Dodie, provided consolation. Moreover, by the mid-1950s, Rogers and Evans internationalized their family by becoming guardians to a young Scottish girl, Marion, and adopting a Korean child, In Ai Lee, who they renamed Debbie.

Shortly before these additions to the Rogers family occurred, a difficult professional issue arose. In the spring of 1951, Roy Rogers's contract with Republic Pictures came up for renewal with negotiations for a new one focusing on the issue of television. The western star wanted to be able to make television appearances and to take advantage of the economic success that his cowboy film competitors, William Boyd and Gene Autry, were having with their television series. Rogers was willing to make an agreement with Republic whereby the studio would produce the television programs, but Republic officials rejected the suggestion. At the same time, and unknown to Rogers or his agent Art Rush, Republic began to prepare the star's feature films for television marketing. Upon learning of Republic's actions, Rogers and Rush obtained an injunction against the studio and then organized a production company to produce their own thirty-minute television Western show.

In October 1951, the federal judge hearing the case ruled in Rogers's favor, and in late December, the initial program of *The Roy Rogers Show* aired on NBC with Post Cereal as its sponsor. Republic Pictures appealed the decision. Finally, in 1954, a federal appeals court, supported by the U.S. Supreme Court, reversed the lower court decision and permitted Republic to edit and market Rogers's Western films for television. By that time, however, Roy Rogers and Dale Evans had established themselves as well-known television stars with a popular network program and sponsor.

The Roy Rogers Show, set in an imaginary Paradise Valley, provided action and excitement for the Baby Boomers of the 1950s. In addition to Roy Rogers and Dale Evans, the show featured their sidekick Pat Brady as well as their horses, Trigger and Buttermilk, a dog, Bullet, and a jeep, Nellybelle. In a little more than five years, NBC aired one hundred episodes of the program. In 1956, Rogers sold rights to the show for more than a million dollars, with reruns continuing to air on the CBS network until the early 1960s. Rogers and Evans controlled the content of the show, emphasizing action and strong doses of morality, yet brutal fistfights spiced the episodes and raised concern about the influence of television violence on children. On the other hand, occasional plots followed Christian themes. Although music was generally not included, except for the closing "Happy Trails" theme song, Dale Evans, for one of the shows, composed "The Bible Tells Me So," a song that crooner Don Cornell put on the pop music charts. Through their television adventure series, Roy Rogers and Dale Evans firmly presented their version of western entertainment for American children and captured a new generation of young fans. Having a family of children the same age as most of their viewers, Rogers and Evans knew the kinds of values they wanted their adventure series to present. Episodes that combined morality plots with basic American and spiritual values fit the conservative Cold War decade of the 1950s.

Roy Rogers's character in the series was that of a settled western rancher and citizen of Paradise Valley. He portrayed the quiet, friendly, and insightful western hero who figured out the schemes of the valley's villains or helped local residents in need. He was peaceful and slow to anger, but if the occasion arose, he used his fists and guns handily, usually two or three times during an episode. He never killed anyone, but he often disabled or disarmed the villain with his fists or with a shot from his trusty six-gun. Roy Rogers, in his television series, assured his young viewers that the mythic cowboy hero was alive and well.

Although Roy Rogers's image reflected the established western hero, that of Dale Evans was less conventional and sometimes contradictory. Her relationship with Roy Rogers in the series was purely platonic. The production decision that excluded romance between the two stars probably resulted from Rogers's past experience with juvenile movie audiences who did not want any "mushy stuff" in their Westerns. In the television series, Rogers and Evans were good friends who talked and worked together to solve local problems but never kissed or showed any overt affection. Dale owned the Eureka Café and served Roy coffee, food, and conversation whenever he was in town. She usually deferred to him in decision making and expressed her feminine nurturing instincts in the stories that featured children, the elderly, and the sick. On the other hand, she shattered that traditional mold by being an independent western businesswoman who had ideas of her own and who on occasion took independent action. Rogers always tried to protect her in hazardous situations, but she was capable of using a gun and frequently came to the hero's rescue with her revolver blazing. In *Ghostown Gold*, Evans shoots the pistol out of a villain's hand when he attempts to gun down Rogers. In *Brady's Bonanza*, she leads a group of townsmen to Rogers's rescue, whereupon a shootout occurs, and she takes the initiative in the gunfight. When the villains are reduced to the use of a single weapon, Dale exclaims, "They're down to one gun. Let's rush 'em." Although Dale Evans portrayed an independent, strong, and fearless western woman, she and the scriptwriters did not abandon the traditional stereotypes applied to American women. The contradictions in Evans's role reflected the changes in American society of the 1950s as more women entered the work force or took increased control of their lives. Regardless of the inconsistencies in her portrayal, Dale Evans created a feminine western character that had lasting appeal.

Both Rogers and Evans's roles in *The Roy Rogers Show* added a family character to the program different from the traditional domestic television sitcoms of the 1950s. Roy Rogers, Dale Evans, Pat Brady, and the local sheriff comprised a western family that regularly met at the Eureka Café to pass the time or decide strategy for solving a local problem. In one sense, *The Roy Rogers Show* was an innocent precursor of *Gunsmoke* with its characters of   the marshal, female saloon owner, doctor, and crusty sidekick. Both shows redefined the family at a time when the American public accentuated the importance of the nuclear family. Ironically, using traditional western plots, the popular show made this redefinition within the context of 1950s values.

Although *the Roy Rogers Show* captured the imagination of young audiences and their parents, the merchandising of more than four hundred Roy Rogers and Dale Evans products entrenched the couple's western image in the minds of American people, young and old. In the mid-1950s, parents bought their children Roy Rogers and Dale Evans products that included lunch boxes, pajamas, bedspreads, lanterns, cameras, toy gun and holster sets, tents, boots, and rocking horses. Two-page layouts of their products appeared in such magazines as the *Saturday Evening Post* and *Life*. Sears Roebuck and Company exclaimed its ads: "It's SEARS for the biggest roundup of Roy Rogers gifts." In the mid-1950s, Roy Rogers Enterprises grossed $35 million annually from the sale of these merchandised products. The two western stars, however, did not stop with endorsement of juvenile products. Businesses used Roy Rogers's face and words to advertise such things as the Magic Chef range, Friskies dog food, and Auto-Lite automotive parts. In 1959, the whole Rogers family, dressed in western garb, appeared in an ad for the Eastman Kodak Company. In addition to the merchandise, Roy Rogers Enterprises sold millions of Roy Rogers, Dale Evans, and Trigger comic books. Businesses and advertisers, capitalizing on Rogers and Evans's celebrity status and western image, recognized the public's nostalgic and positive feelings about America's frontier past. In a time of Cold War uncertainty, any image of the frontier West reassured Americans of their national identity and gave them strength to deal with national responsibilities. With their merchandising, Rogers and Evans took the frontier nostalgia to the youngest members of society and made it a part of their fantasies and their real life. Eight-year-old American children, sleeping in Roy Rogers/Dale Evans pajamas and carrying their colorful Roy Rogers/Dale Evans lunch boxes to school, were never far away from a secure and mythic West.

If their television series, merchandising, and comic books shaped Rogers and Evans's western image, their radio show did likewise. The two stars made their first regular radio appearance together in 1946 on the NBC program *Saturday Night Roundup*, a western musical variety and comedy show. From that program, they moved to a western adventure series on the Mutual Network in 1948 and then in 1951 transferred the show to NBC where it ran for a final four years. Set on a fictional dude ranch, the variety show featured Rogers and Evans's musical talents and the rustic comedy of Gabby Hayes and Pat Buttram. The Sons of the Pioneers added their special western flavor, and guest stars acted in skits that focused on dude ranch life. Although the later episodes of the adventure series were not always set in the West, most episodes included traditional frontier plots with Rogers and Evans over-coming the nefarious actions of western villains. The Republic Westerns had established Rogers and Evans as a western couple, and the radio shows further fixed that image in the public mind.

Rogers and Evans sang on many of their radio shows, and that music as well as their composing and recording advanced their careers as western entertainers. Although Roy Rogers made his first recordings in the early 1930s, Dale Evans did not have a recording contract until the mid-1940s. But together and individually they recorded more than a hundred songs for RCA between 1949 and 1952. These songs ranged from western tunes and children's ditties to spirituals and Christian hymns. A number of them were Dale Evans's own compositions. Even though some people may not recognize "Hazy Mountains" or "T for Texas," millions of Americans know "Happy Trails," which the couple recorded for the first time in 1952. Used as the closing song on their television series, the tune was an instant hit and over the years became as much a part of their western image as Trigger and Buttermilk. Indeed, musical groups as diverse as Van Halen and the Cincinnati Pops Orchestra have recorded variations of the tune. In the mid-1950s, Rogers and Evans added to their western recordings when they released more than fifty songs on Simon & Schuster's Little Golden label. The best of this series is an LP album entitled *Song Wagon: 16 Great Songs of the Old West* (circa 1954–1955), a set of traditional tunes that appealed to a wide audience that accepted the couple's nostalgic and romantic musical interpretation of the West.

Although recordings, radio, television, and films molded and shaped the couple's celebrity image, their numerous personal appearances made them real people to their fans. Over their professional lifetimes the two stars made thousands of appearances at rodeos, state fairs, local festivals, and children's hospitals. They probably made their initial joint tour in the mid-1940s, sometime after their first film together. Month-long tours, covering twenty cities in several states, was a pattern the couple first set in the 1950s. They regularly appeared at Madison Square Garden where they drew enormous crowds. In 1954, Rogers and Evans toured the British Isles doing sixty-five performances. In fact, London possessed the largest Roy Rogers fan club in the world, numbering around 50,000 members. Regardless of where they performed, Roy Rogers and Dale Evans concluded their programs by circling the arena on Trigger and Buttermilk and shaking hands with their fans, an exciting closure that personalized their performances. As with every aspect of the couple's performance career, these personal appearances emphasized the romantic West and reaffirmed their impact on perpetuating the idea of the nation's mythic frontier past.

These public appearances boosted Roy Rogers and Dale Evans's careers in the 1950s when their multifaceted professional lives blossomed. They became superstars with increased moneymaking opportunities. When their television adventure series ended in 1957, the two stars continued to make guest appearances on other television programs, including *The Perry Como Show*, *The Dinah Shore Show*, *I've Got a Secret*, and *The Pat Boone Show*. In 1958, Rogers appeared on an episode of *Bold Journey*, a documentary–adventure show, in which he revealed his skills in speedboat racing and in hunting the Kodiak bear in Alaska. The year 1958 also saw Dale Evans featured in a dramatic role on the NBC series *Matinee Theater*. The following year Rogers and Evans began to host musical variety television shows when they contracted with NBC to emcee the very popular *Chevy Show*. During the ensuing three years, the couple hosted fourteen shows that emphasized their western image and usually featured country-western music or showcased championship rodeos and state fairs. The shows were shot at locations from San Antonio, Texas, to the Cow Palace in San Francisco. One program was even staged at Rogers and Evans's ranch in Chatsworth, California.

Hosting the *Chevy Show* may have had some influence on Rogers and Evans gaining their own variety television show on the ABC network in 1962. *The Roy Rogers–Dale Evans Show* ran for thirteen weeks in the fall of 1962. The two western stars filled their peppy show with a variety of musical and comedy acts that followed specific themes for each individual program. In addition to musical performances by Rogers, Evans, and the Sons of the Pioneers, which provided a regular western component to each show, the series included a broad selection of acts that included tumblers, magicians, and ventriloquists. Although Evans maintained that ABC cancelled the show because it included spiritual music, network executives also paid attention to the program's low ratings. On the other hand, the cancellation did not slow Rogers and Evans's television appearances. Their celebrity status made the couple a natural moneymaking choice as guests or hosts of national television series or specials. In the mid- and late 1960s, they periodically hosted *Hollywood Palace*, a musical variety program, and made guest appearances on such programs as *The Bell Telephone Hour*, *The Andy Williams Show*, and *The Dean Martin Show*.

In addition to their television work in the 1950s and 1960s, Rogers and Evans continued to make recordings, although they shifted recording companies and altered the theme and content of their songs. The late 1950s saw them move from Golden Records back to RCA to record two religious, inspirational albums, *Sweet Hour of Prayer* (1957) and *Jesus Loves Me* (1959). In 1962, the inspirational trend continued as the couple changed recording companies again and made *The Bible Tells Me So,* for Capitol Records. They followed that recording five years later with a holiday album, *Christmas Is Always,* and that same year, Evans cut another religious album, *It's Real.* In the early 1970s, Capitol tried to alter Rogers's image from that of a western ballad singer to a country-western vocalist when it issued three albums: *The Country Side of Roy Rogers* (1970), *Roy Rogers: A Man from Duck Run* (1971), and *Take a Little Love and Pass It On* (1972). Although these recordings may reveal an attempted modification of Rogers and Evans's western image, by that point they had become national icons of America's mythic West. Recognizing that fact, recording companies used the frontier image to market the records.

Rogers and Evans's professional life in the 1960s shifted away from the Westerns and adventure television series that had provided the foundation of their success. Although their television series continued in reruns, the two stars may have thought that Westerns needed a rest since so many aired on television in the late 1950s and early 1960s. Furthermore, the political and social climate of the 1950s changed in the 1960s when it focused on the civil rights movement and the Vietnam War. Within this context, Rogers's Westerns did not seem to fit. Not surprisingly, the hero that Roy Rogers portrayed in his movie, television, and radio dramas lost its appeal as the nation agonized over problems that no single hero seemed able to solve.

Unfortunately, personal tragedy struck the Rogers family in the mid-1960s when two of their children died accidentally. In 1964, their adopted twelve-year-old Korean child, Debbie, died in a car-bus collision while on a church trip in southern California. Their son, Sandy, also adopted, died two years later in an alcohol-related death while serving in the army in Germany. The unexpected loss of two children devastated Rogers and Evans, but their deep religious faith, coupled with a positive outlook, provided them with the strength necessary to cope with the tragedies. Furthermore, the authoring of individual books about Debbie and Sandy helped Evans to deal with the family's grief.

The tragic loss of their children naturally affected Rogers and Evans's professional activities. Even though they slowed their pace a bit, they nevertheless maintained a busy schedule. A trip to Vietnam to entertain the troops put them in contact with both American soldiers and Asians, who reminded them, in a positive way, of their two lost children. About this time Roy Rogers became involved in a Marriott fast food franchise that used his name. Although not directly invested in the management of the chain, Rogers engaged in public relations activities and made personal appearances at store openings. The franchise expanded rapidly, and by the late 1980s when

Marriott sold the franchise to Hardee's, the chain included more than 600 outlets. Revealingly, the removal of Rogers's name from some of the stores caused customer protests, a reaction that prompted Hardee's to reinstate the Roy Rogers logo. The food franchise kept Rogers's name and his western image before the public, thus demonstrating the continuing appeal things western had for Americans.

During the time that Roy Rogers promoted hamburgers and fried chicken, he and Evans moved into their senior years. By the mid-1970s, they were both sixty-five years of age, but being senior citizens did not prompt them to retire. While their professional lives may have become less hurried, idleness was hardly a term that could apply to this couple. They both continued to record music, primarily for Word Records, a company that specialized in inspirational songs. Rogers recorded an album for 20th Century Records, *Happy Trails to You* (1975), that included western tunes and the nostalgic song "Hoppy, Gene, and Me," which climbed to the fifteenth spot on the Billboard country charts. Rogers also generated additional nostalgia when he hosted *The Great Western Cowboys*, a syndicated television program that screened B Westerns from the 1930s and 1940s. He likewise starred in his first feature film since the early 1950s, *Mackintosh and TJ* (1975), a contemporary Western, in which Rogers portrays an aging drifter who helps a troubled Texas teenager. Even though the film received limited distribution and no critical acclaim, it demonstrated that Roy Rogers, at age sixty-four, maintained considerable acting skills.

This film may have provided Rogers with other acting opportunities. In the late 1970s and early 1980s, he appeared in television episodes of *Wonder Woman* and *The Fall Guy*. All of these episodes possessed western themes, and *The Fall Guy* plots closely resembled those of Rogers's old Republic features. Periodically, in this same period, Rogers and Evans appeared on other television programs, ranging from talk shows (*Today, Merv Griffin*) to country and musical variety (*Hee Haw, Barbara Mandrel, Statler Brothers*). Especially important for Rogers and Evans was their nostalgic *Happy Trails Theater*, which aired on the Nashville Network from 1986 to 1989. On this weekly program, the two western stars screened their old Republic features and engaged in nostalgic conversations about their movie-making days. Occasionally, they featured a guest who had worked with them in the films. The popular series introduced a new generation to their films and served to reaffirm the couple's role in perpetuating the concept of the mythic American West.

When Dale Evans was not on television or in a recording session, she traveled the country giving religious concerts and speaking at church gatherings. In the 1980s, she made regular appearances on the shows of televangelists, and in 1985, she aired her own religious talk show, *A Date with Dale,* over the Trinity Broadcasting Network. Evans introduced the show with a song and then interviewed guests that included entertainment figures, religious leaders, or family members. The discussions focused on Evans's spiritual life or that of her guest. Although the show had little to do with the American West, Dale Evans nevertheless capitalized on her cowgirl image by opening the show with clips from *The Roy Rogers Show* or from the couple's Republic Westerns. Furthermore, many of the shows that aired in the late 1990s were filmed in a western setting at the Roy Rogers–Dale Evans Museum in Victorville, California. Interestingly, *A Date with Dale* revealed the reversal of emphases in Evans's career. In the 1950s, she and Rogers accentuated western themes in their performances with a slight touch of the inspirational or religious. In the 1980s and 1990s, Evans focused on Christian and inspirational themes, with regular reminders of her past professional life as Queen of the West.

Both Evans and Rogers reaffirmed those past images in their later musical recordings in the 1980s and 1990s. In 1980, Rogers teamed up again with the Sons of the Pioneers to record "Ride Concrete Cowboy, Ride" for the sound track of the film *Smokey and the Bandit II.* Three years later, the couple made a two-record album, *Many Happy Trails,* with their son Dusty, performing songs that ranged from western and pop to spiritual and patriotic. Although Rogers sang very little in public, in 1989 he recorded a rendition of "Happy Trails" with country-western singer Randy Travis, which was included on his album *Heroes and Friends.* This experience prompted RCA producers to suggest that Rogers cut an album of duets on which he would perform with leading country-western vocalists. When the album, *Tribute,* appeared in 1991, one of the songs, "Hold on Partner," recorded with Clint Black, made the Billboard country charts. Although Rogers, at age eighty, had doubts about whether he could perform well enough to do the album, his natural ability, experience, and strength of voice, combined with modern recording technology, produced a work in many ways reminiscent of his earlier recordings. Moreover, *Tribute,* as much as any recording he made, maintained Rogers's western and cowboy persona, as he performed with other country-western artists such songs as "Tumbling Tumbleweeds," "Little Joe the Wrangler," and "Don't Fence Me In." Within five years from *Tribute*'s release, Rogers and Evans recorded their last album together, *Say Yes to Tomorrow,* a spiritual recording. Both performers were in their mid-eighties, and the frailness of their voices is evident. The only western touch to the album is Rogers's performance of the "Cowboy's Prayer." On the other hand, the couple's duet, "The Best Years of My Life," is a poignant song touching upon the couple's fifty years together as husband and wife.

As Rogers and Evans made this final recording, health problems plagued the couple. Dale Evans suffered a heart attack in 1992 and a paralyzing stroke in 1996. Meanwhile, heart problems had troubled Rogers for years, but other health issues weakened him and depleted his strength, especially in 1996–1997. Despite these physical setbacks, Rogers and Evans continued limited professional activity. When he felt like it, Rogers visited his fans at the Roy Rogers–Dale Evans Museum, and Evans regularly broadcast *A Date with Dale*. Rogers's physical condition deteriorated in 1998, forcing periodic hospital stays. Despite the best efforts of doctors and modern medicine, the ravages of age took their toll, and on July 6, 1998, Roy Rogers died at home in the company of his loving family. His death brought an end to a remarkable individual career as well as a finale to the long-term personal and professional relationship with his wife and partner, Dale Evans.

The careers of Roy Rogers and Dale Evans revealingly represent the romantic and imaginary American West. Through hard work and determination, they captured the imagination and hearts of the American public and audiences worldwide. Through radio, recorded music, films, television, and public performances they entertained generations of Americans, presenting a fantastical, carefree West filled with music and magic. They portrayed the West as a positive place where good always triumphed over evil and justice prevailed. As the familiar singing western cowboy, Roy Rogers focused on that triumph. Dale Evans's portrayal of the strong, independent, properly feminine heroine gave their interpretation of the mythic West a broader dimension than it might have otherwise had. Music lightened this interpretation, as is most evident in Evans's composition of "Happy Trails," which epitomized the couple's approach to the West and to life itself.

The dazzling chemistry between the two performers was apparent from their first joint appearance in 1944, and the magic of that on-screen relationship intensifed when the couple became husband and wife in 1947. Continuing their fictional roles while living and developing domestic and professional realities became a pattern for their half century of marriage. Indeed, the merger of their personal and professional lives achieved a level of success that few performing couples attain. In that achievement they personified and perpetuated the concept and myth of the American West.

three

Gene Autry

Songs, Sidekicks, and Machines

RAY MERLOCK AND JACK NACHBAR

O n October 12, 1987, the ABC show *Good Morning America* included a segment featuring guests Roy Rogers, Dale Evans, and seventy-nine-year-old Gene Autry. Delighted to be interviewing the legendary trio of Western stars, who were dressed in their familiar glittery western garb, anchor Joan Lunden found Rogers and Evans friendly and talkative, especially the hard-of-hearing Rogers, with Autry more quiet and reserved. Actually both Autry and Rogers were at a disadvantage as they had been comparing their hearing aids just before the broadcast and did not have time to reset them properly. Autry, however, who was not accompanied by his spouse, seemed outnumbered and leathery. Seemingly weary of Rogers answering all of Lunden's questions, Autry made a comment by saying, "When I came along as the first singing cowboy. . .," reminding everyone that Rogers was not even locatable in the film business until Autry was firmly established.

Lunden asked Autry about his remarkable success as a businessman. Rogers, not realizing the query had been directed at Autry, blurted out, "Well, I don't know. Just being in the right place at the right time. That's how I feel about it." An obviously irritated Autry shouted back, "Well, I think I learned a long time ago that it's not what you make at the time, but it's how you invest your money."

As time ran out in the interview, which had turned into a mild skirmish, differences between America's two best-known singing cowboys had become apparent. Although Autry had himself occasionally commented that his success was the result "of being at the right place at the right time," that success seems more a result of his knack for being able to extend his fame and fortune from one mass medium to another. His comments also reveal his pride in being an essential contributor in the evolution of the B Western film genre.

As the first "singing cowboy," Autry initiated one of the two most important B Western formulas (the other was the trio Western) of the sound era. The most influential of a second generation of Western heroes, Autry followed in the footsteps of the flashy Tom Mix and Ken Maynard, who both had specialized in fabulous stunts and gaudy clothing. By substituting songs for stunts, and by featuring comic sidekicks and ambiguous time-settings for his stories, Autry and his associates made the B Western palatable to 1930s Western fans, who had gotten used to sound films. These innovations were instrumental in keeping the B Western popular for another generation.

The symbolic roles Autry played in his movies led to his popularity as the top cowboy star of the 1930s and his renewed popularity after his service in World War II. In most of his best films, Gene Autry the movie hero stood between the values of the past and the changing world of the present. By standing between these two time periods, and by heroically triumphing in movie after movie, he suggested to scared Depression audiences and, later, to nervous postwar moviegoers, that they did not have to fear the cultural and technological changes that seemed to be engulfing them. In Autry's Westerns we see cars, tractors, and radios, but we also see traditional family values, the nurturing of children, and help for the downtrodden, all of which is accomplished amidst the confident, comforting warble of memorable, down-home country songs.

The obituaries accompanying Autry's death of lymphoma in 1998 emphasized his role as a popular B Western hero. His initial fame, however, was more closely related to his role as a music performer. Public attention began when the twenty-one-year-old Autry, billed as "Oklahoma's Yodeling Cowboy," secured a job on radio station KVOO in Tulsa and began singing at local high schools, Kiwanis clubs, and parties. The path to Gene's role as a country music singer began with his birth in Tioga, Texas, on September 29, 1907. Autry's autobiography *Back in the Saddle Again* was quite obviously an attempt to create an identity for himself that would compliment his mythic status on the screen. In his autobiography, he presents his childhood as an idyllic, almost Mayberry–like picture of a simple, rural upbringing in small-town Texas and Oklahoma. Orvon "Gene" Autry was one of four children born to Delbert Autry, a footloose horse trader and cattle dealer, and the musically inclined, constantly encouraging Elnora Ozmont Autry. According to Autry, Elnora played the piano, was church organist on Sunday, strummed a guitar in the Latin style, and sang hymns and folk ballads to her children.

Autry's grandfather, William T. Autry, a Baptist minister, gave Gene singing lessons when he turned five and used him as a soprano in his church choir. At age twelve, Gene ordered his first guitar from a Sears and Roebuck catalog. He paid eight dollars for it, money earned baling and stacking hay on his Uncle Calvin's farm. Jobs for young Autry included singing at a local cafe for tips, along with everyday, country-boy chores such as milking cows and slopping hogs. His connection to the movies began when he received a part-time job as a projectionist at the Dark Feather Theater in Achille, Oklahoma. Gene also had an early lesson in selling happy fantasies to crowds. He spent three months traveling with and singing ballads for the Fields Brothers Marvelous Medicine Show where Professor Fields would sell "Fields's Pain Annihilator."

After finishing high school, Gene got a job as a relief telegrapher in the Frisco line, which began his long association with communication technology. In his autobiography, Autry says that when famed cowboy humorist Will Rogers stopped in Chelsea, Oklahoma, to send a telegram one evening in 1927, Rogers heard Gene improvising on a guitar and told him, "You know, with some hard work, young man, you might have something. You ought to think about going to New York and get yourself a job on radio."

The Will Rogers story, as Gene tells it, is an interesting revelation of Autry's own drive and ambition to become a star. Rogers, a legendary cowboy entertainer, passes the mantle on to the young man who would be the next great cowboy entertainer. Whether or not the story is true, it records feelings and hopes Autry had at the time. By 1928 the Frisco Railroad was cutting back its number of employees, and Gene decided his future was as a musician, not as a telegrapher. Using his free railroad pass, the nineteen-year-old Autry traveled first to Chicago, then to New York City.

Although Autry's trip to New York, with $150 savings stored in a sock, proved beneficial, it was not lucrative. His attempts to break into the record industry were unsuccessful, but he did receive good advice from Victor Records executive Nat Shilkret, who told him, "My advice is to go home. Take six months, a year. Get a job at a radio station. Learn to work in front of a microphone."

Autry received a second important bit of advice on his first trip to New York. Oklahoma native and fellow musician Frankie Marvin had just arrived in New York to launch his own music career and shared a room with Autry at the Manger Hotel. Allegedly, during that winter they took turns wearing Frankie's topcoat, the only topcoat between them. Frankie advised Autry to quit the songs he was trying to sing—Al Jolson and other Tin Pan Alley material—and concentrate on country music and emulate Jimmie Rodgers. This is the course Autry chose when he returned to Oklahoma and, at age twenty-one, he found his first paying job on the radio.

Once Autry placed himself firmly in the tradition of "The Singing Brakeman," Jimmie Rodgers, his newly developed blue yodel style earned him increased popularity. He sounded so much like Rodgers that, at one point after the tubercular Rodgers's premature death, a rerelease album collection of Rodgers's vocals inadvertently included one song sung by Gene. By 1931, aware of changing tastes in the marketplace, Autry veered from Rodgers's blues style toward a more sentimental country style. "That Silver-haired Daddy of Mine," sung by Autry and cowritten by Autry and Jimmy Long, with its nostalgic depiction of "a vine-covered shack in the mountains" and an aging father who lives there, became Gene's first big hit. More than 30,000 copies were sold the first month after its release, and, according to Autry's autobiography, it became the first recording in the history of the music industry to earn a gold record, with sales of over one million.

Autry was on his way to fame in two media: recordings and radio. Sears and Roebuck once provided the catalog from which young Autry ordered his first guitar and now was the primary outlet for the Okeh record label, which carried "That Silver-Haired Daddy of Mine." For four years, beginning in 1931, Sears also sponsored *The Gene Autry Program* on WLS in Chicago. At the same time Autry was singing on WLS's *The National Barn Dance*, a program with a national audience. He was also in the process of becoming an exceptionally proficient songwriter. From 1929 to 1959, he applied for copyrights on 338 songs he had either written or cowritten.

The ambitious Autry was ready to ride the range of yet another mass medium: movies. According to film historian Jon Tuska, Nat Levine, the founder of Mascot Pictures, claimed he received half a dozen letters from Autry in 1933 asking for an opportunity to work in pictures. Levine thought Autry to be little more than a local singer, but the persistent Autry wrote continually to Levine until Levine finally relented and put Autry, along with radio coworkers Smiley Burnett and Frankie Marvin, under five-year contracts. Autry's contract called for him to be paid $100 a week.

Levine told Tuska that for the next four months Autry received a primer on being a Western star. Gene took professional dramatic and voice lessons, and, according to Levine, "He wasn't much of a horseman either so I had Tracy Layne and Yakima Canutt teach him how to ride."

Autry's version of his start in pictures differs dramatically from Levine's. It makes him seem more like a heroic savior of B Westerns than Levine's eager-beaver Autry just trying to get his foot in the door. According to Autry, Westerns were in trouble in 1934 because the stars of the silent era were aging, and there was a widespread public movement to cut down on sex and violence in movies. Herbert Yates, owner of a busy Hollywood film lab and soon to be head of Republic Pictures, and Moe Siegel, president of American Records, decided that the straight action Western was a thing of the past and that a new direction for Westerns was essential. Yates then gave Levine the money for a Ken Maynard picture, provided that Autry be brought in for musical interludes in the film.

Whatever the facts about how and why Autry began his Hollywood career, the time was indeed ripe for the emergence of the singing cowboy. The new sound technology in films had set back Western movies in the late 1920s until the first all-talking Western *In Old Arizona* (1929) was a big hit. This film was followed by another all-talking success the same year, *The Virginian,* in which audiences heard Gary Cooper say in his slow drawl, "When you call me that, smile." Westerns had proved to be marketable, and the production of sound Westerns flourished. In 1932, Hollywood released more than one hundred Westerns, and the number would not drop below a hundred until after World War II. Most of these releases were B Westerns, so called because they played second on double features, or were shown on Saturday matinees for young audiences. Most B Westerns ran fifty to seventy minutes in length and were made on low budgets of often much less than $100,000. Singing cowboy Westerns appeared just as the Western genre was regaining popularity, and the musical elements in these films provided wholesome content that took full advantage of the recent developments in movie sound.

Another way Autry and the other singing cowboys that followed his lead were in the right place at the right time was the way in which they were perfect for the tenor of the times. Film historian Andrew Bergman argues that following the inauguration of Franklin Delano Roosevelt in 1933, American movies reflected a renewed faith in the viability of traditional American values within a world of economic uncertainty. Audiences of the day responded to small-town, middle-class, populist values of self-reliance, good neighborliness, and common sense. Screwball comedies, such as *It Happened One Night* (1934) and *My Man Godfrey* (1936), depicted strongly individualistic characters, usually from different economic and social classes, who resolve their differences and fall in love.

Populist hero Will Rogers was the most adored movie star of the early 1930s. He invariably played a wise, folksy sage who reunited lovers, foiled the greedy, made fun of pompous city slickers, and reconciled diverse segments of the small-town community. After Rogers's death in a 1935 plane crash, child star Shirley Temple emerged as the decade's top box-office attraction. A spunky, sweet kid, Temple, like Rogers, specialized in bringing estranged people back together and singing songs of optimism and faith in the future. Meanwhile, director Frank Capra surfaced as another movie icon of the era. Capra created warmhearted, practical heroes such as Longfellow Deeds (*Mr. Deeds Goes to Town*, [1936]) and Jefferson Smith (*Mr. Smith Goes to Washington*, [1939]), who with their simple grass-roots values and Lincolnesque demeanors triumphed over corrupt tycoons and shady politicians.

Gene Autry, the singing cowboy, connected perfectly to this Rogers–Temple–Capra mindset and value system of the late 1930s. He righted wrongs, like other Western heroes, and he radiated confidence, like FDR. Autry was at best a mediocre actor. His slow and wooden delivery of dialogue, however, made him seem relaxed, free of worry, and honest. On top of this there were the songs. Even if he was in jail in one of his movies, he was ready to sing, a symbolic gesture that nothing could really be so bad.

Autry began his movie career with supporting parts in two of aging star Ken Maynard's Westerns, *In Old Santa Fe* and the twelve-chapter serial, *Mystery Mountain* (both 1934). These appearances enabled Autry to observe the great stunt rider Maynard at work. According to Tuska, Autry idolized Maynard and later, when Maynard fell into abject alcoholism and hard times, Autry sent him anonymous monthly checks. Autry's early screen costumes were purposely designed to closely resemble Maynard's. Yet, within a year, Autry would symbolically take over from Maynard in the upper echelon of B Western screen stars. *In Old Santa Fe* mixes big city gangsters and sports cars with stagecoach holdups and galloping horses. This mixing of past and present elements was another aspect of his films that Autry would take over from Maynard. In his first starring film and in most of those that followed, Autry employed the same mixture.

Autry was not the first Western hero to sing on screen. *In Old Santa Fe* includes an opening sequence in which Maynard sings a song on horseback. Earlier Maynard films also included occasional musical numbers as did John Wayne's *Riders of Destiny* (1933) in which Wayne plays a character named Singin' Sandy, who sings a ballad as he walks toward his enemy in a showdown. It has been suggested by some that only after realizing that the tunes in Maynard films had been getting good responses did Levine decide to develop an all-out singing cowboy.

The 1935 twelve-chapter serial *The Phantom Empire*, a project originally considered for Maynard, was Autry's first starring vehicle and would be his only lead role in a serial. Although some critics have found the blend of a contemporary setting, Western characters, and a science fiction plot in the serial "improbable," it proved a fitting beginning for Autry and turned out to be one of Mascot's most popular releases.

The serial is set in present time. The main character, "Gene Autry," and his cowboy musical accompanists live at Radio Ranch where they broadcast on the radio live at two o'clock every afternoon. If Gene fails to appear for a show, their contract will be terminated and the ranch lost. Thus the cliffhanger at the end of most episodes necessitated Autry not only surviving a life-threatening situation but also making it back to the ranch in time for the broadcast.

Autry's friends on the ranch include Oscar (Smiley Burnette) and two adventurous youngsters (Frankie Darro and trick-riding Betsy King Ross). A mysterious group known as the Thunder Riders appears and disappears periodically. They dwell within a futuristic underworld kingdom known as Murania. Gene eventually allies himself with the Muranians, who are being threatened by crooked surface people. In the last chapter of the serial, Gene rides down and captures the chief villain and then proves the crook's guilt by using a Muranian television device.

The Phantom Empire established a number of conventions that became steadfast elements in Autry's later Westerns, which, in turn, influenced a vast number of B Westerns in general. First, Gene Autry's character is named "Gene Autry." Friends call him "Gene," enemies "Autry." The public was already aware that Autry was a performer and radio star. Within the occasionally absurd plot mechanisms, therefore, there was an air of partial reality: Gene, the real person and singer is the same as "Gene," the fictional Western action hero. Republic Pictures, which eventually would absorb Mascot Pictures and become Gene's contracted studio, later used this same ploy of the star and the character standing as the same person in Roy Rogers, Rocky Lane, and Rex Allen films, among others.

The Phantom Empire also was the first of many occasions when an Autry movie cast included children. Frankie Darro and Betsy King Ross portray youngsters who are Gene's devoted friends. Gene, on his part, consistently treats them with respect and concern. Unlike other Western stars who disliked working with children, Autry seemed to enjoy having them in his films and, later, in episodes of his television series.

In the 1940s, Mary Lee, Republic's answer to Shirley Temple and Judy Garland, made nine films with Autry. Autry's Western *In Old Monterey* (1939) includes a sequence where Autry sings at the funeral services of a young boy killed during U.S. Army bombing exercises gone wrong because of unscrupulous anti-American saboteurs. *Prairie Moon* (1938) has a "Dead End Kids" sensibility, and Autry and Smiley Burnette become guardians of three tough Chicago boys whose father was a gangster. Although Gene and Ina Autry never had children, Autry supposedly stated that their children included all the children of the world who idolized the cowboy star and considered him a role model. Besides, featuring kids in his movies gave Gene's Saturday afternoon audiences a way of feeling they were part of the action.

The Phantom Empire and subsequent Republic Autry releases also enlarged the role of the comic sidekick in B Westerns. The sidekick is part of a long-standing literary tradition from Don Quixote's squire, Sancho Panza to Huck Finn's friend, Jim. Earlier western fiction, however, provided no sidekick for Deadwood Dick in dime novels, nor did The Cisco Kid in O. Henry's original short story "The Caballero's Way" travel with a Pancho. Before Autry and Smiley Burnette, sidekicks were also not a fixed element of the B Western. Pat Buttram, a radio and 1940s movie sidekick to Gene, credits Smiley Burnette and his Frog Milhouse character as solidifying the comic sidekick and making it a mainstay of the genre. Throughout Autry's early years at Republic, Burnette, with his strange voice and chubby body, moved right along with him, providing comic relief and funny songs. Together they showed the way for countless other B Westerns, and after the mid-1930s nearly every cowboy star had at least one sidekick to provide slapstick comedy relief.

The rodeo clown was one antecedent for the sidekick. There were others, including characters in medicine shows, vaudeville, and country-western barn dance radio programs.

Autry and Burnette had a successful association in radio prior to their move together to Hollywood, and with them they brought well-developed comic song routines and give-and-take comic exchanges. Burnette made sixty films with Autry and appeared in ninety others. He also supposedly wrote 350 songs, some with Autry, and played more than a hundred musical instruments, despite not being able to read music.

As a classic Western sidekick, Burnett's Frog was stupid, clumsy, and physically unattractive, the opposite of Gene. Yet, like the sidekicks who came later, Frog was passionately loyal, never doubting Gene's innocence if he was unjustly accused. Frog, although generally inept, was also helpful. Autry's movies often ended with Frog, atop his horse, Ring-eyed Nellie, leading a company of riders to assist Gene in his final confrontation with the baddies.

Autry's esteem for sidekicks carried over into his later cordial relationship with Pat Buttram, whom he worked with at Columbia Pictures, on the *Melody Ranch* radio show and on The Nashville Network where the aging pair introduced Autry's films.

An important thematic convention developed in *The Phantom Empire* and used in most of Autry's subsequent Westerns is that the story takes place in a world where past and present time frames are mixed together. This convention had appeared in earlier Westerns. In the plot of *In Old Santa Fe,* Gene's first film, for example, Ken Maynard rides his horse Tarzan but at one point is nearly run over by the heroine's high-powered sports car. In Autry's films, and in many of the Republic Westerns that followed, this mixture of Old West and contemporary ingredients would become a near standard plot device. Autry appeared, to be sure, in Republic and Columbia Westerns that were set in the traditional Old West period from 1870 to 1890, but these Westerns usually proved less interesting than those set in a more mythic time where the past and present intermingled. The usual Autry Western was set in the 1930s or 1940s, the year of the film's release equating to the time when the story occurs. Within this contemporary setting, however, characters still rode horses and wore six-guns.

Many of Autry's films, as in *The Phantom Empire,* took place within a modern show business background, which served to emphasize the mythic time-frame of the story. In *The Big Show* (1936), for example, Autry plays a double role: the good-natured, hard-working movie stuntman, Gene Autry, and the disagreeable leading man, Tom Ford, who cannot sing, is rude, and is being pursued by gangsters because of bad gambling debts. When Ford disappears, Autry agrees to appear as Ford at the 1936 Texas Centennial State Fair. At the climactic scene, Gene rides down and captures the gangsters, and wins the girl and the public's adulation with his singing and his generous attitude.

In his films, Autry often was a radio star who drew on his popularity with the listening audience to convince citizens of a recommended course of action related to the public good, in the same way that FDR sold his New Deal policies via his Fireside Chats. In *The Old Barn Dance* (1938), horse trader Autry's radio appearances enable him to conclude and then to make the argument that tractors are better than horses for plowing. Then, in an Old West way, Gene and his horse Champion ride after, catch up with, and capture the bad guys, who are trying to escape in a fast car. In two other Autry films, *Public Cowboy No. 1* (1937) and *The Big Show,* he initiates a radio broadcast message, "Calling All Cowboys," that assembles the needed forces who jump on their horses and capture the villains.

Gene Autry in The Old Barn Dance *(1938). L. Tom Perry Special Collections,
Harold B. Lee Library, Brigham Young University, Provo, Utah.*

The contemporary elements of modern technology presented in Autry's films perhaps stems from his early jobs as a telegraph operator and radio personality, which ultimately carried over into his movies. For example, in *The Phantom Empire*, as well as in such later films as *South of the Border* (1939), Gene uses his knowledge of Morse Code to relay messages for heroic purposes. Furthermore, he uses radio not merely as an excuse to sing but to inform good people and foil crooks as well.

Other recent technological developments also appear in some of Autry's Westerns. Autry advocates irrigation projects and dam construction in *Red River Valley* (1936). In *In Old Monterey* he communicates the need for military preparedness amidst the devastation in Europe. Television serves as a source of useful information to a group of Native Americans in *The Last Roundup* (1947). Thus, even though Champion can catch up to any train or speed to the rescue when automobiles bog down in riverbeds, overall in Autry films modern technology seeks to improve life, not impede it. Unlike *Stagecoach* (1939), in which the heroic couple is "saved from the blessings of civilization," in Autry Westerns, civilization does bring blessings. The former telegraph operator turned radio and recording artist was a living example of such blessings.

In countless film versions of the western myth, the hero helps vanquish the wilderness, the barbaric, and the greedy. However, because of his proclivity for violence, he cannot remain as part of the new order he helps bring about. *Shane* (1953), Ethan Edwards in *The Searchers* (1956), or Tom Doniphon in *The Man Who Shot Liberty Valance* (1962) are psychologically, spiritually, and physically cut off from the civilized, family oriented West that their guns help secure. Autry, on the other hand, is their smiling, likable, progressive antithesis. Beginning with the Autry films of the mid-1930s, optimism about reconciling the rural and the urban, the garden/prairie and the machine, led to a new kind of Western and a new sociocultural outlook. Children who grew up watching Gene Autry (and, later, Roy Rogers) movies may have dreamed of six-guns and horses, but, perhaps more important, they saw a heroic Gene Autry receptive to technology, understanding how it functions, and amicably convincing others of its potentiality.

It is certainly understandable how the rural and youth moviegoers who were Autry's main audience might have feared the future in the chaotic 1930s and 1940s. By combining a positive attitude toward new technology with material symbols, action sequences, and an espousal of traditional values associated with the Old West, Gene's B Westerns calmed these fears.

The most obvious new B Western ingredients in *The Phantom Empire* and

Autry's later movies were the singing cowboy hero and the inclusion of musical numbers as part of the story. Autry's earnest belief in the power of music made him a workable emissary and advocate for his songs. In one scene in *The Phantom Empire*, Autry, accused of a murder he did not commit, fulfills his contract to perform on a daily afternoon radio broadcast by hiding in a barn and singing a song on a remote hook-up while the sheriff and his men use a battering ram to break down the door and apprehend him. Despite the concerns of his young allies, Frankie and Betsy, Autry refuses to cut short the song even though capture seems imminent. In his first feature film, *Tumbling Tumbleweeds* (1935), Autry's song at a medicine show wagon enchants the crowd except for two hostile, music-hating badmen. Autry bests the two jeering agitators in a fistfight, thus sanctioning the singing cowboy's manly essence and his right to be heard and appreciated.

Country music historian and critic Douglas Green argues that Autry and the singing cowboy elevated what had previously been called "hillbilly music" to a higher plateau, infusing it with the romanticism and purposefulness of the cowboy. Autry's care with a song always involved clear diction and phrasing. He also imparted the comforting sense that he was personally enjoying the act of singing a song. In close-up, Gene would seem to glow with happiness whether he was serenading an attractive woman who had earlier spurned him, performing a comedy number with Smiley Burnette, or singing a song about the wonders of the western landscape.

Music allowed for increased diversity in the Western and a new perspective on the qualities that made for a Western hero. In typical B Western fashion, the capture of the bad guy necessitated the villain getting away on horseback and the hero overtaking him on his own trusty steed. The hero would leap from the saddle, hurling himself and the criminal off their horses into a ravine where, after a few punches, the agile hero would subdue the beat-up evil doer. Autry films included this type of ritualized action, but they added a variety of musical numbers. As a Western hero, Autry was a good-looking young man, but he was not physically tall or imposing. It was while he was singing that he seemed most admirable. In close-ups during a song, Autry exuded an aura of friendly, self-confidence that made firm the value of his music and of his own worth as a singer. He was a man deserving of affection, respect, and admiration. According to historian Douglas Green, it was Autry's amiable singing persona that sold the songs and the hero who sang them.

His gentle, soothing voice created a feeling of intimacy between the singer and his listeners. His guileless honesty was to be particularly effective on film: bashful, sincere, and unaffected, his character was believable, likable, a boy next door. It was a perfect voice for radio and record, intimate and unthreatening, so unlike the stage-trained belters, the slick pop crooners, or the rough-hewn hillbilly (later to be called "country") music of the era.

Many of the songs that Autry sang in his films became not only commercial hits but popular standards as well. "Back in the Saddle Again" from *Rovin' Tumbleweeds* (1939) and used as Autry's theme song on his *Gene Autry Show* (1950–1956), "Tumbling Tumbleweeds" from *Tumbling Tumbleweeds*, "Blueberry Hill," from *The Singing Hill* (1941), and "Mexicali Rose" from *Mexicali Rose* (1939) are only four of dozens of examples.

Ultimately, Autry's historical importance to singing cowboy Westerns is more than his merely being the first singing cowboy hero. His own unwavering position as an advocate as well as a creator/performer of music initially sold the public on singing cowboys and musical sequences in Westerns. For the next twenty years, other motion picture singing cowboys followed in his footsteps. Among these were Tex Ritter, Roy Rogers, Eddie Dean, Jimmy Wakely, and Rex Allen. Singing cowboy Westerns remained popular until television, changing movie markets, and increased budget costs ended the B Western genre in the early 1950s.

The Autry hero straddled the Old West past and the technological present by living in a West where different time periods merged and by creating contemporary musical hits within traditional country-western music. It is not surprising, then, that Autry's relationships with other characters in his movies also revealed both old and new attitudes and perceptions.

Autry was twenty-eight years old when he starred in *The Phantom Empire* for Mascot and in four other 1935 releases for Republic. Yet, on screen he seemed younger, smaller, and more vulnerable than other celluloid Western heroes. Many of his movies in the 1930s exploited these characteristics by having him portray a young man seeking to win his father's respect (*Tumbling Tumbleweeds*, *Yodelin' Kid from Pine Ridge*, [1937]), or help an older father figure who raised him but has fallen into disgrace (*Public Cowboy No. 1, Colorado Sunset*, [1939]).

In these films, Autry displays an old-fashioned respect for his father or father figure, but in being the only person who can help, he becomes the leader of the present such as Autry did himself in his relationships with Will Rogers and Ken Maynard. In *Yodelin' Kid from Pine Ridge*, Autry's father disowns his son, believing that Gene has been a coward and fled from battle. In actuality, Autry had saved his unconscious father's life. The two are finally reconciled when Autry unmasks and captures the rustlers who have been stealing his father's cattle. In *Public Cowboy No. 1*, a sheriff is thought to be too old and out of touch to deal with rustlers who are using airplanes, refrigerated trucks, and two-way radios in their cattle-stealing operation. Autry's usual understanding of contemporary technology (a "Calling All Cowboys" broadcast summons a posse) and the traditional value of a good horse (Champion successfully carries Gene in pursuit of the outlaws who are escaping in automobiles) allows the young hero to outdo city detectives, apprehend the rustlers, and restore his surrogate father's good name and position in the community. In other films, Autry assisted the heroine's troubled father, invariably her sole surviving parent.

Women in Autry's Westerns to some degree conform to their traditional roles in action films, their main purpose being to provide romantic interludes from the action and to be rescued by the hero. On the other hand, in Autry's movies, they were much more than, in the words of Douglas Green, "helpless prairie flowers." They were "modern women" of the 1930s and 1940s, often with the same attributes as their screwball comedy counterparts: wit, sass, defiance, intelligence, and independence. Many of them held jobs or ran their own businesses or labored as their father's chief assistant in his business. Occasionally, the heroine was a dilettante who inherited a ranch and desired only to return to a life of leisure. Under Autry's influence, she realizes that her eastern-bred beau and her previous system of values are inferior to the western values of hard work, community service, and personal responsibility.

Initially, women in Autry's movies tend to find him bumbling or offensive. In a typical scenario, Autry woos a woman with a song especially intended for her, which carries with it an earnest sentiment of personal devotion, and her heart melts. Autry obviously enjoys being with women in his Westerns, and it is not unusual for him to initiate an active courtship. Elements of romance are stronger in his films than in most other B Westerns.

The spunky Gail Davis became Autry's favorite leading lady in the 1940s. She appeared in fourteen of Autry's Columbia releases and later starred as the sharp-shooting, trick-riding heroine in eighty episodes of the television series, *Annie Oakley* (1952–1956) for Autry's Flying A Productions. The program allowed Davis, a skilled rider and a crack shot, to do much of her own stunt work and secured her place in television history as the first woman to star in a weekly Western series.

Ethnic minority characters are also poised between the old and the new in Autry's movies. They often reflect traditional stereotypes and are treated by Autry with some degree of patronizing paternalism. At the same time, they are generally more prominent in Autry films than in other Westerns and often, especially in musical numbers, are treated with admiration and respect. African Americans fare less well than other groups. *Round-Up Time in Texas* (1937), for example, which takes Gene and Frog to Africa, contains some alarming stereotypes of breechcloth-clad Africans hurling spears and capturing white intruders. They are easily won over by music and magic tricks. On the other hand, Autry sometimes featured African Americans in the musical sequences in his Westerns. The talented Cabin Kids appear in two Autry films, *Round-Up Time in Texas* and *Git Along Little Dogies* (1937), providing upbeat, hand-clapping spirituals and boogie-woogie numbers. Another prominent African-American entertainer, Cab Calloway, appeared with Autry in *Manhattan Merry-Go-Round* (1937).

Autry's films were popular in urban ghetto areas, but the only African-American singer–actor to follow Autry's lead and star in singing cowboy B Westerns was Herb Jeffries (billed as Herb Jeffrey), a onetime vocalist with the Duke Ellington Orchestra. Filmed on tiny budgets, *Harlem on the Prairie* (1937), *Harlem Rides the Range* (1939), *The Bronze Buckaroo* (1939), and *Two-Gun Man from Harlem* (1940) embraced many of the same plot components and character types as Autry's Westerns. They provided an African-American Western hero role model for black children, and despite their limited and selected release, the films made money. In the late 1990s, Herb Jeffries and his singing cowboy films were acknowledged and honored with a retrospective at the Autry Museum of Western Heritage.

Latin American characters, settings, and music also are prominent in several Autry films. His movies did well in Latino markets, and on occasion Autry sang in Spanish. The popular hit song "El Rancho Grande" in 1935 was followed by other Autry songs with an Hispanic connection, "South of the Border," probably the best known. The singing cowboy tradition in recordings and films is strong even today in Mexico recordings and films.

Similar to the way women and African Americans were portrayed in Autry's films, the depiction of Hispanic and Hispanic-American characters was mixed. Although Autry's character loves Mexican songs and celebrations, for example, his regard for Mexican culture and ritual in such films as *Down Mexico Way* (1941) and *The Big Sombrero* (1949) seems condescending. Autry receives a comeuppance for this attitude in *South of the Border* (1939), when he falls in love with a señorita but loses her when she becomes a nun to redeem her family's honor after her hot-headed brother, duped by foreign agents, is killed leading an ill-fated revolution.

Native Americans are usually portrayed in a positive way in Autry's Westerns, although Autry's paternalism is once again obvious as it is the heroic Autry who must save the Indians. In an early film, *Ride, Ranger, Ride* (1936), cavalry officer Autry unmasks a corrupt Indian agent who, for personal gain, is inciting Comanches into looting and plundering. In his autobiography, Autry recalls what he witnessed growing up in Oklahoma: "Three of the popular pastimes of the young rogues of the day were drilling for oil, drinking moonshine whiskey, and cheating Indians. They were mostly Choctaw and Cherokee. . . . I had seen the Indians exploited and considered it then, as now, a tragedy. . . . Later, when I made my own pictures, I had no taste for the stock cowboys-and-Indians scripts and we avoided them." This attitude is revealed in Autry's production for Columbia Pictures' *The Last Round-Up* (1947), which was, out of all Autry's films, his personal favorite. In the film, an Indian spokesman (Jay Silverheels) joins Autry in a television hook-up in 1947 to persuade a Native American tribe to relocate to better terrain the government is providing.

In 1996, Vine Deloria, Jr., executive director of the National Congress of American Indians and the author of *Custer Died for Your Sins*, stated during an event in Autry's honor, "If any graduate students are looking for a topic to consider, they should look no further than Gene Autry, a true genius in singing the songs of the people. His songs made us feel better—and be better people. He may be the greatest living American."

Gene Autry's Cowboy Code, also called "The Ten Commandments of the Cowboy," was well known to his youthful fans. If Autry was not always perfect in his gender or ethnic treatments of his characters, his intentions toward these characters are, perhaps, best expressed in the fifth commandment of the Cowboy Code: "He must not advocate or possess racially or religiously intolerant ideas." This lesson is taught in a sequence from the television series *The Gene Autry Show*. Gene overhears a boy complain about a new Mexican student in school and then explains to a multicultural classroom of school children that "Americans," except Native Americans, who were already here, were once all immigrants. He concludes that anyone now living in the United States should be recognized warmly and greeted enthusiastically as an "American." The boys shake hands as their classmates, teacher, and Gene all look on approvingly.

Autry made sixty-three Westerns for Republic prior to enlisting in the Army Air Corps in 1942. On July 5, 1942, at the army's request, he was sworn in on a live broadcast of *Melody Ranch*. During the war, he earned his pilot's wings and flew cargo planes to North Africa, India, China, and Burma. He also experienced the difficulties of subsisting on military pay, which increased his personal ambition to amass a permanent fortune. After returning from the war, Autry made five more films for Republic and then moved to Columbia Pictures where he secured larger budgets, maintained complete control over his films, and received half the profits. His popularity remained when he returned to the screen. Supposedly, when his first postwar film, *Sioux City Sue,* was released in 1946, audiences cheered so rigorously when Autry appeared singing his first song that no one could hear the lyrics. At Columbia he made thirty-two Westerns, and he pioneered the marketing technique of using his television series to prod audiences into also seeing his films.

Long accustomed to working seven-day workweeks making movies, doing his radio series, and making personal appearances, Autry increasingly expanded his professional activities. Now, however, his investments went beyond show business and the mass media into such enterprises as oil, ranches, and hotels. Along the way, Autry's performing interests expanded into a fourth mass medium, television. During the early 1950s, Autry's Flying A Productions was one of the first companies to make half hour television Westerns. Besides the *Gene Autry Show* and *Annie Oakley*, Flying A also made *The Range Rider* (1951–1953), *Buffalo Bill, Jr.* (1955), and *The Adventures of Champion* (1955–1956). These shows were meant for a young audience, similar to the Saturday crowds that earlier had flocked to Autry's B Westerns.

Autry took another new direction toward reaching a youthful audience in the late 1940s and early 1950s with the release of several Christmas songs that have since become children's classics. While riding Champion down Hollywood Boulevard for the 1946 Christmas parade, he heard children exclaim "Here comes Santa Claus!", which inspired the hugely popular song. "Rudolph the Red-Nosed Reindeer" came out in 1949 when Autry's wife Ina talked him into reconsidering the Johnny Marks song that Gene had originally rejected. "Rudolph" became not only Autry's all-time best seller, but one of the most successful music recordings in history. Other holiday tunes, such as "Peter Cottontail," "The Night Before Christmas Song," and "Frosty the Snowman," ensured that future generations would grow up listening to Gene Autry during the holidays. Autry has played an integral part of American childhoods since the 1930s—for those in the 1930s and 1940s through his Westerns, for those in the 1950s through his television series, and for all through his holiday songs.

Autry's long-term influence on adults was in part derived from his consistently being included on *Fortune*'s Wealthiest Men in America list (in the 1990s, his estimated worth was $300 million). No longer was the cowboy hero stereotyped as a penniless drifter wandering the range doing good deeds for nothing. Autry showed that you could walk from the ranch corral into the corporate boardroom. Perhaps Autry's amassing of immense wealth while maintaining public popularity influenced the development in 1960s television of benevolent tycoons in Western series such as Ben Cartwright of *Bonanza* or Victoria Barkley of *The Big Valley*.

Autry's last notable foray into American mass entertainment was his purchase of the Los Angeles (later California) Angels Major League baseball franchise in 1961. When he bought the Angels, Autry closed a major chapter in American mythology. The nineteenth-century mythic American cowboy hero had united with baseball, that equally mythic American ritual of the twentieth century. The Angels retired number twenty-six in honor of Autry (the twenty-sixth man on the club) and in 1999 named their spring training park Autry Field.

Possibly to insure his own legacy, Autry provided millions for the construction of the Autry Museum of Western Heritage in Los Angeles. Modeled after other notable monuments to the West (such as the Cowboy Hall of Fame in Oklahoma City and the Buffalo Bill Historical Center in Cody, Wyoming) the Autry Western Heritage Museum is about more than Autry's life and his films. Exhibits on movie and television Westerns are also included, as well as exhibits on specific subjects such as Native Americans and the historical development of the West. The museum also includes research facilities and support for scholars.

Such a facility was probably not necessary to insure Autry's place in American movie history. As the facts from his life clearly show, in every mass medium he entered, Autry was the most popular and successful of all the B Western singing cowboys. He even led *Motion Picture Herald*'s top-ten list of moneymaking Western stars from 1936 to 1943, when he was out of the movies in the Army Air Corps. When he returned to making Westerns, he was second on the list to his singing cowboy counterpart, Roy Rogers, from 1947 to 1954. During the early 1940s, he was so popular that he even placed high on the overall list of box-office stars, finishing fourth in 1940, just behind Mickey Rooney, Spencer Tracy, and Clark Gable. He was sixth on the list in 1941 a year later. Other than Roy Rogers finishing tenth in 1945, no other B Western star in history has ever made the top ten. Autry's weekly radio program *Melody Ranch* lasted sixteen years, almost to the end of program radio. He had a popular television show for six years and sold millions of records during his era, second in sales only to Bing Crosby. Autry's awards and honors outnumber almost any other entertainer of his era: member of the Country Music Hall of Fame, member of the National Cowboy Hall of Fame, and the only entertainer with five stars on the Hollywood Walk of Fame (one for film, one for recordings, one for radio, one for television, and one for live performances such as rodeos and concerts).

The fall 1998 issue of *American Benefactor* listed Autry as, at the time, number seventeen, among the one hundred most charitable benefactors with $172 million in donations. It was rumored that, at certain times in his life, Autry's public persona differed from his private self. Autry himself admitted in his autobiography to a long-time drinking problem, which he was finally able to control. It is the public Gene Autry, however, that will be his legacy and what he will be remembered for—the shy, friendly young man who valued his past and confidently embraced the future and through that embrace became a hero to millions.

Autry's reputation undoubtedly benefited from the fact that both he and his rival and counterpart Roy Rogers lived such long lives. From the 1930s to the present day, they never faded from the public eye. The question whether one prefers Gene or Roy often seems as much a part of American life as the choice between Pepsi or Coke. Certainly no examination of the Western, or of the forces that influenced popular entertainment in the twentieth century, would be complete without a consideration of Gene Autry, millionaire entrepreneur, multimedia star, and the first singing cowboy.

◆ four ◆
John Ford
Western Mythmaker

RONALD L. DAVIS

irector John Ford, the most honored of Hollywood's old masters, lifted the Hollywood Western to epic proportions. Until World War II inexpensive Westerns were a financial mainstay of the American movie industry, but Ford not only filmed box-office successes, he heightened the nation's creation myth by raising the Western to its fullest potential. "Is there anything more beautiful than a long shot of a man riding a horse well, or a horse racing free across a plain?" the director once asked.

With his instinct for composition, color, action, and storytelling, Ford created enduring cinematic masterpieces that bear his unmistakable signature. He filled the screen with the western landscape and men of action, extending the legends of America's frontier past rather than reconstructing historic facts. He managed to show truth while glorifying personal freedom, adventure, courage, and conquest. Ford captured the spirit of the heroic frontier with grandeur and eloquence. His men of the West spoke a language he understood, and the iconoclastic director identified with his heros' outlook and basic values. "They had a warm, rugged, natural good humor," the filmmaker said of frontiersmen. "Strong people have always been able to laugh at their own hardships and discomforts."

In Western mythology the hero often matures by destroying monsters, and violence remains an essential component in Ford's frontier West. The frontier hero in a Western may not develop emotionally, but he habitually triumphs by slaying whatever demons impede civilization's progress. Although Ford's heros make contributions to society, conflict exists between the heroic individual and society. Ford rarely deals with one's internal turmoil. Rather, it is the external person overcoming obstacles combined with public discord that is a primary theme in Ford's work. His West is primarily a masculine world in which women, albeit strong, are generally depicted as prostitutes, crones, or buttressing forces to their men.

John Ford, Director. Courtesy of Lily Library, Indiana University, Bloomington, Indiana.

Over the course of his career, Ford's view of the individual in frontier society shifted. In general, he glorified the heroic loner at odds with the community he ultimately protects. The director's post–World War II cavalry trilogy focused on a military regime Ford had recently experienced and come to admire during his stint with the Field Photographic Unit, assigned to both the Pacific and Atlantic theaters of the war. By the mid-1950s, the filmmaker recognized the tragic aspect of the man who remained outside society, and by the early 1960s he acknowledged the pitfalls of violence and individual action without legal sanction.

The frontier had closed almost a quarter of a century before John Ford arrived in Hollywood in 1914, but unemployed cowhands still drifted across the western mountain ranges hoping to find jobs as wranglers and stunt performers in the studios' action films. Ford fell in love with moviemaking and enjoyed the companionship of motion picture cowboys, who told him stories of the West and represented a hardy breed the director admired. Ford capitalized on the current popularity of Westerns and tried to bring an element of authenticity to Hollywood's depiction of the frontier by working in remote on-location areas, particularly Monument Valley. His Westerns are a blend of myth and reality, filled with celluloid images often compared with the paintings of great western artists such as Frederic Remington and Charles M. Russell.

Born in 1884 outside Portland, Maine, of Irish parents, Ford understood the plight of the outsiders he depicted in his films. Young Jack followed his brother, actor–director Francis Ford, to Hollywood, and began his movie work as a stuntman and occasional actor. From the outset, the youth was fascinated with the camera, and in 1917 he was given an opportunity to direct his first film, *The Tornado*, a two-reeler, at Universal. The scenario, which Ford wrote, centered around a cowboy, played by the director himself, who rescues a banker's daughter from a gang of outlaws and uses the reward money to bring his mother over from Ireland. The filmmaker later dismissed the movie as "just a bunch of stunts," but it contains a combination of action and sentimentality that became Ford's signature.

The Soul Herder, also made in 1917, was the first of the director's twenty-six Westerns starring Harry Carey. Time and again in these films Carey played a saddle-tramp, Cheyenne Harry, a man who looked like a working cowhand and was at odds with the law. The actor dressed for the part in an old flannel shirt, a vest, patched overalls, and a gun stuck in his belt with no holster. Although Cheyenne Harry was a hard-riding, fast-shooting cowboy, he was human enough to appear disheveled and lose fights in which he was outnumbered.

In contrast to the intensity of William S. Hart's good badguys, Carey played his hero in a lighter, more natural vein, performing routine chores such as putting out rock salt and mending fences.

Ford concurred with Carey's realistic approach to making Westerns, and together they extended the concept. "Louse up your hero," became an early Ford dictum. "Get him thrown in jail if possible. Have him arrested for stealing a horse or something. Heros shouldn't be holier-than-thou and namby-pamby. Heros shouldn't be clay statues, but they should have feet of clay." The young director thought that Carey's depiction was not only truthful but would win wide acceptance with mass audiences.

Most of Ford's pictures with Carey were shot at the actor's ranch, near Saugus, just north of Los Angeles. Although there was a three-room house on the property, the two men wanted to emulate real pioneers while they worked and slept in bedrolls out in an alfalfa patch. At night they sat around the kitchen table with a wood fire in the stove, drinking and talking until the wee hours of the morning, with Ford taking notes. The next day they would shoot what they had discussed the night before. If they needed a leading lady, Harry's wife, Olive, was recruited; otherwise she was in charge of cooking.

Crews on the first Cheyenne Harry pictures consisted of Ford, Carey, a property man, an assistant director, and a writer to put a rough continuity on paper after the movie had been shot—enough to satisfy the story department at Universal. The first pictures the team made were one- and two-reelers, shot in four or five days. Eventually, the Cheyenne Harry movies proved popular enough that they quickly grew in length to five reels.

During the three years he worked with Harry Carey, Ford developed many of the characteristics that would remain his hallmarks: a hero uncomfortable with social responsibility; a cinematic eye for landscape; a straightforward approach to storytelling; romance combined with authenticity; artful composition with minimal movement of the camera; and, above all, forceful imagery. Although Ford and Carey relied on dime-novel plots, they blended action, plausible characters, and compelling situations in an artistic way. Women played marginal roles in their films, and their male heros were gentle and redeemable, although far from perfect.

In 1921, after directing twenty-nine features for Universal in less than four years, Ford signed a long-term contract with the Fox Film Corporation for more money. Soon after joining Fox he made two pictures with Tom Mix, a flashier Western star than Harry Carey. Mix's approach was unrealistic and full of show business tricks, but the actor started a trend that continued throughout the 1920s. Unlike his older brother, Ford adjusted to the current vogues in Westerns. In 1924, he was catapulted to the top of his profession by his silent masterpiece, *The Iron Horse,* an epic that chronicles the building of the nation's first transcontinental railroad, which Ford saw as symbolic of the Anglo-American conquest.

Studio executives awarded the director the largest budget of any Fox picture to date — $450,000. For the movie's star the filmmaker chose George O'Brien, an athlete and former property boy who had worked at Fox as a stuntman and assistant cameraman. Ford approached the project with enthusiasm, viewing the story as a grand milestone in the young nation's progress: through the wonders of technology, the United States had reached its inevitable destiny and spanned the continent. To enhance the spectacle, Fox sent the company to Wadsworth, Nevada, near Reno, where most of *The Iron Horse* was filmed. Since there were no housing facilities on the location selected, the studio hired a train with sleeping cars from the A. G. Barnes Circus. A railroad construction town was built for the picture, and some of the workers moved into the shacks constructed as sets and slept there. "We all lived exactly like real railroad tracklaying crews did fifty years earlier," wrote Hollywood Indian actor Iron Eyes Cody. "We slept in tents and ate out of tins and had a wonderful, miserable time of it."

Since the plot called for "the largest band of Indians" the director could gather, Sioux, Pawnee, Cheyenne, and nearby Paiute were brought in and told to wear traditional tribal dress for the picture. During the filming of crowd scenes, Indians played Chinese laborers, and the forty Chinese crew members played Indians. For the joining of the rails at Promontory, the Central Pacific lent the company the original "Jupiter" locomotive, whereas the Union Pacific lent "Old 119," a twin engine used on the early transcontinental line.

The Iron Horse was the first movie to play at Grauman's Egyptian Theater in Hollywood and opened in New York at the Lyric Theater, where it played for almost ten months. Film celebrities, as well as leaders from the railroad world, attended the premiere. Despite its melodramatic plot, the epic exhibited effective dramatic composition and embodied characteristics for which Ford would become famous: broad humor, Irish references, adoration of Abraham Lincoln, Indians grouped along the crest of a hill, dogs barking, and intense action. Perhaps the greatest shot in the film comes with the Indian attack on the train, when Ford shows their shadows against the cars, poetry in motion achieved with a second camera. The Native American is depicted in the film as a hazard, standing in the way of civilization's progress. Immigrants, on the other hand, band together, overcome deficiencies, and are transformed in the service of their adopted country. Ford punctuates his story with heroic images, and there is no hint of the capitalistic motives behind railroad building. Heros have triumphed, and the expanding nation has had its boundaries joined.

The director's last silent Western, *Three Bad Men* (1926), mixed courage with greed and climaxed with a land rush that involved 150 wagons dashing into unsettled territory. Much of the picture was photographed near Jackson Hole, Wyoming, at the foot of the Grand Tetons, although the land rush was shot on a dry lake bed outside Victorville, California. To add humanity at the height of the action, Ford placed a baby on the ground, with wagons racing past at a terrific speed before the infant is rescued just in the nick of time. "Several of the company had been in the actual land rush," the director claimed. "They'd been kids and rode with their parents. So I talked to them about it. The incident of snatching the baby from under the wheels of a wagon actually happened."

With the introduction of sound, outdoor filming that involved dialogue was difficult at first. By the late 1930s, Westerns had fallen out of favor with the American public, except for the inexpensive double-bill oaters churned out by Republic, Columbia, and Monogram. Ford did not return to the genre until 1938, when he began work on *Stagecoach*.

Based on "Stage to Lordsburg," a story by Ernest Haycox that had appeared in *Collier's* magazine, the movie is peopled with Bret Harte–like characters who journey across Arizona by stagecoach toward New Mexico amid an Apache uprising. Dudley Nichols, one of Hollywood's most respected screenwriters, constructed a script for the picture in close consultation with Ford, who insisted that a Western should be intelligent and contain a basic moral quality. "The people who coined that awful term 'horse opera' are snobs," the director said. Ford urged Nichols to write the way people speak and to keep dialogue to a minimum. The result was an adult script to which the director would affix a dramatic sweep and intimate human touches that were uniquely his.

Stagecoach not only prompted a resurgence of the big Western; it propelled John Wayne into major stardom. Wayne played a young gunslinger called the Ringo Kid in the picture, while Claire Trevor was cast as a prostitute, Thomas Mitchell as a drunken doctor (a role for which he won an Academy Award), and John Carradine as a southern gambler. In addition to excellent casting, the film elevated the western landscape into a panorama of beauty and symbolic importance. During the 1930s, most movies were shot in the studios rather than on location. *Stagecoach* was the first sound film to exploit Monument Valley as its principal location, a site Ford would return to six more times over the course of his career. A wonderland of cathedral-like buttes and mesas in a remote section of the Navajo Reservation on the Arizona–Utah border, Ford used Monument Valley as a metaphor for the untamed American wilderness populated by "hostile" Indians.

What makes *Stagecoach* memorable is the interaction of its striking characters played against Ford's visual panorama. The director employs the landscape as a dramatic device for thrusting his Western into the realm of legend. "I think you can say that the real star of my Westerns has always been the land," Ford said. The Native American is portrayed as the child of this mythic wilderness, not so much bad as angry at invaders. The Indians who terrorize the band journeying to Lordsburg are seldom individualized; they are seen as part of the land. Only Geronimo emerges briefly from the background, and although he is viewed as a menace, he is also a leader with dignity.

Ford's focus in the film is a theme he would return to throughout his career—society's outcasts in times of danger mustering the strength to overcome the demon that threatens the very community which rejects them as misfits. The Ringo Kid has broken out of jail to avenge his father and brother's murder by the Plummer Gang. The prostitute Dallas and the alcoholic doctor have been cast out of Tonto by the town's Law-and-Order League. Yet, when Lucy Mallory, an aristocratic southern lady, prematurely gives birth to her baby, the outsiders become the activists in the moment of crisis, prove themselves pillars of strength, and earn the respect of members of the establishment. Ringo, a primitive individualist and a loner by necessity, demonstrates courage and nobility a short time later during an Indian attack, and he eventually rids the territory of the Plummer Gang and restores order to a town he is forced to flee. In the end Dallas and Ringo turn to one another for love and a sense of belonging. They plan to ride off to the Kid's ranch south of the border to start a new life, while the imbibing doctor expresses relief that they have been "saved from the blessings of civilization."

Ford's personal ambivalence toward society is close to the surface in *Stagecoach*. As did historian Frederick Jackson Turner, the director imbues the wilderness with regenerative powers. If the West in its natural state was spiritual and pure, urbanity brought corruption; cleansing came through the healing effects of nature. Like Ralph Waldo Emerson, Ford worried that the human race might die from too much civilization.

Yet the director, true to his Irish heritage, continued to idealize family and community values and depicted them with affecting sentiment. The tension between these two viewpoints permeates Ford's work, constituting a central issue that he never resolved. Again and again the director's camera peers through doors, windows, gates, porches, and canopies, contrasting indoors and outdoors, refuge and danger, civilization and wilderness, but the opposites are never reconciled. Despite his love for the natural, Ford's upbringing in the tight-knit Irish enclave of Portland, Maine, remained too strong for him to dismiss human society. At the same time his identification with the outsider as a constructive, creative force made him antagonistic toward a collective order.

In 1939, Ford directed his first movie in color, *Drums Along the Mohawk*, based on Walter Edmonds's novel. Filmed partly in the Wasatch Mountains of Utah, the story deals with pioneer farmers in the Mohawk Valley at the time of the American Revolution. Ford devised rituals that fit the period, yet bore his own signature—dances, family meals, military drills, a wedding, a birth, a death, moments of communal suffering and joy. Both home and wilderness were depicted in the film in images that are pure Ford. The farmers of the Mohawk Valley become representatives of the agrarian myth, examples of what frontier scholar Henry Nash Smith called "the yeoman ideal."

The Indians in *Drums Along the Mohawk* are portrayed as devilish marauders, a threat to white settlers, yet they rarely come into the foreground enough to become believable characters. When one does step forward, he is usually played for laughs. Blue Back, a Christian Indian, acted by Chief Big Tree, remains loyal to the film's hero, played by Henry Fonda, but the Iroquois are depicted as bloodthirsty enemies who burn homes and fields and attack American forts.

The Mohawk Valley farmers see their wheat and cabins destroyed, but they survive their losses and keep on pioneering. Their tribulations become tests for American democracy, but an agrarian utopia triumphs in the end. *Drums Along the Mohawk* leaves no doubt that the American dream is intact; God and nature are on the side of the small farmers, who have rejected eastern artifice and dedicated themselves to tilling the soil of a solidifying America.

Ford's next project, *The Grapes of Wrath* (1940), turned to the contemporary West. Based on John Steinbeck's controversial novel, the picture would be hailed as a masterpiece and earn the director his second Academy Award. (The first was for *The Informer* in 1935.) Ford became intrigued by the similarities between the dispossessed Okies during the Dust Bowl of the 1930s and the Irish peasants evicted by landowners and left to wander and starve during Ireland's famine in the nineteenth century. He could understand the breakdown of the family and their mourning the loss of the sharecropped land they had worked for generations. He updated the westward movement to include the Okies' migration to California in search of a Promised Land. With his affinity for the outsider, the director could identify with Tom Joad, played by Henry Fonda, as he lashes out at an unjust economic system and strikes out on his own to forge a more equitable social order.

Working with cinematographer Gregg Toland, Ford achieved a documentary look in photographing the dying America of the Dust Bowl's victims. The film presents haunting glimpses of abandoned farms and empty houses. Tom Joad first appears walking through a ruined landscape, juxtaposed against a line of telephone poles. Always the poetic visualist, Ford captures Ma Joad's anguish over leaving the only home she has known by picturing her before a broken mirror, holding a pair of cheap earrings up to her face and then tucking them into her pocket. Defeated Hooverville occupants later walk in front of the Joad's jalopy, fatigued and hungry. The movie's realism is laced with a visual poetry that elevates the work to enduring artistry.

Ford volunteered to head a field photographic unit and was assigned to the navy during World War II. Since the mythic West still held undiminished fascination for moviegoers in 1946, Twentieth Century-Fox production head Darryl Zanuck suggested in 1946 that the director remake the story of Wyatt Earp during his time as sheriff of Tombstone, Arizona, concluding with the famous gunfight at OK Corral. Ford liked the concept and even claimed to have known Earp, who late in his life lived in Pasadena and was eager to have his story told by Hollywood. An added incentive for Ford came when Zanuck consented to shooting the film in Monument Valley.

The resulting Western, *My Darling Clementine (1946),* starred Henry Fonda as Wyatt Earp, Victor Mature as Doc Holliday, and featured Walter Brennan as Old Man Clanton. Ford wanted Earp to be played in a restrained, dignified manner that contrasted with the brusqueness of the Clantons, and Fonda proved an ideal actor for that approach. The marshal's slow walk with Clementine down the street to the unfinished church has been viewed by critics as Earp's gradual acceptance of organized society, and his awkward dance with Clementine has been construed as the outsider's reluctant union with the community. "Without quite realizing what he has done," wrote Joseph McBride and Michael Wilmington, "Wyatt Earp has hewn a garden out of the wilderness." Yet, *My Darling Clementine*'s screenwriter, Winston Miller, denied that he and Ford had any such intent. Still, the director turned western lore into a film classic with a social commentary.

The ingredients of *My Darling Clementine* fit the Ford mold to perfection. The story's simplicity allowed the moviemaker plenty of opportunities to digress and develop a pivotal theme at the same time. Wyatt Earp, the mediating hero, is morally strong and fearless. His first step toward refinement is to visit Tombstone's barbershop, an indication of his latent impulse toward civilization. Earp possesses the western hero's commitment to law and order, yet is reluctant to bind himself to an established society. He finally accepts the job of sheriff to find his brother's killer, but in doing so makes decency and social progress in a rough town possible. Once he has seen the commitment through to a conclusion, he returns to the wilderness, preferring to live apart. But there are darker implications to his accomplishment; the name of the town he rescues is Tombstone, which symbolizes death.

For all of his lip service to community, family, and organized religion, Ford championed the loner who was free of society's shackles. He feared that communal pressures would weaken the outsider's power and independence. The Wyatt Earp portrayed in *My Darling Clementine* is the classic mythic hero, from whom something has been taken and who becomes involved in extraordinary adventures, yet reverts back to his original status in the end. Earp rescues civilization from primitive forces through superior frontier skills. An element of legend exists in all of Ford's Westerns, but *My Darling Clementine*, despite its deceptive simplicity, is among his most complex and open to interpretation. The movie mirrors the stress within American civilization, pitting freedom against social responsibility.

Ford's next Western, *Fort Apache* (1947), was an attempt to put his own production company, Argosy Pictures, on a firm financial footing. *Fort Apache* was the first segment of the director's cavalry trilogy, which portrayed an idealized frontier, more myth than history, and gave the filmmaker an opportunity to exalt a military camaraderie he had experienced during World War II and to teach moral lessons at the same time. As cinematic drama, the trilogy stands close to the center of Ford's greatness, and the pictures reflect male bonding on a rewarding and productive level.

All three cavalry movies — *She Wore a Yellow Ribbon* and *Rio Grande* after *Fort Apache* — were based on short stories by James Warner Bellah, which had appeared in the *Saturday Evening Post*. Bellah believed that although the public was tired of modern warfare, they fundamentally liked war and found combat exciting. What Bellah created was a romantic struggle against an enemy, the nomadic Indians of the Southwest, who could not fight back politically or economically. He wrote terse, forceful dialogue that was easily adapted to film and lent an authenticity to the depiction of military life in the Old West.

Although the names and setting were changed, *Fort Apache* became Ford's version of the George A. Custer legend. Filmed in Monument Valley, the movie cast Henry Fonda as Colonel Owen Thursday, a self-absorbed cavalry officer who refuses to listen to the advice of Kirby York, a more seasoned frontiersmen played by John Wayne, and leads his men to defeat in battle. Despite the friction between Wayne's and Fonda's characters, *Fort Apache* is primarily an adulation of male relationships, in which the harshness of a military regime in a frontier outpost is overshadowed by the warmth of life under regimental discipline. Women at the fort are depicted as dutiful yet pale, little more than appendages of their men. What is important is the tight-knit community of males, bound together by military tradition and ritual—men drinking, smoking, bathing, marching, fighting, and dying together. The cavalry becomes a self-contained unit, in which responsibility and sacrifice are essential to manliness. Honor, loyalty, and gallantry distinguish Ford's military heroes, but they are not textbook soldiers unwilling to bend the rules when necessary. Ford's cavalry outsiders, many of whom are Irish, have found a comfortable haven, a place where their worth is accepted, a forum in which they can distinguish themselves and contribute.

James Warner Bellah depicted the Apache as a savage, marauding enemy, but Ford gave them dignity. Cochise's people have a legitimate complaint against white encroachers; the villain is not the Apache chief, but a corrupt agent who cheated the Indians. Kirby York respects Cochise and accepts the truth behind his grievances, and the two leaders are able to negotiate as equals. Unlike the Native Americans in *Stagecoach*, who serve as a counterforce to civilization, those in *Fort Apache* are seen through sympathetic eyes. Owen Thursday, the martinet, may view Cochise as a "breech-clouted savage, an illiterate, uncivilized murderer and treaty breaker," but York insists that the Apache warrior is behaving as any honorable man would if herded onto a reservation and abused. Even though Ford has been branded a racist, his position in *Fort Apache* is an argument for peaceful coexistence.

It is the self-consumed Colonel Thursday who cannot adjust his absolute standards to a new environment, and *Fort Apache* ultimately revolves around a crisis in leadership. Thursday stupidly leads his men to their death, yet York covers up the blunder by lying to the press, insisting that "no man died more gallantly nor won more honor for his regiment." With this lie, York permits Thursday to become a legend to protect a greater truth—the loyalty of his men to their country and to each other. Ford believed that a nation needs its myths, as a cohesive thread amid inevitable change.

The second film in Ford's cavalry trilogy, *She Wore a Yellow Ribbon* (1949), was the filmmaker's first experience with photographing Monument Valley in Technicolor. He intended for his camera to capture the troopers as Frederic Remington might have painted them. The director tried to establish a format for each of his films, and before shooting *Yellow Ribbon* he studied Remington's groupings and composition and recreated the painter's imagery with striking accuracy.

The plot of *She Wore a Yellow Ribbon* centers on an attempt to avoid another Indian war after the defeat of Custer. The old chief in the picture, Pony That Walks, is as sensitive and well-intentioned as Nathan Brittles, an aging cavalry officer played by John Wayne, and the two have enormous respect for one another. Both have lost control of their young subordinates, who crave excitement. The two leaders admit that they have grown too old to fight and acknowledge the folly of continued warfare. Their scene together is a tender exchange between two veterans whose time is past.

Nathan Brittles knows that the Old West is vanishing, yet even in the face of his own retirement, he cannot bring himself to return to the restraints and pretensions of the East. A quintessential man of action, whose sense of community rests within the military, Brittles is a proven leader, but his command is limited by regulations that duty forces him to accept. The film's tension stems from a conflict between individual freedom and communal control, yet harmony is the issue.

Rio Grande (1950), the third of Ford's cavalry pictures, paired John Wayne with Maureen O'Hara on the screen for the first time and found Wayne back in the role of Kirby York. Estranged from his wife and family, York now stands on the verge of becoming a martinet himself. Filmed around Moab, Utah, this final installment of the cavalry trilogy departed from the conciliatory mood of its predecessors. In *Rio Grande* Kirby York no longer proposes negotiation with the Indians and argues against the diplomatic restraints put on the military to defeat aggression. The picture was released five months after President Harry Truman committed American forces to a limited war in Korea. York's position, which was to stop Apache raids into Texas by not allowing warriors to retreat into Mexico and gather the strength to strike again, is similar to that of General Douglas MacArthur, who favored bombing north of the Yalu River during the Korean War and persisted in that view until he was fired by Truman. *Rio Grande* demonstrates that Westerns not only draw on historic material, but also reflect the time in which they were made.

Earlier in 1950, Ford had shot *Wagonmaster*, a small, inexpensive Western without big stars, near the Mormon town of Moab. Making the picture proved one of the director's happiest experiences, and *Wagonmaster* ranks among his most lyrical movies. The story deals with a band of Mormons who set out across the Utah desert in 1879, intending to establish a home in the San Juan Valley. Ford admired the Mormon people, respected their sense of community, and viewed them as a society of outcasts. A square dance sequence is included in the film as an expression of Mormon oneness, but the dance is interrupted with dramatic effect by the arrival of the villains, who threaten the community with violence.

Wagonmaster is well paced and contains engaging action, but it is a more personal movie than most of Ford's Westerns. The story is reminiscent of the silent movies the director made with Harry Carey, and the film is more optimistic than the Westerns Ford made later, after he became disturbed by a world growing more troubled and complex. The Mormon pioneers face a series of dangers in their search for a Promised Land, but along the way they deal with the obstacles, and their leaders keep the group intact. Ford still saw the American frontier as a garden where dreams and ideals could be harvested, but his tone would soon take on a sadness, as his concept of contemporary American society darkened.

Busy with other projects, the director did not return to Westerns until 1955. In late January of that year, he and screenwriter Frank Nugent began work on the script of *The Searchers*, which many critics have hailed as Ford's masterpiece. Based on a novel by Alan LeMay, *The Searchers* eventually won a cult following that has outlasted any of the director's other pictures, for the movie demonstrates a psychological complexity Ford had not achieved before and would never equal again. Despite its visual beauty, the picture tells a brutal story, and its characters are not the romantic figures the public had come to expect in Westerns. Ford thought the subject called for a more realistic look and for this project chose the works of cowboy artist Charles M. Russell as his model.

Although *The Searchers* begins in Texas during 1868, Ford shot most of the picture in Monument Valley. In the film John Wayne plays Ethan Edwards, one of the actor's strongest characterizations. This time the story deals with the tragedy of the loner, which Ford by 1955 was prepared to recognize. Ethan Edwards returns from the Civil War, after undisclosed adventures in Mexico, unable to accept or understand domesticity and the demands of society. He cannot embrace family life and has allowed the woman he loves to marry his brother, even though she continues to love him. Ethan is hostile to civilization's rituals, easily becomes impatient and claustrophobic, and is doomed to remain a wanderer. He is the son of the frontier but belongs neither to the white nor the Indian world. His is a masculine, repressed, celibate existence, and through the years he has become brutalized, as savage as his enemies. His very presence threatens to destroy the stability of his brother's household. The door of their cabin, which introduces and closes the film, is symbolic of the central conflict—family versus the eternal loner.

When his brother and members of his family are massacred by Comanche and the frontiersman's two nieces are abducted, Ethan's desire for revenge estranges him from society even further. With his mixed-blooded, adopted nephew, Martin Pawley (deftly played by handsome Jeffrey Hunter), Ethan spends the next seven years looking for his niece, Debbie, driven more by racial hatred and vengeance than a desire to rescue the kidnapped girl. When he realizes that Debbie has come of age and become an Indian's squaw, Ethan's search turns destructive. Driven by psycho-sexual fears, he is determined to kill the girl, who by mating with an Indian has become debauched and ceases to be white in his mind. As the search continues, the similarities between Ethan and the Comanche chief who led the raid and mated with Debbie become clear, as both are driven by a determination for revenge.

With every year of the quest Ethan's racism grows more fanatic, until the frontiersman is exposed as a maniac, his mind clogged with bigotry and sexual repression. He scalps the Comanche chief and attempts to carry out his threat to kill Debbie. In the end he relents, probably for two reasons, although the question remains open-ended. Through their journey together Ethan has come to accept and emotionally bond with Martin, himself one-quarter Indian, and to some degree surmounts his racism. Also, Ethan at last remembers that Debbie is the daughter of the woman he once loved, and in the original script he comments on their similar appearance. In the last scene of the film, Martin and Debbie are welcomed into the home of a neighboring family, while Ethan, the immutable outsider, stands framed in the doorway, then turns and walks away without entering the house.

Ford captured profound truths in *The Searchers*, reflecting tensions so complex, so haunting, and so subliminal that critics have called the movie "the story of America." No longer are his cavalry troops the knightly protectors of an underdeveloped society, nor is there community on this frontier. Each family in *The Searchers* fights to hold its own homestead against overwhelming odds. The film depicts neither a civilized order nor the wilderness in idealized terms. To live in harmony with the realities of a raw frontier necessitates compromise, sacrifice, and change; there are no alternatives it seems.

Although *The Searchers* was hailed as a popular and critical success upon its release, the greatest praise came later. French director Jean-Luc Godard, a Marxist, was among the first to label the picture a masterpiece, and in time the film earned Ford the respect of what would be termed "the new Hollywood." The director continues to be greatly admired by such contemporary filmmakers as Steven Spielberg and Peter Bogdanovich, and academic conferences frequently ponder the layers of meaning in John Ford's work.

Since Westerns still commanded a loyal following in the early 1960s, the director, after three lesser attempts, created his last undisputed classic, *The Man Who Shot Liberty Valance* (1962). Saddened by the death of a number of his close friends, disgusted with the current movie business, and sickened by what he considered the breakdown of American society, Ford began working on *Liberty Valance* in mid-January 1961. The director was determined to have his protégé, John Wayne, as the feature's star. Ford insisted on shooting the movie in black-and-white as he wanted a dark, anachronistic look, since the picture incorporated his deteriorating faith in American values. No longer did the director feel like celebrating the course of civilization, which he accepted, but did not necessarily see as progress. "For a change, no locations," Ford wrote Wayne in July 1961 about *Liberty Valance*. "All to be shot on the lot." The filmmaker wanted a claustrophobic feel to the picture and photographed all but three days of the footage inside the Paramount studio.

As *The Man Who Shot Liberty Valance* opens, Tom Doniphon, the frontier hero played by John Wayne, lies dead; his coffin establishes the mood of the film. Senator Ransom Stoddard, who reputedly shot the notorious gunman Liberty Valance, has returned to Shinbone with his wife, Hallie, to bury Tom. They arrive by train (the Western symbol of progress) to find the landscape tamed and the frontier town they once knew orderly and depersonalized. Although the town's violent past was horrendous, its tepid present seems sterile. The film's dialectic is encapsulated in the image of a cactus rose, which symbolizes the contradiction between desert and garden. Stoddard, a man of books and compassion, has led the frontier toward civilization through his successful political career, whereas Tom (the actual slayer of Valance) had begun to act as wild as Liberty had, tossing chairs around, breaking glass, and creating havoc—an anachronism amid changing times.

Ford mourned the passing of the mythic frontier, as he lamented the corrosive forces of progress. By the time he made *The Man Who Shot Liberty Valance* the iron horse for him had become an iron monster, yet he remained convinced that change could not be stopped, no matter how much cultural dislocation resulted. Tom Doniphon, whose fast gun epitomized the Old West, appears to have lived a meaningless life. He lies dead in a pine box in a cluttered stable—a pauper at the end of his life, his boots stolen by an avaricious undertaker. Yet Tom knew his world was coming to an end. He allowed Stoddard to take credit for killing Valance so that a new order could emerge, and he willingly accepted anonymity for himself.

Since the conquest of the wilderness had been founded on myth, the progress achieved rests on shaky ground. At the end of the film, as Stoddard and his wife leave Shinbone, Hallie looks out the train window at the grassy plains and remarks wistfully, "Look at it. It was once a wilderness. Now it's a garden." Ford suggests that the Old West and its values survive in the legends its heros helped create. To have exposed what the frontier symbolizes as fraud would have destroyed its meaning in history, and the public would not have accepted the truth anyway. Therefore, the newspaper editor says in the fadeout, "When the legend becomes fact, print the legend."

In *The Man Who Shot Liberty Valance* Ford confronted the losses of the past—his personal and professional losses, as well as broad historical sacrifices. The picture makes a melancholy and troubling statement yet one that remains consistent with the dark side of Ford's romanticism. Toward the end of his career the director questioned the mythology he himself had invented over four and a half decades of filmmaking. Even though Ford admired Tom Doniphon and regretted the passing of frontier individualism, he saw value in Ransom Stoddard as a modern and more flexible male who could wash dishes and don an apron (which the character does in one scene) without eroding his masculinity.

For his final Western, Ford decided to tell the Indians' side of the conquest of the frontier. *Cheyenne Autumn* (1964), inspired by Mari Sandoz's book, deals with the heroic flight in 1878 of three hundred Northern Cheyenne from a reservation in Oklahoma back to their ancestral lands near the Yellowstone River. Based on a true story, it portrays a tragic people at the mercy of a heartless majority—a theme in harmony with the rising Native

American rights movement in 1964. "I've long wanted to do a story that tells the truth about them [the Indians]," said Ford, "and not just a picture in which they're chased by the cavalry."

Cheyenne Autumn took a viewpoint opposite that of the Westerns drawn from the James Warner Bellah stories. Rather than glorifying an expanding American empire, as Bellah ("the American Kipling") had done, *Cheyenne Autumn* concentrates on the victims of Anglo-American expansion. In that regard the picture was a forerunner of New Western history. The Cheyenne faced starvation, disease, and death on the fifteen-hundred-mile return to their homeland, pursued along the way by the cavalry, with only eighty of the Indians surviving. "I've killed more Indians than Custer," said Ford. "This is their side."

The filmmaker's association with the Navajo in Monument Valley had sensitized him to some degree to Native American cultures, and he had become sympathetic to their plight. "They are a very dignified people," Ford remarked about the Indians with whom he had worked through the years. The director claimed that he caught Jack Warner, head of production at Warner Bros., in a weak moment, and the mogul agreed to a budget of $5.1 million with the proviso that *Cheyenne Autumn* be loaded with stars.

Although Ford took liberties with Sandoz's book, he remained sensitive to the story and helped screenwriter James R. Webb shape it into a big outdoor spectacle. He returned once more to Monument Valley for much of the footage, although life on the Navajo reservation had changed considerably since the director's initial visit there for outdoor filming on *Stagecoach*. From the outset it was clear to veteran members of the John Ford stock company that the aging director was no longer operating at full capacity. His sight and hearing were failing, and Ford soon grew bored with the project. "Uncle Jack still had the talent with the camera," said Harry Carey, Jr., "but not how to tell the story. He couldn't keep it all in his mind." As the weeks in Monument Valley wore on, Ford sometimes opted to shoot scenes right in front of Goulding's Lodge, where the company was housed, since that required the least effort. "I think the same thing happened on *Cheyenne Autumn* that happened on a number of the Old Man's later films," said cinematographer William Clothier. "He just got tired and lost interest. You could see his energy flagging. After a while he just wanted to wrap the picture up."

Cheyenne Autumn unquestionably turned the cavalry story around, giving what hope there was to a minority culture at the mercy of their conquerors.

The Indians are no longer the savage enemies of an advancing civilization; they are the tragic heroes, the dispossessed. The cavalry was viewed as the pawn of a remote and vindictive government, and Ford appears to have lost faith in the individual's capacity to right society's wrongs. Secretary of the Interior Carl Schurz fears that his benevolence toward the Indians will give his political opponents "the false move they are waiting for." Society's leaders have become powerless, in contrast to Ford's lifelong hero, Abraham Lincoln, in whose framed portrait Schurz's face is reflected during a pivotal scene. But the Cheyenne are doomed to defeat, too. The Indians not only face starvation and annihilation, but they also splinter from within.

The Dodge City sequence in the film stands as a controversial and confusing interlude. Ford claimed that he added the episode for comic relief, a light touch after the intermission, in what otherwise was a tragic story. Others have viewed the insert as Ford's reflection on the degeneracy of the Old West, a counterpoint to the plight of the Native Americans. Wyatt Earp, the idealized western hero in *My Darling Clementine*, has become a parody, a menace to decent values. At best the Earp depicted in *Cheyenne Autumn* is a middle-aged buffoon, with Doc Holliday as his side-kick; at worst the gambler is a selfish cynic and a decadent capitalist, caring only for his poker game. Whatever its intent the Dodge City sequence reduces heroism to clowning.

When Ford's last Western was released in the fall of 1964, most critics were not impressed. "*Cheyenne Autumn* is a rambling episodic account," *Variety* maintained. Stanley Kauffmann, reviewing for *New Republic*, found the cast, which had Ricardo Montalban, Dolores Del Rio, Sal Mineo, and Gilbert Roland playing Indians, "beyond disbelief." *Newsweek*'s assessment of the picture was even harsher: "Ford has apparently forgotten everything he ever knew, about actors, about cameras, about Indians, and about the West."

At seventy years of age, the director acknowledged the disintegration of everything he once believed in. He became a recluse, spending most of his time in bed, reading or watching television. In 1971, he was diagnosed with cancer and soon moved to Palm Desert to be near Eisenhower Hospital. He died on August 31, 1973.

John Ford's career spanned Hollywood's formative years and decades of maturation. He was of a pioneering breed, a man who talked with visual action. Matchless as a storyteller, Ford ranks high among the cinema's legendary filmmakers, an artist who painted with the camera. A complex, enigmatic personality, Ford created motion pictures of lasting significance.

His vision of the American frontier embodied much of the evolving mythology of the West, yet Ford gave the myth sweeping action, indelible heroes (particularly those played by John Wayne), and a philosophical complexity that continues to spark discussion.

Although literature, painting, and sculpture had captured parts of the western saga before the frontier closed, its most dynamic expression awaited the twentieth century and the arrival of motion pictures as a popular art form. John Ford stands at the apex of western mythmakers, for he blended legend and reality into a sophisticated art form that combined the visual, complex character development, and the fundamental issue of individual rights in a changing society. Perhaps more than any other filmmaker, Ford lifted America's creation myth to epic proportions, giving it a tension of lasting significance, and posing questions about heroic deeds, assertive violence, and social responsibility that remain relevant in the modern world.

◆ five ◆

John Wayne

An American Icon

JOHN H. LENIHAN

A birthday celebration in March 1956 included my choice of any first-run movie playing in downtown Seattle. Being an avid fancier of wide-screen epics that were fashionable at the time, I quickly narrowed the options to *The Conqueror* and *Helen of Troy*. The former won out, and for no other reason than it starred John Wayne—and whoever heard of Rosanna Podesta or Jack (Warners' translation of "Jacques") Sernas featured in *Helen of Troy*. After sitting through the nearly two-hour Genghis Khan epic, I felt comfortable with the choice I had made. It was not vintage Wayne in familiar frontier garb and setting, but the film was adequately exciting and colorful, and Wayne seemed a reasonably credible medieval easterner as he slashed his way through Tartar hordes. The deluge of critical pans mattered not at all—even *The Searchers*, which came later that year, seemed dull by comparison, no matter that Wayne was back to packing a six-gun and battling "savage" Indians.

The years have not been kind to my earlier judgments about "cinema." *The Searchers* is now considered Wayne's best film and indeed among the best films of all time, whereas *The Conqueror* remains by virtual consensus the embarrassment that critics sensed it was in 1956. But it is not the critics who made John Wayne the most popular star in the history of motion pictures or, arguably, America's greatest cultural icon in the twentieth century. The millions who flocked to his films from the late 1930s to the mid-1970s took care of that—joined by the countless television and video watchers who keep his memory alive. In today's world of White House sex scandals, indecision regarding petty (but dangerous) foreign tyrants, affirmative action, or the environment, Wayne remains for many the sturdy model of American individualism and right-thinking, which he represented on screen for more than four decades and in his political outspokenness during the troubling years of Vietnam and Watergate.

Those of a more liberal persuasion, including much of the nation's intelligentsia, have been less effusive. Theirs is a reactionary Wayne whose films and politics reflected an undying racism, sexism, and militant anticommunism in postwar American life. As Randy Roberts and James Olson argue in their recent biography *John Wayne: American,* perhaps it is because America's largely liberal cultural elite could never see beyond Wayne's politics that "serious biographers" heretofore dismissed his importance as a subject worthy of their attention.

Scholars had not totally neglected Wayne, particularly in connection with the movies he made. With the publication of Roberts and Olson's 600-plus page biography in 1995, followed shortly by book-length studies from historians Garry Wills (*John Wayne's America*) and Ronald Davis (*Duke: The Life and Image of John Wayne*), John Wayne is at last receiving his due as a legitimate subject for professional historical inquiry. This recent surge of scholarly literature has greatly contributed to explaining Wayne's cultural importance and why he has captured the imagination of so many Americans.

John Wayne was born Marion Robert Morrison on May 26, 1907. "Robert" became "Michael" four years later when his parents Clyde Leonard Morrison and Mary Alberta Brown decided to name their second child Robert. Clyde was a pharmacy clerk whose repeated change of jobs and intermittent income was a source of considerable marital tension and financial uncertainty for the Morrison family. In 1914, Clyde brought his unhappy wife, "Molly," and their two sons to southern California's Antelope Valley where he tried farming on property homesteaded by his father. It was desert land with little agricultural promise, particularly given Clyde's lack of sufficient capital and experience.

With a desperately unhappy spouse now threatening divorce, Clyde moved the family two years later to Glendale, a community that, like Los Angeles just to the south, was attracting many other mid-westerners. Clyde was again working in drugstores and with little more success than in Iowa. Despite the more hospitable environment, life was still a financial struggle. The Morrisons changed residences several times, with Clyde drinking too much and Molly taking out her frustrations on both Clyde and her first son. When not in school, young Marion spent much of his time away from his troubled household, working paper routes and other odd jobs and joining groups such as the YMCA and Boy Scouts. Years later John Wayne remembered frequenting the movie theater in Glendale and hanging around film crews that were then shooting footage in his hometown.

In grammar and high school, young Morrison was both popular and a top student. At Glendale Union High School he also proved himself on the gridiron and upon graduation accepted the offer of a two-year football scholarship at the University of Southern California. Having been turned down as an applicant to the U.S. Naval Academy, Morrison embraced this new opportunity to escape a deteriorating family environment and to acquire the means for the material success that had eluded his father.

Morrison enrolled as a pre-law major at USC in 1925 and played first-string guard on the freshman football team. He earned his board and room as a member of Sigma Chi, washing dishes and waiting on his fraternity brothers. Suffering a shoulder injury from a surfing accident and relegated to second and third strings on the varsity team during his sophomore year at USC, he was informed at the end of that school year that his football scholarship would not be renewed. The loss of his fraternity job at the beginning of his third year spelled the end of his college career.

After dropping out of college for lack of financial support in the fall of 1927, Morrison went to work full time at the William Fox Studios where he had been employed the two previous summers. Early he was assigned as a prop man to director John Ford, who also used him as an extra in several of his films. It was the beginning of a personal friendship that would sputter on and off for years to come. But, as of the late 1920s, the relationship did not extend professionally beyond Ford offering young Morrison spot appearances on screen and the accompanying extra pay to supplement his income moving props.

It was not John Ford but a directorial colleague at Fox, Raoul Walsh, who "discovered" John Wayne. Walsh was searching for someone to cast in the lead role of a big-budget Western he planned to direct and one day caught sight of the 6-foot-4 Morrison gracefully hurtling furniture. Impressed with his physique and the way he carried himself, Walsh called for a screen test. Given the lavish budget slated for *The Big Trail* (1930), signing an unknown for the lead role was a considerable risk. At a reported $75 per week, however, Morrison would come much cheaper than Tom Mix or Gary Cooper, whom Walsh initially wanted but who were unavailable. For Morrison, $75 was a king's ransom not only by comparison with what he had been earning but also in light of the recent stock market crash. More important was the promise of sudden stardom and a whole new career. The only remaining obstacle for an image-conscious studio was the name Marion (or even Duke) Morrison. There seemed little inclination to replace "Marion" with "Duke," the name young Morrison had embraced since his grammar school days in Glendale, when local firemen began calling him after the name of the family dog that often accompanied him. And so, on the eve of America's worst economic calamity, by executive decision, twenty-year-old property man and sometimes extra for Fox studios Marion Mitchell Morrison became movie star John Wayne.

A single starring role does not guarantee stardom, however, as John Wayne soon discovered. *The Big Trail* remains one of Hollywood's most visually spectacular epics for all of its dramatic awkwardness, episodic plot, and overblown "Manifest Destiny" rhetoric. Its unknown leading man cut an impressive figure as the buckskin clad scout guiding a wagon train of pioneers through both natural and human hazards. Even though his acting in retrospect appears uncharacteristically stilted, his physical presence perfectly captured the innocence and agility of the natural man celebrated most famously in James Fenimore Cooper's "Leatherstocking" tales. Except for hiring Wayne on the cheap, the studio spared no expense to include multiple location footage, extravagant stunts, and 70mm wide-screen photography, which the studio touted as revolutionary as the recent introduction of sound to movies. Unfortunately, because all but two of the nation's theaters could not afford the larger screens and projection equipment and because Depression audiences could not afford the higher admission price where the innovation was available, *The Big Trail* was a financial disappointment for a studio already near bankruptcy.

After subsequently starring Wayne in two minor films, the ailing Fox studio dropped his contract. Inexplicably, John Ford refused to help, or even talk to, his supposed "friend." Instead, Columbia's Harry Cohn signed Wayne for a series of nondescript films, only the first of which afforded him a starring role. Perhaps it was because Cohn wished to humiliate Wayne for allegedly making a pass at one of the mogul's personally coveted starlets that Wayne was reduced to playing a corpse in *Columbia's Deceiver* (1931).

Faced with the prospect of unemployment as the Depression worsened in early 1932, Wayne accepted producer Nat Levine's offer of making cheap serials for his Mascot Pictures. This job was Wayne's introduction to Hollywood's "poverty row" of studios, which mass-produced inexpensive action films. Except for six B-films (mostly remakes of Ken Maynard's silent Westerns) made for Warner Brothers, most of the four dozen or so films Wayne starred in for the remainder of the 1930s were Poverty-Row Westerns produced by Monogram and Republic. Wayne became understandably weary of churning out as many as seven undistinguished Westerns a year. Yet the work was steady in an otherwise depressed economy, and his name above the titles made him a public fixture, if only as a second-string cowboy star. He was also in the company of experienced craftsmen who helped hone his skills at delivering a line, riding a horse, and learning stunt skills that would serve him well in later years. Stuntman Enos (Yakima) Canutt was particularly important in developing Wayne's horsemanship, his characteristic swagger, and an unparalleled ability to fake a punch. It was from Canutt, according to Garry Wills, that Wayne "learned the importance of making difficult things look easy."

In the spring of 1933, with unemployment wreaking havoc on American families, Wayne was secure enough financially to marry the Hispanic debutante he had been courting since his days at USC. The WASP son of a druggist who had gone "Hollywood" was not what the status-conscious Roman Catholic parents of Josephine Saenz wanted for a son-in-law, and in fact the marriage proved less than idyllic. Four children would be born over the ten years of their marriage, but the long hours Wayne spent before the camera, combined with his penchant for male carousing in his off time, did not mix well with Josie's world of church work and polite society.

Professionally, Wayne seemed unable to rise above the pack of competitive B-movie cowboy stars. Gene Autry remembered that "Duke and I were the first two players under contract when Republic was formed." That was 1935 and by 1938 Autry was Hollywood's top money-making Western star. Ranked fifth were "the Three Mesquiteers," the role name for a trio of Republic players that from 1938 to 1939 included John Wayne. Meanwhile, by the end of the 1930s, feature Westerns were enjoying a revival after a half-dozen years of being eclipsed in popularity by comedies, gangster thrillers, and social-problem melodramas. Then, in the summer of 1938, the powerful director for whom Wayne had worked as a prop boy at Fox offered Wayne the role that would return him to Hollywood's big league.

Having turned a cold shoulder to Wayne following his failed attempt at stardom in *The Big Trail*, John Ford rekindled the relationship in 1934. Friendship finally turned professional when Ford cast Wayne as the Ringo Kid in *Stagecoach* (1939). Without a Western to his credit since *Three Bad Men* thirteen years earlier, Ford delivered the most acclaimed Western since the 1931 multiple Oscar winner *Cimarron*. Under Ford's artful direction (augmented by stunning location shots of Monument Valley), the still youthful-looking Wayne unexpectedly stood out in what was basically an ensemble piece about an assortment of social outcasts and respectables who reveal their true character in the course of a hazardous stagecoach journey. That *Stagecoach* managed to win two of five Oscar nominations (supporting actor and music score) was remarkable given the unprecedented competition from classics such as *Gone with the Wind*, *The Wizard of Oz*, *Mr. Smith Goes to Washington*, *Ninotchka*, and *Wuthering Heights*.

With the favorable notices he received for his role in *Stagecoach*, Wayne was, at age 32, finally in demand for feature films. At the peak of his physical attractiveness, Wayne proved adept as a romantic lead opposite top-billed actresses such as Joan Crawford, Jean Arthur, and Marlene Dietrich (with whom he costarred in three films and for a time romanced offscreen). After *Stagecoach* and four more "Mesquiteer" films released in 1939, over the next half decade less than a third of Wayne's prodigious output of four films a year were Westerns, and most of these were routine fare under a renegotiated contract with the minor-league Republic studio. Although Wayne was Republic's biggest star in the 1940s, he did not always command top billing in major productions for other studios. Paramount's top producer–director Cecil B. DeMille cast him as the adventuresome antagonist (though redeemed at the end) opposite star Ray Milland in the sea-faring spectacle *Reap the Wild Wind* (1943), and even John Ford provided Robert Montgomery the lead role in his naval epic for MGM, *They Were Expendable* (1945).

They Were Expendable was one of four combat films that Wayne made during the war years, beginning with *Flying Tigers* (1942), which Republic rushed into production after the bombing of Pearl Harbor. In these and subsequent war films Wayne came to personify American military bravura and sacrifice. His less-flattering role in *Pittsburgh* (1942), however, as an unscrupulous entrepreneur whose hunger for success overrides social responsibility, may have captured something of his real-life situation in these years. In the movie, Wayne's character ultimately redeems himself by joining in the nation's defense effort to meet production demands for wartime mobilization. Although in the abstract Wayne undoubtedly shared the film's propagandistic appeal for national unity and sacrifice, his preoccupation with furthering his career during World War II bore an uncomfortable resemblance to the character he plays through most of *Pittsburgh*. By 1942, Wayne was 34, married, the father of four children, and therefore legally deferred from military service. But exemptions did not stop bigger stars like James Stewart and Henry Fonda from enlisting. Although Wayne wrote John Ford of his interest in joining his photographic unit for the Office of Strategic Services, he never took the decisive step of ending his deferment.

Meanwhile, Wayne's single-minded pursuit of Hollywood stardom and off-time carousings continued to strain his marital life. No sooner had his affair with Marlene Dietrich broken up than Wayne struck up a romance with Mexican beauty Esperanza Bauer (Chata to her friends). Josephine Wayne sued for divorce in October 1943, and within two-and-a-half years Chata became the new Mrs. John Wayne.

At the end of the war, Republic and RKO signed Wayne to nonexclusive contracts that guaranteed him higher salaries and, at Republic, a 10 percent profit share of his films. More importantly, Republic presented him with his first opportunity to produce. For *Angel and the Badman* (1947) Wayne assembled a crew of friends and former associates, including screenwriter and drinking buddy James Edward Grant, cinematographer Archie Stout, and stuntman Yakima Canutt from Wayne's poverty-row days at Monogram, and former coplayers Bruce Cabot and Harry Carey. Carey, who died a year after shooting was completed, was a much-respected Western film star from the silent era, a longtime friend of John Ford, and with his wife, Olive, provided Wayne a second family when his own was deteriorating in the early 1940s. Although Wayne allowed Grant to direct his own screenplay, he remained the controlling influence of this modest curiosity of a Western. The decidedly pacifist story of an outlaw who is redeemed from his violent ways by the love of a Quaker woman was different from anything Wayne had done before and a conspicuous departure from the combative type of screen heroism popular during the war years. With the onset of the Cold War and Wayne's own political turn to the anticommunist right, *Angel and the Badman* would remain a thematic anomaly.

The role of Tom Dunson, which Wayne agreed to play next for producer–director Howard Hawks in *Red River* (1948), was the antithesis of the gentle badman in his own production. Here was a Western with an epic theme comparable to that of Wayne's failed debut film *The Big Trail,* but with an acting challenge unlike anything he had encountered. Wayne was not yet forty when filming began, and he was to play a character in his fifties. Contrary to the likeable heroes Wayne typically played, Tom Dunson is an obsessed, empire-building cattleman who in the course of a long cattle drive becomes hardened and tyrannical to the point of alienating those closest to him. Although the film's storyline credits Dunson with being instrumental in laying the foundation for a prosperous civilization, it also shows him emotionally self-destructing under the pressure of preserving the domain he has built—the cattle drive he leads is essential if he and other Texas cattlemen are to survive economic devastation

John Wayne in Red River *(1948), with newcomer Montgomery Clift. Here Wayne displays a tougher image in the postwar years. Courtesy of MGM CLIP & STILL.* Red River © *1948 United Artists Corporation. All Rights Reserved.*

and if the nation is going to be fed in the aftermath of the Civil War. As it turned out, Wayne was perfectly cast, his towering physical presence conveying both the toughness necessary for building and preserving an empire and the menace that results from desperation and uncontrolled rage. Wayne was frighteningly credible with the darker elements of his complex character and at the same time made effective use of his established screen persona to register Dunson's more heroic qualities.

When John Ford saw *Red River,* he reportedly told Howard Hawks, "I never knew the son of a bitch could act." Indeed it was a revelation, though few other than Ford took notice when the film was released in July 1948. Reviewers were generally favorable toward the film and the performances of Wayne and newcomer Montgomery Clift. *Red River* ranked third in annual box-office returns and catapulted Wayne to the top level of Hollywood stars.

Wayne's jump in stature owed much to the popularity of *Red River* and was reinforced by the respectable work he did in John Ford's *Fort Apache* (1948), released four months previously. *Red River* had been shot earlier but delays and overruns had delayed its release. *Fort Apache* was the first of three majestically framed cavalry–Indian Westerns that forged the artistic relationship between Wayne and Ford, which began with *Stagecoach*. Although the lead role of an Indian-hating Custer facsimile went to Henry Fonda, Wayne's understated performance as the level-headed Captain York represents the film's moral center. Helpless to prevent his glory-seeking superior from leading the regiment into an Apache massacre, York, in a much-discussed final scene, publicly pays him tribute in order to preserve the regiment's honor. Filmed as a Western, *Fort Apache* was also for Ford an unabashed love poem to the American military.

After casting Wayne as one of the *Three Godfathers* (1948), a beautifully photographed but belabored Western nativity parable, Ford starred his now-favorite actor in two more cavalry–Indian Westerns. *She Wore a Yellow Ribbon* (1949) again had Wayne convincingly playing an older man, although the elderly career soldier Nathan Brittles is a wiser and gentler soul than the irascible cattleman Wayne portrayed in *Red River*. Wayne plays closer to his own age in the third and most interesting of Ford's cavalry films, *Rio Grande* (1950). There is the usual barracks humor and sentimental comradery, and Ford is again obviously paying tribute to American military efforts to safe-guard the nation. Unlike the first two cavalry Westerns in which Wayne's character exhibits respect for his Indian adversaries (in *Fort Apache* the Indians are clearly exploited by an encroaching white civilization), in *Rio Grande* he is frustrated by diplomatic obstacles that prevent him from defeating Indians who raid helpless Texans and then escape across the border to Mexico. Wayne's Colonel York is also burdened emotionally by the appearance of his estranged wife, who still carries the bitterness of his having destroyed her southern home fifteen years earlier in the Civil War and now pleads that her husband discharge their son who has recently enlisted in his outfit. Ford skillfully integrates the theme of familial reconciliation with York's defeat of the Indian menace—he has been secretly authorized by General Sheridan to bypass state department restrictions and "cross the Rio Grande, hit the Apache, and burn him out."

The film's release in November 1950 was timely. Later that same month China's intervention in the Korean War set the stage for a major dispute between General Douglas MacArthur and President Harry Truman as to whether U.S. forces should strike the "aggressor's" homebase across the Yalu River. General MacArthur's outspoken frustration with Truman's policy of containing the war to the Korean peninsula mirrored the sentiments expressed in Ford's Western. "The state department could do something," Wayne's Colonel York complains early in the film about surmounting the diplomatic impediment to his attacking the Apache's homebase across the Rio Grande River.

The release of the Ford–Wayne military Westerns coincided with a new round of World War II combat films. Among the first was the Republic's *Sands of Iwo Jima* (1949), which earned Wayne his first Oscar nomination. A spectacularly staged reenactment of the Marine assaults on the Japanese-infested islands of Tarawa and Iwo Jima, the film permanently fixed Wayne's screen image as America's quintessential military hero. As he mercilessly disciplines his recruits, Wayne's Sergeant Stryker reveals a manic edge that recalls Tom Dunson's brutal leadership in *Red River*. Indeed, both men's tortured psyches are related in part to guilt over a failed romance (Dunson is unable to save the woman he loves from an Indian attack, and Stryker is estranged from his wife and son). Unlike the socially detrimental consequences of Dunson's rage, however, Stryker's disciplinary toughness is shown to be essential for survival against an implacable enemy. In the three years that elapsed since the making of *Red River*, the Cold War had obviated any need to qualify a hero's ruthless demeanor.

Sands of Iwo Jima was a pivotal film in Wayne's meteoric rise at mid-century to becoming America's biggest movie star. Furthermore, his Oscar nomination affirmed what the postwar Westerns of Hawks and Ford had already revealed concerning his acting ability. Having broken into the top ten of box-office favorites as America's fifth most popular star in 1949, Wayne captured the number-one spot in 1950. Despite the inferior quality of his two war films released in 1951 (*Flying Leathernecks* and *Operation Pacific*), Wayne was number one again that year and would remain on the top ten list for an unprecedented 24 years.

By 1950, Wayne's iconographic link with America's frontier heritage and combat heroism in World War II had special meaning for an anxious public engulfed in the most feverish period of the Cold War. Congressional hearings in 1947 and 1951 brought Hollywood into the forefront of the Red Scare, and John Wayne became a political activist for the first time in his life. Serving a term as president of the right-wing Motion Picture Alliance for the Preservation of American Ideals, Wayne aligned himself with Hollywood conservatives who openly supported the congressional hearings and blacklisting of unrepentant leftists in the industry. In Howard Hughes's *Jet Pilot* (filmed in 1949 but not released until 1957) and his own productions of *Big Jim McLain* (1952) and *Blood Alley* (1955), Wayne also battled communists on screen. These propaganda-laden adventures did little to enhance Wayne's standing with critics, but they scarcely detracted from his popularity and reinforced his reputation as one of Hollywood's most outspoken anticommunist hawks.

Big Jim McClain and *Blood Alley* also typify the bad-to-mediocre quality of most films that Wayne produced from 1952 to 1954 with business partner Robert Fellows and thereafter under his own Batjac banner. Republic had not provided Wayne the control he wanted over the films he starred in, and after the studio refused to back Wayne's plans for a film about the Alamo, he and studio head Herbert Yates parted ways. Ironically, Wayne's last film for Republic, *The Quiet Man* (1952), was second only to *Sands of Iwo Jima* as the biggest money-maker in the studio's history and was vastly superior to anything Wayne would produce for himself. In this Irish battle-of-the-sexes comedy, John Ford again coaxed one of Wayne's better performances and reunited him with Maureen O'Hara with whom he had sparred romantically in *Rio Grande*.

The temperamental clashes that Wayne and O'Hara played out in their five movies together (usually as estranged spouses), plus his many other films since *Red River* that make a point of his character's failed domestic relationships, had their real-life counterpart in Wayne's own troubled home life. Wayne's marriage with Chata proved more tempestuous than his first with Josephine and ended in a highly publicized, bitter divorce hearing in October 1953. In November of the following year, he married Peruvian actress Pilar Palette whom he had met two years earlier while scouting locations in Peru for the Alamo project he had planned with Republic. She bore him three children from 1956 to 1966 and, despite Wayne's continued preoccupation with work and penchant for socializing with longtime associates like John Ford, she provided an element of domestic stability for most of their years together until the couple eventually separated two decades later.

Notwithstanding the proliferation of Westerns in the 1950s, they comprised only a fourth of Wayne's output in that decade. But they were among his biggest hits and included what is now widely considered his greatest film and performance, *The Searchers* (1956). To critics at the time, however, *The Searchers* seemed at best a competent "rip-snorting Western" and at worst "meandering" and "very confused." Assessments of Wayne likewise varied from "the saddle-worn star can act" to his "glum moroseness" in playing a character "who behaves like a dangerous lunatic." If some of today's academic adulation of *The Searchers* borders on hyperbole, reviewers in 1956 grossly underestimated the complexity of the film and Wayne's performance.

As in *Rio Grande*, the setting (this time evoked by Ford's signature locale of Monument Valley, brilliantly shot in Technicolor and VistaVision) is the post–Civil War Texas frontier in a fierce struggle against rampaging Indians. In *The Searchers* Ford explores the racial underpinning of that struggle, which in the person of Ethan Edwards reaches psychotic proportions. The strength of Wayne's portrayal lies in making Edwards alternatively menacing and aggrieved, fiercely independent and lonely, cruel and tender. The film's dramatic tension in effect hinges on Wayne's mastery in conveying both the danger and pathos of his racially obsessed character.

In terms of quality, Wayne's next two collaborations with Ford, *The Wings of Eagles* (1957) and *The Horse Soldiers* (1959), were letdowns despite his credible performances in the type of military roles with which he had become identified in the public mind. It may well have been Wayne's popular image as an authoritative leader that explains the commercial success of his portrayal of Genghis Khan in Howard Hughes's critically panned eastern horse opera, *The Conqueror* (released less than a month before *The Searchers*, it made nearly as much money). By contrast, audiences turned thumbs down on Wayne playing a nineteenth-century diplomat in the actionless *Barbarian and the Geisha* (1958).

Feeling betrayed by director John Huston's conception of his part in that film, Wayne welcomed the opportunity to make another profitable Western with Howard Hawks. *Rio Bravo* (1959) did not disappoint. As modestly plotted and leisurely paced as *Red River* was spectacular and intense, *Rio Bravo* offered an engaging blend of crisply staged action and character interaction dominated by Wayne's reassuring presence as a town sheriff defending his authority against lawless cattlemen. With *Red River* Hawks had significantly toughened Wayne's western image and invested it with the kind of psychological complexity that became a fixture in the postwar genre and would reemerge notably in Wayne's performance in *The Searchers*. With *Rio Bravo*, Hawks again departed from convention by countering the antisocietal perspective that *High Noon* had made fashionable in 1950s Westerns. Wayne believed the latter film to be un-American, owing to blacklisted screenwriter Carl Foreman's jaundiced depiction of a community's cowardly failure to support its marshal. *Rio Bravo* renders the question of communal responsibility a moot point as it focuses on the courage and professional expertise of Wayne and his deputies. It was a premise that Hawks and Wayne would repeat almost literally in *El Dorado* (1968) and *Rio Lobo* (1971), and which would inform other subsequent Westerns.

Rio Bravo was no sooner completed than Wayne immersed himself in producing, directing, and starring in *The Alamo* (1960). Wayne believed that an epic celebration of American courage and sacrifice in the face of despotism was needed now more than ever as America's commitment to fighting Communism appeared to be floundering with the decline of the Red Scare, policy shifts toward "peaceful coexistence," and the beckoning of Kennedy liberals at the White House door. In deference to prominent Texans who protested earlier plans to film in Mexico, Wayne took the more expensive course of constructing an elaborate set near Brackettville, Texas, not far from the Alamo's historical locale in San Antonio. The emotional strains of over-seeing every aspect of this large-scale production (compounded by John Ford's uninvited intrusion on the set) were exacerbated by cost overruns that stretched Wayne's own financial resources to the limit.

The resulting film delivered on the level of visual spectacle but nearly self-destructed under the weight of pompous rhetoric. In addition to receiving generally unfavorable reviews, *The Alamo* was awarded only one of six Oscar nominations following an embarrassingly solicitous campaign to curry the favor of Academy voters. Disappointing box-office returns failed to compensate Wayne's considerable personal investment and, on top of disclosures from other failed investments, left the popular 1950s star financially strapped.

Wayne quickly rebounded with a steady succession of profitable films that, for every consecutive year over the next a "decade-and-a-half", kept him in the ranks of America's top-ten moneymaking stars. Ironically, it was only after the postwar boom in movie Westerns had run its course by the early 1960s that the genre began to dominate Wayne's prolific output for the first time since his early days on Poverty Row. Without discounting the importance of directors Sam Peckinpah, Sergio Leone, and star-director Clint Eastwood for the revisionist strain that breathed new life into the Western in the late sixties and early seventies, the name John Wayne became virtually synonymous with a more traditionally heroic vision of the Hollywood West, which many Americans believed was worth preserving in these troubled times of antiwar protests and profound social discord.

Increasingly, Wayne played roles commensurate with his advancing years and, particularly in his own productions, his characters mirrored his own social and political conservatism. Overweight and wearing a toupee to cover his thinning hair, Wayne was less inclined to perform romantic scenes with a woman less than half his age as he did in *The Alamo*. Beginning with *The Comancheros* (1961), in which a romantic subplot is played out by the younger Stuart Whitman and Ina Balin, fewer Wayne films engaged the star with a love interest. Even his reunion with Maureen O'Hara in *McLintock* (1963) was played more for comical effect compared with their earlier pairings. The mudsliding slapstick in *McLintock*, duplicating the earlier and funnier *North to Alaska* (1960), revealed a penchant for rambunctious comedy that further endeared Wayne to audiences.

On a more serious level was Wayne's next-to-last performance for John Ford in the now classic Western, *The Man Who Shot Liberty Valance* (1962). Wayne claimed to be at a loss as to what do with the part of a tough, mind-your-own-business cattleman in a story that centered on a conflict between the civilizing efforts of a young lawyer (played by a not-so-young James Stewart) and the lawlessness of the title character (Lee Marvin). But the poignance of Ford's tale of civilization versus savagery does in fact hinge on the sympathy Wayne registers as a frontier individualist who, in shooting *Liberty Valance*, makes possible the modern social order that in turn will render him obsolete. This melancholic portrayal of the darker implications of Frederick Jackson Turner's 1890s acknowledgment of the closing of America's frontier epoch was John Ford's last great film and the last Western he made with his most famous Western player.

Wayne had just finished shooting Otto Preminger's World War II opus *In Harms Way* (1964), when medical X-rays revealed the cause of a worsening incessant cough. John Wayne had lung cancer. Surgery removed the tumor that apparently had not metastasized, and soon Wayne went public with the news that he had licked "the Big C." Within four months of having half of his left lung removed, Wayne was on location in Durango, Mexico, for his next Western, *The Sons of Katie Elder* (1965). The thin mountain air exacerbated the star's breathing difficulty, which is still audible on parts of the film's soundtrack.

After finishing two more profitable Westerns (*El Dorado* and *The War Wagon*, both released in 1967), Wayne produced, directed, and starred in another film statement of his concerns about America's resolve in the unending war against Communism. The *Green Berets* (1968) enraged many of the country's movie critics with its naked endorsement of the Vietnam War and assault on antiwar sentiment. Audience response was considerably more enthusiastic (the film was the tenth largest box-office draw of 1968), an indication that Wayne was far from alone in his feelings about America's most controversial war.

With *True Grit* (1969) Wayne won back many of the same critics who lambasted *The Green Berets*. His tour de force performance as the crusty one-eyed marshal, Rooster Cogburn, also earned Wayne his only Oscar nomination since *Sands of Iwo Jima*. Not unexpectedly, given the Academy's tendency to favor nominees whose longstanding contributions have been unacknowledged, Wayne won the coveted Oscar for best actor.

True Grit was not Wayne's best Western, but it was the perfect vehicle for exhibiting the comical self-parody he had begun to manifest in *North to Alaska* (1960), (also for director Henry Hathaway), combined with a warmth of feeling that prevented his Rooster Cogburn from lapsing into sheer caricature. There is humor but also something deeply moving, for example, in a scene where the tired, drunken, overweight marshal drops from his horse; unable to pick himself off the ground, he tells his two younger companions, "We'll camp here for the night."

For all of the eccentric qualities of the story and main character that derive from Charles Portis's novel, *True Grit* abounds with what were becoming familiar traits of the screen persona Wayne had been cultivating over the years. Rooster's melancholic reference to having lost a wife and family life because of his independent ways recalls any number of Wayne roles—including his other Oscar-nominated Sergeant Stryker in *Sands of Iwo Jima*. The paternalistic feeling Rooster exhibits toward Matty (which she reciprocates in the final scene by offering him a burial plot next to hers) recalls the Wayne–Clift relationship in *Red River* and reappears with greater frequency in Wayne's later films. In *The Cowboys* (1973), Wayne shepherds an entire crew of young boys on a harrowing cattle drive.

Perhaps most indicative of the mature Wayne image is Rooster's single-handed, fierce enforcement of justice and his impatience with the legalistic obstructions that Wayne in real life associated with soft-headed liberalism. He is no longer the team player of Ford's cavalry films or the maladjusted loner of *Red River* and *The Searchers* who must ultimately reconcile with the good of the community. Whatever divides Wayne from society in his later films, to include *True Grit,* implies not his but society's maladjustment.

In a sense Wayne never stopped playing the anachronistic "man who shot Liberty Valance." But rather than reenact this character's tragic displacement by modern civilization, Wayne's subsequent characters usually triumph in their refusal to succumb to modernity. As the cattle tycoons in

McLintock and *Chisum* (1970), Wayne defends his property and traditional way of life against pompous bureaucrats, grasping land agents, and undeserving homesteaders who are part of the new encroaching social order. As the former cattle baron in *Big Jake* (1971), who is asked by his estranged wife (Maureen O'Hara in a brief reprise of virtually the same role she played in *Rio Grande* and *McLintock*) to take charge of the rescue of their kidnapped grandson, Wayne asserts the same ruthless but right-minded "grit" that sets Rooster Cogburn above and apart from the ineffectual modern order. If George Washington McLintock, John Chisum, and Jacob McCandles are windier and more direct than Rooster in articulating their portrayer's conservative beliefs and more closely approximate the actor's status as a self-made success figure with strong, albeit dysfunctional, family bonds, they were also characters scripted specifically for Wayne's own Batjac production company.

Wayne strayed little from character types that virtually replicated the conservative image he exhibited in numerous interviews and public appearances. He could be irascibly blunt, as he was in a much-discussed 1971 *Playboy* interview, about sex and violence in current movies, the continuing threat of Communism in the nation's schools, as well as in Vietnam, liberal welfarism that favored society's undeserving elements, and the irresponsible dissidence of the younger generation. His pronouncements on these and other issues were of obvious appeal to those of the so-called "silent majority," whose discontent would find a political voice in Ronald Reagan's bid for the presidency in 1980. But Wayne's candor could also attract respect from those otherwise adverse to his political slant. Such was the case in 1974 when he entered Harvard Square atop an army tank to accept a Harvard Lampoon award and then proceeded to win over his student mockers in a good-humored exchange of barbs.

Prior to his Harvard visit, Wayne had finished work on *McQ* (1974), a critically and commercially failed attempt to cash in on the urban-crime genre and particularly the popularity of Clint Eastwood's "Dirty Harry" character. Wayne had no more success with the equally banal cop thriller *Brannigan,* released the following year. These films remained the only departures from a steady output of mostly formulaic Westerns following his award-winning performance in *True Grit*. Much was made of the badguy (Bruce Dern) killing off Wayne at the conclusion of *The Cowboys* (1973), but even this was not without precedent since Wayne had met a fatal end in six previous Westerns.

Wayne's films in the 1970s lacked the creative spark of *True Grit,* not to mention the best of his collaborations with Ford and Hawks. Still, the star's iconic legacy owes much to the sheer repetitiveness with which these largely mediocre films identified him as the venerable frontier patriarch ill at ease with the restrictive, compromising nature of modern progress even as he defeats the savage impediments to that progress.

The self-reflectiveness of Wayne's later Westerns turned somber in what was to be his last film, *The Shootist* (1976). Wayne's health was again fragile (breathing problems in particular weakened him) when shooting began on this story of the final days of a legendary gunman who is dying of cancer. Although no one could predict with certainty Wayne's own imminent encounter with a return of the "Big C," the film scenario was uncomfortably close to his worst fears about his declining physical condition. From the opening clips of earlier Wayne Westerns, audiences could not help identifying the star with the terminally ill character he plays and with the unfolding, now familiar theme of modern times supplanting the frontier world he represents.

Unlike "the shootist," who goes down in a final heroic gunfight rather than suffering nature's prolonged agonizing course, John Wayne would have to contend with another three years of physical deterioration. In March 1978, he survived open-heart surgery to replace a defective mitral valve. Less than a year later, in January 1979, he underwent a more debilitating surgery to arrest stomach cancer. Wayne's painfully thin appearance at the 1979 Oscar ceremony seemed to belie press accounts of a full recovery. Within two months he was back in the hospital for colon surgery, but at this point the cancer was incurably malignant.

Newspapers around the world carried the announcement that John Wayne had died in the early hours of June 11, 1979. President Jimmy Carter was among the first to pay respects: "John Wayne was bigger than life. In an age of few heros, he was the genuine article." Three weeks earlier Maureen O'Hara had sounded a similar note in testimony before a congressional subcommittee that was considering (and would approve) a special gold medal for Wayne: "John Wayne is the United States of America. . . . He is a hero and there are so few left." These are lofty tributes to someone who had opted out of military service in America's greatest war, endorsed congressional witchhunts and blacklisting, and had little truck with movements for racial and gender equality. But such adulation does speak to how inseparable America's greatest movie star had become in the public mind from the screen image he had cultivated over the span of five decades.

As a subject for biography, there is little about Wayne's personal or public life that is terribly remarkable, let alone heroic. His importance, rather, lies in what he projected in the many films he made, which in turn made him

America's most enduring movie star and a cultural icon. Were it not for the Vietnam War and the acrimony surrounding his production of *The Green Berets*, he might be more fondly remembered as the model of combat heroism that so impressed General Douglas MacArthur when *Sands of Iwo Jima* was released. Significantly, *The Green Berets* was Wayne's last war film, and for the remaining eight years of his career he confined himself to the genre with which he began his filmmaking career. Accordingly, John Wayne remains today primarily identified with the Hollywood West.

That is not to say that either the Hollywood West or its most famous star were unchanging in the sense that there was an archetypal John Wayne Western. There was to be sure the definable Wayne gait and voice inflection that he consciously began to fashion during the years on Poverty Row. But these stylistic peculiarities were continually refitted for characterizations that could vary considerably depending on the demands of a given script scenario and whether Wayne was being directed by John Ford, Howard Hawks, or a lesser talent contracted by Republic. There is also the fact that script narratives and directorial visions were affected to some degree by changes in the prevailing cultural climate. The Hollywood West that featured John Wayne as the Ringo Kid for Depression audiences was not the same as the Hollywood West of Wayne's Kirby Yorke in the post-World War II years or his John Chisum in the aftermath of the Great Society. If John Wayne retained throughout the decades a familiar behavioral code on screen that evoked a tradition of frontier individualism, that same persona endured in large part because of films that kept pace with the times.

six

Gary Cooper

Cowboy, Actor, Gentleman

LOUIS TANNER

G ary Cooper's Hollywood film career (1924–1961) ran from the innocence of silent movies to the disillusionment of the Cold War cinema. Cooper usually played super-masculine characters, but with a touch of sensitivity and uncertainty that set him apart from the run-of-the-mill cowboy hero. A childhood spent partly in American cow camps and partly in an exclusive British boarding school helped him to develop a range of mannerisms that broadened his screen appeal, so that his work was not restricted to Westerns or other action films. Westerns, in fact, were a small percentage of Cooper's total output. Still, his best movies were Westerns, and those few were among the best Westerns ever made.

With his diverse personal background and flexible style, Cooper could be equally effective in a 1920s action Western that cheerfully celebrated traditional American ideals, or a 1950s "adult" Western that reflected this period's preoccupation with betrayal, pessimism, and doubt. In his thirty-seven years acting before the American people, Cooper crafted an image of the western hero that incorporated the best and the worst of our frontier legacy.

Even in his private life, Cooper exhibited many traditional mannerisms of the quiet, undemonstrative cowboy largely because he had been a cowpuncher long before he became a successful actor. Born Frank James Cooper on May 7, 1901, in Helena, Montana, Cooper's earliest memories were of the family's nearby Seven-Bar-Nine cattle ranch, bought in 1906. His father, Charles H. Cooper, was a British citizen who left his wealthy Bedfordshire family to explore the American West. In 1894, he married Alice Louise Brazier, another native Briton, who was visiting relatives in Helena. Charles Cooper settled into a law practice, hoping to become a judge, while running the ranch as a sideline.

Young Frank spent his every free moment on the ranch, hunting, fishing, and learning cowboy skills from the hands, many of whom remembered Montana's wilder past. He later claimed to have gotten his first riding lesson when he was four years old from "a tall, angular, silent man who wore his hair long after the fashion of Buffalo Bill." To a degree, Cooper later used these old-timers of his childhood as models when portraying western figures in his films. They also, at least as a romantic ideal, helped to shape his private character as well.

Cooper's mother did not always approve of the old timers' influence on her young son. She was particularly upset when he copied their imaginative profanity, and she decided he needed a more cultured environment. In 1909, she took her two sons, Frank and his older brother, Arthur, back to the Cooper ancestral home in Bedfordshire and enrolled them at the Dunstable School, an exclusive private academy attended by generations of Coopers. Frank was an indifferent student who much preferred the western outdoors to the classroom, but in his three years rubbing shoulders with the English privileged class he acquired a slight British accent and a social polish that he would never lose and that contributed to his versatility as an actor. He returned to the United States in April 1913 and happily resumed his life on the ranch.

About three years later Cooper was badly injured in an automobile accident, suffering "a broken leg and other complications too numerous to mention," as he later recalled. One of those complications was a broken hip, which no one diagnosed at the time. The doctor recommended vigorous horseback riding to work out the "stiffness" in the hip, advice that Cooper followed despite great pain. On the positive side, Cooper reported, he had been forced at this time to develop exceptionally good riding skills. To avoid sharp bursts of agony, he had learned to anticipate the horse's every move. But this ill-advised therapy apparently did permanent damage to a hip that would bother him for the rest of his life. Particularly in his later movies, he can be seen hunched to one side in the saddle, his left leg pushed out straight in front to help relieve the chronic pain from his teenage injury.

When Cooper returned from England, the Montana schools refused to give him full credit for his work at Dunstable, so he had to fall back a year. His education was further interrupted by his automobile accident and then by America's entry into World War I. Young men across Montana rushed to enlist in the army, leaving ranches with a labor shortage. Cooper, too young for service, dropped out of school for two years to help his mother run the ranch while his father continued his law practice in the city. In these adolescent years, doing the work he loved, Cooper grew tall and thin, reaching a height of six feet, three inches and a weight of only 160 pounds.

When Cooper returned to school, he towered over his much younger classmates and finally graduated from a Bozeman, Montana, high school in 1922. During the previous two years he had taken drawing courses at Montana Wesleyan College and at Montana Agricultural College (now Montana State University). He admired the western paintings of Montana artist Charles M. Russell, a family friend, and thought he might like to pursue a similar career as an illustrator. He enrolled in an art training program at Iowa's Grinnell College, where he remained for a little over two years. At Grinnell he repeatedly tried to get involved in school theatricals, but was turned down for lack of experience. He left college in 1924, never to return, and went home to live with his parents.

Charles and Alice, however, had moved from Montana to Hollywood. Confused and unemployed, Cooper took long walks around the unfamiliar California town, pondering his future and wondering if he might get a start in show business.

In December 1924, wandering near Poverty Row where low-budget Westerns were being made, he met some cowboy friends from Montana. They were working in movies as stuntmen and extras and invited him to join up. Jay "Slim" Talbot, a rodeo champion and rising stuntman, was hiring riders who could look good falling off a horse. So Cooper began his movie career falling off horses for $10 a day, plus lunch. At Fox Studios he rode in Tom Mix Westerns, and at Paramount he worked in several movies based on Zane Grey novels. His first appearance was probably in Grey's *The Thundering Herd* or *The Vanishing American,* both released in 1925.

Falling off horses was hard, dangerous work, however, and Cooper began brooding about the thousands of dollars a week the big stars were making. He hired a horse and a photographer, decorated his face with powder, lipstick, and mascara, as was then the style in these silent films, and produced his own screen test for about $65. He rode the horse straight at the camera, dismounted in a cloud of dust, and finished with a smiling close up. He showed his twenty-second screen test to anyone who would watch it, hoping for the legendary big break. At about this time he hired an agent, Nan Collins, to help him get started. Collins disliked the name Frank Cooper and convinced him to adopt Gary as a first name. She liked it better since she had a fondness for her hometown of Gary, Indiana.

Several Hollywood figures have circulated stories describing, and taking credit for, the "discovery" of Gary Cooper. According to scriptwriter Frances Marion, who has the best story, Cooper got his big break because he had been dating the secretary of studio mogul Samuel Goldwyn. Marion spotted

Cooper loitering outside the office window and immediately thought him perfect for one of the supporting roles in Goldwyn's *The Winning of Barbara Worth* (1926), for which she was preparing a screenplay. When her male bosses insisted they already had superior candidates for the role, Marion suggested they show screen tests from all the candidates to Goldwyn's female employees and let them decide. The women trooped in and watched silently until Cooper appeared, then the room filled with "Aahhs." Although Cooper still did not get the part, the studio powers soon would remember him when a chance opening appeared.

Those who only know the Gary Cooper of *High Noon* (1952), with his rugged, seamed, outdoorsman's face, would hardly recognize the Gary Cooper of the 1920s. He had an ethereal beauty, emphasized by the standard makeup, that was more feminine than masculine. Some critics have since called his face "androgynous" and suggested that this ambiguity of sexual identity, perhaps even in his most "masculine" roles, gave each performance a submerged complexity that attributed to his extraordinary popularity and sex appeal. Whatever the explanation, women found him irresistible, both on the screen and in person, and his affairs with successful Hollywood actresses aided substantially his early career in films.

For *The Winning of Barbara Worth*, as the result of Marion's efforts, Cooper went on location to the Nevada desert as an extra. When a featured actor failed to show up, he was cast in the character of Abe Lee, a young engineer who discovers that a dam is about to collapse. Lee makes an exhausting, suicidal ride through the desert just in time to warn the male and female leads, after which he dies in melodramatic fashion. Cooper was brilliant or at least memorable in this relatively small part, and movie critics went out of their way to praise his inspired performance.

Now modestly in demand, Cooper signed a five-year contract with Paramount for $175 a week, after turning down Goldwyn's offer of $65 a week. With money of his own and with an increasingly complicated love life, Cooper moved out of his parents' home and into his own apartment.

In his first weeks with Paramount, he began an affair with Clara Bow, one of the studio's rising stars. Bow was scheduled to play the lead in *It* (1927), the film that would give her lasting fame. Hoping to assist her most recent sexual conquest, Bow demanded a small part for Cooper. He played, for his few seconds of film, a reporter trying to interview the "it" girl. When word of Bow's arrangement got around, to his disgust, Cooper was dubbed "the 'it' boy." No one complained about his performance, however, which was excellent while it lasted. Then, with Bow's assistance, he had a brief appearance in one of the year's most successful films, *Wings* (1927), the story of two young fighter pilots during World War I. Cooper plays an avuncular older pilot who inspires the hero worship of the two youngsters, then flies off to his death. His brief appearance was riveting, and when *Wings* won the first Academy Award for Best Picture, he shared in the glory.

Also in 1927, Cooper got his first starring role as "the cowboy" in the low-budget Western *Arizona Bound*. Cooper looked good on a horse, did his own stunts, and generally pleased the studio brass, who were then certain he could carry a Western despite his clumsy handling of love scenes. Paramount immediately cast him in Zane Grey's *Nevada* (1927) with Thelma Todd and in *The Last Outlaw* (1927) with Betty Jewell and Flash, the Wonder Horse. Drawing upon his experiences with Slim Talbot, Cooper again did his own stunts and was widely believed to have given better performances than the screenplays merited.

In his first year as a serious actor, Cooper had demonstrated professional talent and the precious ability to captivate an audience. But Paramount used him poorly the following year in a series of ill-conceived costume dramas and love stories that did nothing for his career.

In 1929, Cooper returned to a Western role in *Wolf Song*, in which he played a fur trapper operating out of Taos, New Mexico. This film was Cooper's first "partial talkie," in which 1,000 feet of dialogue and singing were spliced into a typical silent film. *Wolf Song* was a melodramatic romance with a controversial nude swimming episode and several heated love scenes featuring Cooper and Mexican actress Lupe Vélez, real-life lovers at the time. The chemistry between the two stars, a hit theme song, and a determined publicity campaign helped to make this film financially successful, but reviewers were unenthusiastic. Cooper's career seemed locked in mediocrity.

But later that year, he starred in his first blockbuster for Paramount, *The Virginian* (1929), and his reputation skyrocketed. *The Virginian* was the third film treatment of Owen Wister's ground-breaking cowboy novel and Cooper's first all-sound movie. Cooper was well cast as the quiet, bashful cowboy with hidden strengths and unshakable integrity. In the classic formula that Wister's novel had created in 1902 and other Westerns had then imitated, the Virginian woos the new school marm (Mary Brian) and has fun with his friend Steve (Richard Arlen) until he finds Steve putting his own brand on somebody else's cow. The Virginian reluctantly lynches Steve and finally kills the head rustler, Trampas (Walter Huston), in a main street shoot out.

Cooper handled this role successfully partly because the script had changed the Virginian from the mature, supremely self-confident figure he had been in the novel into a bashful youngster trying to find himself, an interpretation more suited to Cooper's acting skills at the time. But here, as in his best performances in later years, he was rarely guilty of overacting. He uses only his eyes, for example, to convey the Virginian's internal chaos as he helps to execute his friend Steve. Overcoming dialogue that generally works against him, Cooper is able to communicate his character's growing maturity as he learns to accept the burdens of responsibility.

He also did well underplaying the action scenes. At one point early in the story, Trampas starts to call the Virginian a "son of a bitch," but the Virginian pushes his pistol into the villain's belly and says, in what became a classic line, "If you want to call me that, smile." Walter Huston as Trampas then smiles a big toothy grin that seems to fill the screen. Cooper was appropriately serious in this scene while carefully letting Huston "steal" it, which made the most artistic sense. Huston was the highest paid actor in the film, receiving $20,000. Cooper got $3,400. The film was shot in 24 days in Sonora in the High Sierra and featured impressive outdoor shots such as a panoramic view of cattle swimming a swift-flowing river.

The success of *The Virginian* established Cooper as a star in the eyes of the public, but Paramount still wanted him to grind out a lot of movies in a hurry. The studio soon paired him with Fay Wray in *The Texan* (1930), based on an O. Henry short story. Cooper played an irresponsible young bandit, the Llano Kid, who matures while witnessing other people's tragedies. With larceny in mind, he pretends at first to be the long lost son of a wealthy elderly woman. But the Kid soon decides to go straight and to help punish the real crooks. Reviewers noted that Cooper did well speaking Spanish in this film; probably he had been coached by Lupe Vélez.

At this time, Cooper was working particularly hard, putting in fifteen to twenty-three hours a day, often making two movies at once. He lost 30 pounds, became anemic and jaundiced, and suffered bouts of depression. In addition, his relationship with Lupe Vélez began to disintegrate, which only added to his stress. Velez was hoping for marriage, but she later said that Cooper's overprotective mother had intentionally broken up the relationship. Exhausted by work and caught in this crossfire between the two women in his life, Cooper finally realized he needed a break to recover his emotional and physical health. "I felt like an old man," he later said. "Hollywood had burned me out and I hadn't even begun to act."

He told reporters he wanted to return to his cowboy roots and relax. He thought he might even retreat to the wilds of South America where he could forget the predatory atmosphere of Hollywood and come to terms with his own celebrityhood. But in 1931, at this crisis point in his life, he did not go to Montana to commune with nature. Instead, he put his Paramount contract on indefinite hold and headed for Europe to frolic with the rich and the well-born.

At that time and in the future, Cooper frequently promoted himself as just a good old Montana cowboy, but in fact he had a taste for the high life, for upper-class companions, and for conspicuous consumption. He had become one of the best-dressed men in Hollywood, buying handmade suits from the most exclusive shops in London. Fashion magazines like *Flair*, *Women's Wear Daily*, and *Esquire* wrote features about his stylish clothes, and fashion designers claimed he would have made a wonderful professional model. As befitted a country gentleman, he raised high-priced show dogs and once appeared with his champion pet, he and the dog both perfectly groomed, on the cover of *Western Kennel World*.

Like a good Montanan, Cooper enjoyed simple outdoor sports like hunting, fishing, archery, and tennis. But he also liked fast, expensive cars. In 1930, he bought the most expensive car made, a Duesenberg, and a few years later had a Mercedes built to his specifications. When he could get away with it, he liked to see how his cars handled at 125 mph on city streets.

In short, he liked expensive things and the kinds of people who could afford them. When Cooper walked off the Paramount lot in 1931, not sure if he would ever return, he soon began an affair with the rich American wife of an Italian count and became a member of her exclusive social circle. It was something of a trend at the time for suddenly rich American heiresses (now hungering for social respectability) to link up with penniless European noblemen (always hungering for money). In this case, the heiress was Dorothy Taylor of New York, said to have $12 million, and the nobleman was Count Carlo Dentice di Frasso. The count, thirty years older than his wife, did not object to her romances outside of marriage, so that husband, wife, and lover often attended social gatherings as a congenial threesome. Using his wife's money, the count rebuilt the moldering family estate, the Villa Madama, which the countess then tried to keep constantly full of important personages. She frequently entertained, for example, England's Duke of York (later King George VI), various members of the Greek and Italian royal families, and the odd duchess or duke.

Being a descendant from English lineage, Cooper fit in well with this company, not only because he had the proper bloodlines and table manners, but also because he truly admired the idle rich and wished to learn their ways. The countess taught him about fine wines and French cooking. She introduced him to Italy's artistic treasures and helped him test his riding skills against Europe's most accomplished horsemen. Cooper discovered to his surprise that many European aristocrats admired and envied him in turn, which helped to boost his shaken self-confidence.

In the fall of 1931, the countess took Cooper on a luxurious safari in Africa, hunting big game in Kenya and Tanganyika. Cooper later said he had the time of his life. "I love Africa. I love its bigness, its toughness, the savagery you can feel all around you at any place in the continent," he said. Cooper killed truckloads of game. An amateur taxidermist, he later stuffed his own trophies and filled his Hollywood house with them.

This year among the high born brought out the latent British gentleman in Cooper, a process that his years at Dunstable School had only begun. His experiences in real drawing rooms gave authority to his performances when he played sophisticated characters on the sound stage. Of his eighty-five feature films, he played Old West figures in approximately twenty-five of them depending on definitions, which was less than a third of his total. For most "cowboy" stars of his day, the proportion would be reversed and for some, such as Roy Rogers and Gene Autry, a non-Western would be a rare exception to their usual work.

But Cooper's handsome English face, his refined speech, and his visible comfort in high-society settings gave him a versatility that few other cowboy actors could match. Among his best films were the non-Westerns *Morocco* (1930) and *Desire* (1936), both with Marlene Dietrich. In addition, *Mr. Deeds Goes to Town* (1936) earned him an Academy Award nomination, and in *Love in the Afternoon* (1957) he played an autobiographical role as a polished but aging playboy who seduces young women. He was also the determined architect in Ayn Rand's *The Fountainhead* (1948) and the flawed hero in adaptations of two novels by Ernest Hemingway, *A Farewell to Arms* (1932) and *For Whom the Bell Tolls* (1943). He won a best actor Academy Award for his work in *Sergeant York* (1941), a patriotic war film. Respect for Cooper's versatility was so great that he was offered the role of southern aristocrat Rhett Butler in *Gone with the Wind* (1939), which he turned down, incorrectly predicting that it would be "the biggest flop in Hollywood history."

From 1929 to 1950, his two most productive decades, he starred in only six noteworthy Westerns: *The Virginian* (1929), *The Texan* (1930), *The Plainsman* (1936), *The Westerner* (1940), *North West Mounted Police* (1940),

Gary Cooper in The Plainsman *(1936). L. Tom Perry Special Collections, Harold B. Lee Library, Brigham Young University, Provo, Utah.*

and *Along Came Jones* (1945). By the strength of his performances in these roles, he became permanently identified with the western hero. He established his western image so firmly that in the last period of his life, from 1950 to 1961, he intentionally manipulated this conventional image for artistic effect, shocking his audiences by portraying a character more cowardly or more sadistic than they had come to expect.

After returning to the United States in 1932, Cooper broke with Countess di Frasso and soon became interested in another wealthy and stylish woman, Veronica "Rocky" Balfe, stepdaughter of Wall Street millionaire Paul Shields. Balfe, who had attended finishing school but had never earned a high school diploma, was attempting to break into the film industry under the name Sandra Shaw, but she felt no urgency and soon gave up this career. On December 15, 1933, the twenty-year-old Balfe married thirty-two-year-old Cooper, a marriage that would last until Cooper's death in 1961 and produce one daughter, Maria, born in September 1937. Cooper told *Picture Play* that he was attracted by Balfe's purity and virginity, saying he had not wanted "damaged goods." Certainly he was excited as well by her upper-class mannerisms and her ability to provide access to the exclusive reaches of American society.

The Montana cowboy was a persona to which Cooper returned intermittently throughout his life, usually on a hunting or fishing trip. When burdened with work, he often expressed a desire to go back to his small-town roots. But his most powerful ambitions pointed in the other direction—toward the East and the cities, toward conspicuous wealth and sophistication—as his choice of a wife revealed.

In 1936, Cooper worked for the first time with the legendary director Cecil B. DeMille in *The Plainsman* (1936), a fictionalized biography of James Butler "Wild Bill" Hickok, famed western lawman and gunfighter. The film compresses history a bit, since it historically begins in 1865 and ends in 1876, whereas the storyline's action takes, at most, a few weeks. Here Hickok is an army scout who tries to keep smugglers from selling modern rifles to Indian warriors. The evil Yellow Hand and Painted Horse plan to use the weapons against Colonel George A. Custer's Seventh Cavalry.

Hickok's best friend is retired scout Buffalo Bill Cody who has married and now wants to settle down. Cody represents the new, civilized man of the West. Hickok, in contrast, is the old-time frontiersman, a "two-gun plainsman," as he calls himself, who can exist only on the frontier and who now must pass away. In keeping with this symbolism, Hickok dies at the end, shot in the back while playing cards, as happened in real life.

The pedestrian plot of *The Plainsman* limps along, and Cooper does not get much help from the supporting cast. Jean Arthur as the love interest, Calamity Jane, is entirely too perky, and James Ellison as Buffalo Bill is unconvincing. The best supporting performances come from Victor Varconi and Paul Harvey as genuinely scary Indian villains.

Cooper, however, is superb, underacting perfectly, masterfully using the small hand and eye movements for which he is famous, and injecting his own subtle brand of light humor whenever the script permits. His face has matured. He is no longer the beautiful youth, but he is not yet the craggy-faced, middle-aged, fading hero of his last and perhaps best-known movies.

Several directors, DeMille among them, thought Cooper's acting dull and wooden as they first watched him on the set and wondered how they could liven him up. But then they saw the rushes of the day's shooting and realized he had actually been playing brilliantly to the camera, using small movements of eyes, lips, and hands to give his character depth and complexity. Making full use of these techniques, Cooper brought *The Plainsman* to life as few other actors could have.

In the 1930s, with these now well-developed acting skills and favorable roles, Cooper became one of the most popular actors in America, and the best paid. Still working mostly at Paramount, he had also agreed to make one movie a year with Samuel Goldwyn for a minimum $150,000. In 1939, the U.S. Treasury Department announced that Cooper was the country's highest-paid individual taxpayer. Earning $482,826 that year, he made more than the heads of General Motors Corporation, Lever Brothers, or International Business Machines.

In 1940, Goldwyn cast him in *The Westerner* with Walter Brennan, Cooper's close friend since the mid-1920s. The two actors brought out the best in each other and eventually made seven movies together. To some degree, *The Westerner* was designed to showcase Brennan's talents, despite his supposedly supporting role. Cooper later claimed that when he first read the script and saw the weakness of his own role he refused to do the movie. "I couldn't see that it needed Gary Cooper for the part," he wrote in his published memoirs. When Goldwyn flourished their contract and threatened to sue, Cooper finally agreed to do the movie under protest.

Brennan played Judge Roy Bean, a historical figure who once called himself "the only law west of the Pecos River." Brennan's Bean is cranky, idiosyncratic, bloodthirsty, and passionately in love with the actress Lily Langtry, whom he has never met. Cooper plays cowboy Cole Hardin who comes before the judge for stealing a horse and who is certain to be executed until he notices the judge's obsession with Langtry and cunningly uses it to his advantage. Hardin pretends to have a lock of Lily Langtry's hair, which he offers to the judge in exchange for his release.

Hardin and Bean slowly become good friends despite being on opposite sides in a range war between cattlemen and crop farmers. The range-war conflict brings them to a climactic gunfight in a theater where Lily Langtry is about to perform. When Bean collapses, Hardin lifts the dying judge in his arms and carries him to Langtry so that he can have one happy moment before he expires.

Generally, this plot follows a tradition set by *The Virginian* as the central character must choose between friendship and justice: the Virginian had to hang his friend Steve; Hardin has to kill the murderous Judge Bean. But perhaps foreshadowing themes of the following decade, the moral conflict in *The Westerner* ends in ambiguity. The judge had ordered his henchmen to burn out the sodbusters and drive them from the territory. In doing so, he established himself as a classic western villain. But nothing could be more tender than Hardin's treatment of the judge just before his death. Clearly Hardin's affection has not abated, and viewers are left with the image of the judge as a lovable eccentric rather than as a ruthless villain.

The Westerner permitted Cooper to exercise his full range of talents; his sensitivity and humor again were prominently on display. In his best scene, he appears with a huge pair of scissors to clip a lock of hair from the head of his sodbuster sweetheart so that he can pretend the hair is Langtry's. His playful use of the prop and his expertise with subtle hand and face movements rivet the audience's attention and demonstrate again his mastery of light comedy. Despite Cooper's initial reservations, this film was a critical and commercial success. Brennan won an Oscar for supporting actor, and Stuart N. Lake, the biographer of Wyatt Earp, received a nomination for best original story.

Cooper then returned to Paramount for *North West Mounted Police* (1940), in which he played a Texas Ranger helping out the Mounties in Canada. This was Cooper's first Technicolor film, lavishly directed by Cecil B. DeMille. Today's critics usually admit that the color photography was superb, but otherwise express little respect for this film. *North West Mounted Police* was popular when released, however, and received one Academy Award (for sound) and four other nominations. Although the Ranger in this film was not the morally complex figure Cooper had played in *The Westerner*, the role again presented Cooper as the independent, taciturn western hero and helped him fix that basic image in the public mind.

In the 1940s, Cooper found other major roles that were not western, but that promoted the same basic image. He always sought stories, he said, western or nonwestern, that "were credible, that fitted my personality on the screen, and that didn't clash with the beliefs people held of me." These personal requirements naturally took him in the direction of Westerns, where such characters were standard, but other "action" films offered similar opportunities. During this decade, *Sergeant York* (1941), *The Pride of Yankees* (1942), and *For Whom the Bell Tolls* (1943) won Cooper flattering praise from his peers, proved again he could make commercial hits, and firmly embedded his chosen image in the public mind.

In 1944, hoping to continue such successes under his own control, Cooper formed a production company, International Pictures, with partners Leo Spitz, William Goetz, and Nunnally Johnson. The company's first effort was *Casanova Brown* (1944), a contemporary light comedy with Cooper as lead actor and producer. For his next feature, Cooper chose *Along Came Jones* (1945), a parody of cowboy movies with a comic reversal of his own western persona. In the film, a bumbling cowboy who cannot do anything right is mistaken for a famous gunfighter, which puts him in constant peril. Continuing the theme of reversed roles, the love interest (Loretta Young) frequently rescues the cowboy from his own ineptness and even shoots the villain at the end. Cooper later said he was not a very good producer, but *Along Came Jones* was finished on time, cost less than budgeted, and pleased audiences, which are the usual measures of success. Cooper clearly did not enjoy the double duty as both actor and producer, however, so after these two films he merged his company with Universal Pictures to form Universal–International Pictures, Inc., and returned to full-time acting.

As part of his plan at this time to take more active control of his image, Cooper toyed with the idea of linking himself publicly to Republican Party politics and to anti-communist activism. In 1944, he joined the conservative Motion Picture Alliance for the Preservation of American Ideals, which hoped to purge Hollywood of all communist influences. On October 31, 1944, entering directly into that year's presidential contest, Cooper bought his own radio time to support Republican presidential candidate Thomas E. Dewey against incumbent Franklin D. Roosevelt, and on November 6 he bought ad space in *The New York Times* to endorse Dewey. Cooper said he had supported FDR at one time, but no longer would, saying that the president had broken too many promises, whereas Dewey was efficient and honest. Cooper continued this policy of political identification for a year or two, but as the postwar attacks on communists became more vicious and more damaging to his friends in the movie business, he began to back away from a close association with the most radical conservatives.

In 1947, at the urging of the Motion Picture Alliance, a committee of the U.S. House of Representatives conducted hearings on alleged anti-American activities in Hollywood, investigating charges that subversives were using movies to promote communist ideas. The House Un-American Activities Committee (HUAC) called many prominent Hollywood figures to testify about communists in Hollywood. Those named as communists or communist sympathizers or those who refused to testify when called were blacklisted by the movie industry and prohibited from future work in Hollywood films. Anyone associating with blacklisted persons risked being branded as disloyal and being likewise cut out of filmmaking.

Cooper testified as a "friendly witness" before the committee October 23, 1947, but when asked to identify specific persons or scripts that promoted communist ideas, Cooper was intentionally vague. He testified that he believed there were communists at work in Hollywood, but he did not know any personally. He carefully put himself in a position safe from all criticism. He cooperated with the committee, expressing his hatred for Communism, while making sure no one in Hollywood would be hurt by his testimony.

Rejecting this opportunity to link his public image to right-wing causes, Cooper apparently gave up the idea that political activism could further his career. Thereafter he avoided conspicuous statements about politics. Occasionally he remarked that actors should not publicly discuss things they knew nothing about. In future years, he refused to endorse the continuing congressional red hunt when other prominent actors such as John Wayne did so proudly. Wayne, for example, helped promote the red hunt by playing a heroic HUAC investigator in *Big Jim McLain* (1952), whereas Cooper publicly supported blacklisted colleagues despite threats of being shunned himself. In the 1950s, when Cooper made Westerns whose themes reflected the moral ambiguities of the Cold War, he could draw upon his own personal struggle to find a middle ground during the Red Scare hysteria.

By the early 1950s, despite his increased concern with his public image, Cooper saw his popularity slipping. He no longer ranked among the top ten Hollywood money makers. Believing that his reputation was again being damaged by bad scripts and inappropriate roles, he began to look for a project that could reinvigorate his career. He liked the script for a low-budget Western being planned by producer Stanley Kramer and writer Carl Foreman called *High Noon* (1952). Cooper liked the script so much that he offered to cut his fee, an unusual move for a man who felt poor no matter how much he made. He had been collecting $250,000–$275,000 for each film, but now he settled for $60,000 and a percentage of the profits.

Cooper later said he saw in this film the western values that his father had taught him in Montana: the importance of taking a stand for what was right regardless of who stood with you. "It was a challenging role—and I loved it," he said. Fred Zinnemann agreed to direct for the same financial deal offered to Cooper. The unknown actress Grace Kelly, twenty-one at the time, was picked to play Cooper's wife, partly because her youthful blond beauty contrasted so sharply with Cooper's aged and ill appearance and partly because she would work cheap. The future Princess Grace of Monaco received $500 a week.

In the film, a loose adaptation of the story "The Tin Star" (1947) by John Cunningham, Cooper plays Marshal Will Kane of Hadleyville, a small dusty town in New Mexico Territory. On his wedding day, he learns that a murderer he had sent to jail has been pardoned and will come on the noon train seeking revenge. Kane's wife, a Quaker, says he must flee or she will leave him.

Kane decides he must stay and begins looking for a posse to help him defend the town. The townspeople refuse to help and suggest it would be better if Kane were to leave their quiet village so that the murderer could run him down somewhere else. The aging marshal, clearly terrified, scratches out his last will and prepares to face, by himself, the returning murderer and his three-man gang. In a wild fight through the town, Kane kills three of the gang, and his bride, casting off her Quaker scruples, kills the fourth. With the bodies lying around, the husband and wife embrace in the street as the townspeople gather. Then Kane takes off his badge, throws it to the ground as a sign of contempt, and the couple drives off.

In addition to this archetypal story line with its suggestions of universal conflicts, several production innovations also gave the movie a unique feel and undoubtedly contributed to its success. The movie was in "real" time; that is, film time matched the story's action, which presumably began about ten forty-five in the morning and climaxed with the arrival of the noon train. Frequent shots of clocks built suspense. Kramer and Foreman also chose to film in black-and-white to emphasize starkness and despair. They filmed Cooper with the least flattering makeup and lighting to make him look old and tired. He had recently suffered with ulcers, hernias, and a bad back, and his health problems showed on his face. Always the professional, he still managed a brutal fight scene largely without a double.

Marshal Kane was a role designed specifically for Cooper's minimalist acting style. Kane did not say much, and there was little action before the last gunfight. But Cooper brilliantly projected just the right look. As intended, he appeared worn by dust and time, beaten down by a hostile environment. And in deliberate contrast to his well-established image as the iron-nerved western hero, Cooper showed to surprised audiences a vulnerable public servant tormented by fear and shocked by his community's indifference. By this time Cooper's face had already become an American icon, expressing with perfection one image of the western hero. But with this performance he added an element of the tragic to that image, and his face reflected not only the end of the mythic West but also the end of simplistic faith in American innocence.

When Kramer viewed the first cut of the film, he was disappointed and suspected that he had produced a flop. He had missed the tension for which he had striven. Film editor Elmo Williams then recut, eliminating a subplot and tightening the suspense. Williams's new cut restored everyone's confidence, and, with other small changes, they took the movie to preview audiences. Their confidence promptly crashed again; the audiences hated it. But after trade screenings, professional critics wrote complimentary reviews, so United Artists agreed to release the film with a major publicity campaign. All was not lost.

After a slow start, *High Noon* grew into a box-office hit, making money, spawning imitations, and reviving Cooper's career. The film grossed $3.75 million in America and $18 million worldwide. Cooper reportedly made $600,000. The film was nominated for six Academy Awards and won four: Cooper for best actor, Elmo Williams and Harry Gerstad for editing, and Dimitri Tiomkin (2 awards) for theme song and musical score. The theme song, "Do Not Forsake Me Oh My Darlin'/On This Our Weddin' Day," sung by Tex Ritter for the movie, was redone by Frankie Laine and became a hit record.

Many viewers recognized in *High Noon* references to contemporary politics. Scriptwriter Carl Foreman later said he had intentionally created a parable of the Cold War and the Red Scare based on his own experiences. In April 1951, while working on the script, Foreman was subpoenaed in the latest round of HUAC hearings. Called in September, he testified that he was not then a member of the Communist Party, but refused to name any communists he might have known. Foreman knew months earlier that he would be black-listed for this "uncooperative" testimony and that his Hollywood career would soon end. He later recalled that he rewrote *High Noon* to represent his view of Hollywood in the clutches of the Red Scare. He wished to show how fear caused otherwise good people to do disgraceful things and how anyone who challenged Washington's fanaticism would have to do so alone.

Foreman said that after his subpoena was announced there was a strong "underground" movement to force Cooper off *High Noon*. Cooper refused to leave, however, despite these threats of blacklisting and even announced publicly at one point that he would form a new production company in partnership with Foreman. Finally, afraid he might permanently damage Cooper's career, Foreman dropped plans for the partnership and migrated to England where he could work in relative peace. He later said that Cooper was the only "big one" with the courage to support him during the Red Scare and to stand up for what he thought was right. Foreman was dropped from the picture's credits as associate producer but retained credit as scriptwriter, for which he received an Academy Award nomination despite these controversies.

Foreman's testimony about his intentions, however, has not ended specu-lation as to what *High Noon* meant to contemporary audiences. Some critics, such as historian John H. Lenihan, have pointed out that the movie could support the conservative position on the congressional hearings as easily as it might support Foreman's view. In this opposite interpretation, the heroic Marshal Kane could represent the most passionate red hunters who struggle to save society from the communists (the gang of murderers in the movie) while the weak-spined, liberal American public (i.e., the town) refuses to come to their aid.

Nothing in the movie demands that we accept one or the other of these opposing interpretations, and the final script (perhaps at Zinnemann's urging) intentionally avoided identifying the lawman hero with any specific person, political party, or set of policies. The filmmakers wished instead to por-tray archetypal conflicts that might exist at any time or place and expected their audience to fill in the blanks. Still, in the kinds of questions it raises, *High Noon* departs from movies Cooper made early in his career and demonstrates typical features of Cold War films.

For example, although *The Virginian* at the beginning of his career and *High Noon* near the end have sev-eral similarities in their basic structures and in the functions of the central characters, there are thematic differences between the two which reflect the change over time of public concerns. The films are similar in that both have strong central figures who must confront evil at risk to their lives. In both films the wife or fiancée tells the hero that she will not condone violence and that if he fights the crook she will leave him. The hero (at the mercy of his masculine code) goes out to fight anyway. In both films the woman changes her mind, and the couple is reunited. Also in both, to emphasize the hero's lonely courage, the showdown with the villain happens in the street with all the townsfolk watching from indoors.

But the two films have radically different views of the relationship between the hero and the society in which he lives. The Virginian and his community work together toward common goals. When the shooting ends, the Virginian has a supportive wife, a good job, and the respect of his neighbors. Harmony prevails. Kane, by comparison, breaks with community leaders at the beginning and succeeds despite their opposition. When the villains are defeated, Kane and his wife leave in disgust, permanently ending their ties to the town. The story ends pessimistically with disharmony and separation, and with the suggestion that frontier democracy was chronically infected with cowardice and greed.

The difference between these movies illustrates how Westerns of the 1950s typically questioned the moral complacency of earlier films. A 1920s Western like *The Virginian* took for granted that taming the wilderness was a good thing and that "civilization" resolved all frontier conflicts. In these early stories, white adventurers moved into the West to displace Indians, kill anyone else who threatened life or property, and build new outposts of the American republic.

In the 1950s, Westerns questioned the value of civilizing the wild places and pointed out that civilization (government, in effect) could be bad or good. If early Westerns were content to bring "law" to the frontier, later Westerns asked, "what kind of 'law'" and "whose interests will be protected?" Were the criminals really absolutely bad and society absolutely good, or did the distinctions crumble under closer inspection? Would killing people resolve all social conflicts as seemed to be *The Virginian*'s message? Although Cooper's Westerns of the 1950s were not as blatantly political as many of the period's films, they frequently asked these kinds of questions and similarly challenged the simple and optimistic moral codes of the Western's earlier days.

Cooper's later Westerns also reflected indirectly America's growing anxiety over the international threat from the Soviet Union. His films often employed "revolution" plots in which democratic freedom fighters tried to unseat a totalitarian dictator or, conversely, an established democracy defended itself from antidemocratic insurgents. These story lines mirrored the chief concerns of U.S. foreign policy at that time as the country strove to contain world Communism. After making *High Noon*, Cooper starred in *Springfield Rifle* (1952), *Garden of Evil* (1954), *Vera Cruz* (1954), *Man of the West* (1958), *The Hanging Tree* (1959), and *They Came to Cordura* (1959). Each of these films illustrates to some degree the Western's postwar concern with moral ambiguity and communist threats.

Adding contemporary relevance did not necessarily improve these movies, however, or bring out the best in Cooper. To his own disappointment, his roles after *High Noon* failed to make full use of his talents and he often felt he was letting his audiences down. In 1961, as he prepared for his unavoidable death from cancer, he wrote, "Nothing I've done lately, the past eight years or so, has been especially worthwhile. . . . Some of the pictures I've made recently I'm genuinely sorry about." Earlier in his career, for example, Cooper had used light comedy to give a character depth and complexity. But his films in the 1950s, perhaps reflecting the seriousness of their contemporary themes, often were devoid of humor, thus causing his performances to emerge as one-dimensional and wooden. His public tended to forgive him, however, and many of these mediocre offerings were commercially successful.

In *Springfield Rifle*, Cooper played a Civil War officer who goes under-cover to identify a traitor in the Union ranks. In its concern with counter intelligence, subversives, and revolution this movie qualifies as a Cold War film. But unlike *High Noon*, which questioned the virtues of the American political system, *Springfield Rifle* generally endorsed the standard patriotic line, including the importance of warm family values. *Springfield Rifle* was a popular action film among moviegoers, but critics found little good to say.

Vera Cruz, with Burt Lancaster, was one of several films Cooper made in Mexico during the 1950s in an effort to reduce his U.S. taxes. *Vera Cruz* is about two American mercenaries who hope to get rich somehow from the Mexican revolution of 1866. The Mexican people are trying to overthrow a totalitarian dictator, a theme reflecting the political conditions in Eastern Europe after World War II. Cooper's character, Benjamin Trane, con-verts to the people's cause. When he and his partner Joe Erin (Lancaster) capture one of the dictator's gold shipments, Trane wants the gold to go to the revolutionaries; Erin wants to keep it. As in *The Virginian* and *The Westerner*, the hero has to kill his friend to ensure that society's interests will be served. But here the issue is not the protection of individual property rights, as in the earlier films, but the success or failure of a democratic revolution.

Cooper's most unusual film of this period was *Man of the West*, costarring

Lee J. Cobb and Julie London, and directed by Anthony Mann. Cooper plays Link Jones, a reformed killer trying to go straight. By coincidence, he and two innocent bystanders fall in with Jones's former gang, and he must pretend still to be a killer to save his companions' lives. Lee J. Cobb, who spends most of his time screaming and wailing in the manner of King Lear, plays the insane leader of this gang of sadistic degenerates, whose crimes range from robbery to rape. Jones manages to kill all the villains, but then wonders if he has only proven himself to be a better predator than his enemies and equally in love with violence. Although *Man of the West* has the hero win at the end in conventional fashion, it leaves the audience with disturbing questions about that hero's motives and, by extension, the frontier's legacy in America's continuing fascination with violent death. Some critics found this film to be an interesting experiment in moral ambiguity; others called it "a waste of time" for Cooper and London.

The Hanging Tree, with Maria Schell and Karl Malden, was Cooper's greatest critical success after *High Noon*. Cooper plays Joseph Frail, a doctor running from his past who lands in a small mining town in Montana Territory. He rescues a woman from an attempted rape by killing her attacker, but then is nearly lynched by townspeople who call him a murderer. The woman (Maria Schell) stands up to the mob and eventually buys the doctor's freedom by giving the town her gold mine. As in *High Noon*, this film shows two agents for evil: a predatory criminal and a dysfunctional society. The resolution brought about through individual courage shows that the criminals can be simply destroyed by force, but that a diseased community cannot be cured with the Western's traditional six-gun therapy.

This movie is sometimes called a "sleeper" whose success exceeded anyone's expectations. Critics found the acting and directing superb, and the title song eventually received an Academy Award nomination. *The Hanging Tree* was Cooper's last successful film. Again, he played what he called his ideal role: the quiet, courageous man with whom the audience could identify.

During the 1950s, Cooper's health began to deteriorate. In 1960, he was diagnosed with cancer. He underwent surgery for prostate cancer in April and soon after had an operation for colon cancer. Fighting acute pain, he worked steadily until just a few months before his death. His last performance was as host and narrator for an NBC television special called "The Real West," which aired March 29, 1961. On April 17 he received an honorary Academy Award, his third Oscar, which he was too ill to accept in person. He died on May 13, 1961, at age 60.

Despite his long and persistent popularity among moviegoers, Cooper often doubted his ability and downplayed his achievements as an actor. A few months before his death, Cooper reported that he often thought of himself as "a fraud" who pretended to be something he was not. "I became an actor by accident," he wrote, "and stayed with it only because of the forbearance of the people who pay good money at the box office. . . . I'm still groping around."

But in expressing these doubts, Cooper was excessively modest. During his long career making Westerns, Cooper had a profound impact on how Americans interpreted their national myths. Most importantly, he created a distinctive interpretation of the western hero. He brought to the already rich tradition his own background as a cowboy, his secondary identity as a British gentleman, his extraordinary physical presence, and his carefully crafted minimalist acting techniques. With this combination of authority, personal charisma, and understated style, Cooper invented a personalized image of the West and of the western hero that could express the best and, at times, the most troubling qualities of America's frontier past.

seven

Barbara Stanwyck

Feminizing the Western Film

GLENDA RILEY

B eginning in the mid-1930s, film star Barbara Stanwyck increasingly portrayed women of the American West as "tough broads." Stanwyck eschewed such traditional figures as the wife, the civilizer, the schoolteacher, and the soiled dove. In so doing, Stanwyck not only challenged the film industry, but also asked the viewing public to accept more compelling interpretations of women's contributions to the development of the American West. Ultimately, she spearheaded the movement to feminize Hollywood Westerns by bridging the gap between Victorian male-centered Westerns of the early 1900s and feminist Westerns of the late twentieth century. Along with other leading ladies, such as her good friend Joan Crawford, Stanwyck achieved this modernization by replacing male heros with female heroines. Gradually, her public acceptance and numerous awards made Barbara Stanwyck the undisputed queen of the female-centered Western.

Stanwyck's western heroines captured audiences, not by becoming pseudo males, but rather by accentuating their feminine sides, combining courage with compassion, guts with grace, and spunk with sensuousness. These women fell in love and cared deeply about husbands and children. Stanwyck's visual images of indomitable western women appealed to all types of people: young and old, liberal and conservative, male and female. Stanwyck especially provided for female audiences an element heretofore missing in Westerns. She offered women a form of liberation through film fantasy. In the 1930s, when women envisioned but not always seized new roles, Stanwyck showed women what it could feel like to be forceful and even formidable.

In Stanwyck's view, the West, symbolic of Americans and their young nation, was no longer male-dominated. Women now exercised more than a marginal or behind-the-scenes influence. In Stanwyck's Westerns, women were not simply adjuncts or satellites. They could, and did, express their own wills and take action for themselves. Moreover, a strong woman did not have to choose between the worlds of work and love. She could have a ranch *and* a man.

Stanwyck's women regarded the West as a place that provided redemption, fulfillment, or gratification to a man or woman willing to endure its tests. Although earlier audiences had become accustomed to men starring in Westerns, Stanwyck demonstrated that women also had quests in their lives rather than giving in easily to love and domesticity.

In helping to bring about such a revolution in Westerns, Stanwyck proved the genre could be adaptive. In the years before and after World War II, Americans were growing accustomed to thinking of women as full of energy, initiative, and personal agency. It was an easy step to believing that women might have exhibited those very qualities in the Old West. The movie industry responded to these new ideas.

In reality, of course, many western women were people of influence and action. But during the early and mid-twentieth century, the "beleaguered female pioneer" myth as put forth by many books and poems held sway with the general public. Not even scholars of the American West had begun delving into western women's lives and their many endeavors. Only recently has research illustrated that women were indeed movers and shakers in the frontier West.

How did Barbara Stanwyck anticipate such revised thinking about the larger roles of women in the West? She always admired strong women in films. She once explained that during the 1910s her idol was silent film star Pearl White, especially known for her role as Pauline in *Perils of Pauline*. "I came from very poor surroundings," Stanwyck continued, "and had to work my tail off just to get a penny, a penny so that I could see her. She's influenced me all my life."

Stanwyck also loved the West and its peoples. She envisioned western men and women as America's aristocracy, heros and heroines all. To her "the immigrants coming over on the covered wagons and atop the trains, the little Jewish peddler with his calicos and ginghams on his back, the good men, the bad men, they all made this country." As a forceful woman, Stanwyck felt unfairly shut out from the adventure and seeming freedom the West offered men.

In addition, throughout her early stage and film years, Stanwyck developed into a savvy businessperson with an eye for "the bottom line"—what would sell theater tickets. She recognized that the time was right during the 1930s for the emergence of the dynamic heroine who enlarged the usual female images.

Perhaps most importantly, Stanwyck lived a difficult life that provided her own personal odyssey and developed her toughness. In addition, she learned firsthand the tensions involved in trying to combine career and family. Stanwyck would have agreed that, in her words, "life and experience" made the best acting teachers. Accordingly, as Stanwyck's experiences accrued, and as she not only survived but blossomed, so did her heroines increase in texture and assertiveness.

Barbara Stanwyck's early life gave her the capacity to empathize with the heroines she would one day play. Born Ruby Stevens on July 16, 1907, in Brooklyn, New York, she was the last of five children of Byron and Catherine McGee Stevens. Stanwyck grew up living with adversity, instability, and poverty. When she was two years old her mother died in a trolley car accident. Shortly afterward, her grief-stricken father deserted his children to enlist on a merchant steamer, where he too died.

Mildred, Ruby's eldest sister, finding herself unable to support her younger siblings, sought foster homes for them. Not surprisingly, young Ruby grew up with mixed feelings about life in Brooklyn. "I was boarded out and always being changed from one boarding place to another," she recalled in 1932. "I never knew what it was to have anyone cuddle me or fuss over me or mother me, except when my sisters came to see me." Young Ruby filled in the many holes in her life with dancing (learned from sister, Mildred), attending the Pearl White serials that showed a courageous woman fighting adversity and even foiling attempts on her life, and spending days fighting and dancing on Brooklyn's streets. Religion also sustained her, as church services helped her through especially bad times.

At thirteen, after finishing sixth grade at Brooklyn's P.S. 121, Ruby started a series of jobs, working as a file clerk, bundle-wrapper, pattern-cutter, and receptionist, before trying out as a dancer for the Remick Music Company's new revue at the Strand Roof in New York's Times Square. She borrowed Mildred's resume as her own and obtained employment as a chorus girl at thirty-five dollars per week. One of Mildred's vaudeville dancer friends, James "Buck" McCarthy, taught Ruby new steps, but the dance director at the Strand Roof, Earl Lindsey, remained unimpressed. Lindsey demanded Ruby's immediate improvement or her resignation. After Lindsey's ultimatum, Ruby progressed so rapidly that he moved her to the front row. When the Strand Roof show closed, Lindsey found Ruby another job. He later helped place her at such Manhattan nightclubs as the Club Anatole and the Silver Slipper.

The mid-1920s provided myriad opportunities for Ruby. In 1924, she moved on to the dance review *Keep Kool* and to a spot in *The Ziegfeld Follies*. The following year she appeared in more reviews, including *Gay Paree*. In

1926, director, producer, and writer Willard Mack hired Ruby for a dancing and speaking part in *The Noose*. Mack also changed her name to Barbara Stanwyck, which he derived from faded theater programs in the Green Room at the Belasco Theater.

Stanwyck excelled in the opportunity Mack offered her. After *Theatre* magazine described Stanwyck as a "real discovery," she took several screen tests, which resulted in the 1927 silent film *Broadway Nights*. Meanwhile, she continued her New York career dancing and occasionally acting.

On the verge of stage stardom, Stanwyck felt ecstatic yet insecure. "It is very satisfying to have attained one's dreams," she remarked. "If only one could feel that it is permanent. Personally, I'm always afraid that it won't last—that something will take it away," she said, an understandable sentiment for a woman who had grown up on the brink of poverty, never knowing when one foster family would be replaced by another.

In 1927, romance revolutionized Barbara Stanwyck's life. Vaudeville star Frank Fay, despite a reputation as a hard drinker and superficial person, attracted and kept Stanwyck's attention. On August 26, 1928, the couple married in St. Louis. Barbara was twenty to Fay's thirty-one; it was her first marriage, whereas Fay had two previous unions. Determined to make the marriage work, Barbara joined Frank on the vaudeville stage and soon followed him to Hollywood.

In 1929, while Fay hosted *The Show of Shows*, Barbara made her first real film, *The Locked Door*. The *New York Times* reviewer remarked that Stanwyck "presented herself admirably." Meanwhile, Fay starred in two successful films, purchased an expensive mansion to celebrate his achievement, and increased his drinking and carousing.

Fortunately for Barbara, now unemployed and growing disillusioned with marriage, director Frank Capra chose her for a leading role in *Ladies of Leisure* (1930). Other films followed, including *Ten Cents a Dance*, *Night Nurse*, and *The Miracle Woman* in 1931, and *Forbidden*, *Shopworn*, *So Big*, and *The Purchase Price* in 1932. That same year, a *New York Journal* reporter described Stanwyck as "one of America's finest actresses" who refused to become affected by "the adulation of hundreds of thousands of fans throughout the world."

Stanwyck appeared to have it all—stardom, marriage, and motherhood when on December 5, 1932, she and Frank adopted a ten-month-old boy they named Dion Anthony. Although Stanwyck turned her attention to the child, she continued to make films, including *The Bitter Tea of General Yen* (1933) and *The Woman in Red* (1935).

Despite the couple's seemingly fulfilling life, their marriage was disintegrating. Although Stanwyck made more films for Columbia Pictures and Warner Brothers, Fay's career declined. As his drinking worsened, his behavior became erratic. Stanwyck left the Fay mansion with Dion in 1935 and purchased a ranch in the San Fernando Valley. She bought Dion a pony and, even though she was once afraid of horses, learned to ride herself.

When Stanwyck played in her first Western, *Annie Oakley* (1935), she could easily understand the trying life young Annie had led. Annie had been born in 1860 as the fifth child of a poor Ohio farm family. When she was six years old, Annie's father died of pneumonia. To help her mother support the other children, Annie spent parts of the following years living and laboring in the county infirmary and working as a hired girl for a farm family. Unable to garner much education for herself, a situation that always distressed her, Annie turned to her Quaker beliefs for emotional sustenance during such crises as the death of her stepfather. Later, Annie met and married shooter Frank Butler, whom she joined on the vaudeville stage.

The parallels between the lives of Annie Oakley and Barbara Stanwyck were remarkable. As children, the two had seen parents die, lived poverty-stricken childhoods, and bounced from one substitute home to another. As teenagers, both attempted to earn badly needed money, endeavors that later turned into show business careers. Both were poorly educated and very religious. Both fell in love with vaudeville stars named Frank and followed their husbands onto the stage.

In playing the Annie Oakley role, Stanwyck must have felt like she was acting herself on screen. As a result, although the film's promoters advertised Stanwyck as "Queen of the Roaring 80s" and promised viewers that the film would "thrill" them with "drama of fighting men and romance," Stanwyck characterized Oakley as winsome, clean-cut, and intelligent. Stanwyck also improved her riding skills for the part and learned to shoot so that she could do her own stunts, which, like her paragon Pearl White, she increasingly insisted on doing as her film career progressed. In *Annie Oakley*, Stanwyck showed the beginnings of the earthy, yet powerful heroines she gradually became in later Westerns.

Stanwyck also understood Hollywood images of the West. She recognized that a movie version of Annie Oakley's life had to present a pretty woman interested in romance and able to win her man, whatever the cost. In addition, the film had to picture an Old West of freedom and prosperity rather than the Depression-era 1930s reality of destitution and Dust Bowl.

Furthermore, it had to enlarge Annie Oakley from her usual modest self into a flamboyant Western heroine.

Stanwyck realized there was little she could do to alter the script. She played opposite Preston Foster as Toby Walker, who represented Annie's real-life husband, Frank Butler. When Stanwyck's Annie fights her famous shooting match against Toby Walker, she purposely loses the match rather than winning it as she had in real life. Just as Stanwyck's Annie is about to defeat Toby, her mother whispers that Annie would not want to cause the "nice young man" to lose his job. Annie duly throws the match and, contrary to reality, lets Toby win.

Thus, Annie not only saves Toby's pride but also his job with Buffalo Bill's Wild West. Annie accepts a position with the Wild West so she can be near Toby. Although William F. Cody introduces Annie to his all-male troupe as a "high-minded" and "uplifting" woman, the type who helped "civilize" the West in thousands of other Westerns, Stanwyck's Annie is not a typical lady. Unlike Annie herself, Stanwyck wears short skirts and rides astride. She also reveals that she had let Frank win the match between them and continues to outshoot him at every opportunity.

Only toward the end of the film does Annie prove herself a "true" woman and wind up in Toby's arms. Despite this conventional conclusion, Stanwyck's Annie retains her dignity and strength of character. As a result, audiences were taken with Stanwyck's Annie. A viewer in Annie Oakley's hometown of Greenville, Ohio, even declared Stanwyck to be "just like" Oakley.

The making of *Annie Oakley* marked a turning point in Stanwyck's views of western women. During the course of filming, Stanwyck had come to like and respect Oakley. "Modern women could learn a great deal from her," Stanwyck said. "She was a woman of all ages, deeply feminine in spite of her shooting ability—which she developed to support her family." When Stanwyck heard that the citizens of Greenville planned to erect a bronze plaque in Annie Oakley's honor, Stanwyck mailed a one-hundred-dollar check to Mayor Frazer Wilson of Greenville.

Certainly, as a result of *Annie Oakley,* Barbara Stanwyck was one of the hottest actresses in Hollywood. She could pick her own roles and move from studio to studio. She appealed to Hollywood's top directors, from Frank Capra to Billy Wilder, and she widened the genres in which she could appear, ranging from dramas and comedies to Westerns.

On the personal side, however, the situation was not so bright. In 1935, Stanwyck survived a divorce from Fay, including a bitter custody trial over

Dion, which she won. Although the divorce became final on December 31, 1935, Barbara and Frank would periodically return to court for the next three years in disputes about visitation rights. In these difficult circumstances, Barbara began the year 1936 on her own with a young son to raise.

Despite the professional prominence Stanwyck enjoyed, she found it difficult to find good Western scripts that featured convincing heroines rather than the usual stock female figures. Hollywood's 1930 production code also hampered script-writers, who had to bear in mind ethical issues and to avoid treatments of sex and crime. To show deviancy of any sort in films, it was believed, would teach American children violent or antisocial attitudes. Thus, during the 1930s, Western heroines had to watch not only their manners, but their female demeanor as well.

Meanwhile, Stanwyck was busy with her personal life. On one hand, she was unable to create a close relationship with her son and felt like a failure because of her 1935 divorce from Frank Fay. On the other, she received an Academy Award nomination for her 1937 film *Stella Dallas*. Moreover, Stanwyck became romantically involved with film idol Robert Taylor, whom she costarred with in *His Brother's Wife* (1936). Throughout the late 1930s, Stanwyck played additional roles opposite Taylor, and he purchased a ranch adjacent to hers. Taylor also made friends with Dion, who called Taylor "Gentleman Bob," and included the boy in such activities as riding and swimming when filming schedules did not interfere.

On May 13, 1939, Stanwyck and Taylor—ages thirty-one and twenty-seven respectively—eloped to San Diego and married. The next morning the couple returned to their individual film projects. Soon Taylor sold his ranch and moved in with Barbara and Dion. In November, Stanwyck and Taylor spent a delayed honeymoon in New York. After she returned to what one observer called a "grueling" filming schedule, however, the couple took up residence in separate bedrooms.

The Stanwyck–Taylor union proved to be a difficult one. The pressures of two top Hollywood careers and the contentious relationship between Stanwyck and her former husband over their son tore at their marriage. Biographer Axel Madsen believes that the marriage was a sham from the beginning, that film moguls engineered the marriage of Stanwyck, a lesbian, to Taylor, a gay man, to reassure audiences of the stars' heterosexuality. No solid evidence exists, however, indicating that either Stanwyck or Taylor was homosexual.

Despite the tensions of Stanwyck's marriage, the events in the year 1939 were special to her. Not only had she wed Taylor, whom she vowed to love forever, but she had also landed a role in her second Western, *Union Pacific*, in which she plays Mollie Monahan opposite Joel McCrea's Jeff Butler and Robert Preston's Dick Allen. Wielding his usual lavish hand, Cecil B. DeMille produced and directed the film, in which Stanwyck performed her own stunts. McCrea remarked that Stanwyck had "more guts than most men," whereas DeMille once declared that he had never "worked with an actress who was more co-operative, less temperamental, and a better workman, to use my term of highest compliment" than Barbara Stanwyck.

Stanwyck equally adored DeMille. In *Union Pacific*, Stanwyck's character serves as postmistress for the men laying track for the Union Pacific railroad as the line snakes its way across the West to meet up with the Central Pacific. The combined roads would form the first transcontinental railway in the United States. As the tomboy daughter of the Union Pacific's Irish engineer, Stanwyck's Mollie joins forces with trouble-shooter Jeff Butler and his opponent Dick Allen to fight off the Indians determined to stop the road's progress. Despite an atrocious Irish accent, Stanwyck is endearing as Mollie. She also nods to conventions concerning western women by being a "civilizer" in that she unites all sides and by becoming romantically involved with McCrea's character.

The key to Stanwyck's Mollie, however, is that as a woman, she makes the decisions and directs events. With alacrity, she issues orders to her father, her suitors, and her employers. Her confidence never wanes, even in the face of her father's and husband's deaths. At the same time, Stanwyck's physical strength serves her well. She never falters or falls into the trap of acting like a "weak woman." Wearing trousers, she operates a gandy dancer's conveyance early in the film. Later, wearing skirts, she shoots at Indians with equal aplomb.

After the film's worldwide premiere on April 29, 1939, in Omaha, Nebraska, an occasion that drew 400,000 people, including the governors of three states, reviewers hailed DeMille's production as everything from a "colorful" epic to a "spectacular" Western. Stanwyck received kudos as well. The reviewer for *The New York Times* commented that Stanwyck gave "a lively and surprisingly convincing characterization of the Irish spitfire." Another, writing for *The New York Daily News*, called Stanwyck's performance "the best work of her screen career." *Variety* added that Stanwyck, despite limitations of the script, sustained "the femme interest" and "more than impressed" her viewers.

By the beginning of the 1940s, Barbara Stanwyck had risen to the top in Hollywood. She was also among America's highest paid women.

On June 11, 1941, Stanwyck, along with Taylor, put her handprint in the sidewalk in front of Sid Grauman's Chinese Theatre on Hollywood Boulevard. Barbara wrote, "To Sid, We Love You." She signed on the left side, Taylor on the right.

The following year, Stanwyck received a best actress Academy Award nomination for her role in *Ball of Fire* (1942). Although she did not win the award, Stanwyck still had her pick of scripts and accepted the lead in *The Great Man's Lady* (1942), directed by William A. Wellman for Paramount Studios. Once again starring opposite Joel McCrea, Stanwyck played Hannah Sempler, who aged from sixteen to one hundred and nine during the course of the story. At age thirty-three, Stanwyck had achieved the personal maturity and acting experience to carry off the age change with assurance. She also portrayed Sempler as a woman of spirit and high character, who chose to give up McCrea so that he could pursue politics. Again, Stanwyck's female character made decisions for herself and decided people's fates. She wore trousers for her wedding and shot rabbits for dinner. Playing the strong woman behind the weak man, Sempler had a backbone that was notable because she kept it concealed.

Stanwyck's performance in *The Great Man's Lady* demonstrated that she had achieved mastery in her art. Stanwyck also explained that she truly enjoyed playing the part of Sempler: "I loved that film. I was just crazy about it. I loved the challenge." Still, Stanwyck's characterization of Sempler resonated less clearly with the public. Although *The Great Man's Lady* comes across today as a brilliant film, especially in light of the contemporary feminist movement, it did not do well at the box office in 1943. Perhaps Americans, involved in World War II, needed to see strong male figures who would presumably save the nation. Stanwyck was crushed: "It was never very successful, and that kind of broke by heart."

World War II, besides creating new attitudes among Americans, disrupted Stanwyck's personal life. In 1943, Taylor joined the U.S. Navy to serve as a flight instructor at the Great Lakes Naval Training Station in Illinois. In Hollywood, Barbara volunteered at the local canteen and continued making films, including *Lady of Burlesque* and *Flesh and Fantasy*, both in 1943. She also tried to simplify her life. Because of gas rationing, Stanwyck rode a motorcycle to the studio. The next spring, she sold her ranch and horses.

As the war came to an end in 1945, Stanwyck's life continued to include bad and good elements. On the down side, she failed to receive yet another Academy Award (for *Double Indemnity* in 1944) and noticed strands of gray in her auburn hair. Despite studio pressure, however, Stanwyck refused to color her hair. On the up side, Stanwyck earned well, a total of $323,333 in 1944, which she used to help such institutions as the Los Angeles Orthopedic Hospital and a number of orphanages. Similar to her earlier heroine, Annie Oakley, who also gave generously to hospitals and orphanages, Stanwyck became a supporter of organizations meaningful to her.

Stanwyck also welcomed home her husband, Robert Taylor, who returned from the war to resume making films. Stanwyck's agent and close friend, Helen Ferguson, noted that during the immediate postwar years the couple enjoyed having quiet dinners together and sharing "a consuming interest in their jobs and the industry."

Meanwhile, World War II had changed the lives and attitudes of American film audiences. Stanwyck soon discovered that Americans had become more amenable to strong women on the screen. For the four years of U.S. involvement in the war, the nation's women had served on the front and at home, keeping factories and offices going and maintaining homes and families. Although postwar U.S. government propaganda urged women to forsake jobs and return home, many women held onto their jobs—and to their newly found self-confidence and enlarged self-image. To maintain their profits, Hollywood studios had to reflect the new trends. Film scripts, including those of Westerns, adapted to the changed thinking. This transformation pleased Stanwyck, who as a mature woman and seasoned actress was more anxious than ever to strengthen her portrayals of women, especially western women.

Stanwyck's opportunity came in 1947 with the film *California,* her first venture in Technicolor. John Farrow directed Stanwyck in the part of Lily Bishop and Ray Milland as Jonathan Trumbo. Card sharp Lily meets Union deserter Jonathan on the road to California. After a series of mishaps, through which events in western history loom large, a reformed Lily waits while Jonathan serves a prison term for desertion.

Unfortunately, reviewers were unenthusiastic. One thought the film "better" than "most Westerns," whereas another commented that the movie "quickly loses its stirrups and ends up caught by its chaps in a clump of cactus." All regarded Stanwyck's performance as solid, but none analyzed her rendering of Lily Bishop as far more than the usual "bad" western woman. For example, before recognizing Trumbo's nice side, Stanwyck says in her indomitable style, "If I live long enough, and I will, I'm going to pull you off your fancy horse and shove your face in the mud." Perhaps because *California* annoyed the critics by cramming in nearly every possible stock situation known to the Hollywood Western, they seemed blind to the implications of Stanwyck's character and the way she chose to represent her.

In 1950, Stanwyck tried again as Vance Jeffords in *The Furies*. Produced by Hal B. Wallis and directed by Anthony Mann, this film offered the opportunity to depict perhaps her toughest western woman thus far. Stanwyck's Vance Jeffords is a stubborn woman who runs her father's Arizona cattle ranch, The Furies, with verve and near-genius. When her father, played by Walter Huston, marries a conniving widow, Vance turns jealous and vindictive and subsequently attempts to ruin her father. Although her revenge is satisfied, she sees her father fall to a gunman's bullet.

Filmed in stark black-and-white, *The Furies* was dubbed an "adult" Western. The script contained overt Freudian interpretations and elicited a superb performance from Walter Huston in his last film. Stanwyck proved a match for this great actor, turning in fine scene after scene. Adorned in a blond wig and as slim as ever, Stanwyck came across as a willow tree, swaying but never breaking in the strongest prairie wind.

In the meantime, Stanwyck's marriage was not going as well as her career. Some of Stanwyck's contemporaries blamed her problems with Taylor on her strong will. Some called Barbara outspoken, whereas others said she was manipulative and self-centered. Many listed her penchant for work as the culprit. Certainly, she seemed to have more interest in work than in family and motherhood.

Still others criticized Taylor, who spent innumerable hours flying his plane "Missy." In 1949, Stanwyck had reportedly said, "Taylor lives in the airplane—lives in it. Oh, there are times when I go up with him with a tight grip and a tight lip to keep the family together. But it's his life and none of my business, and I wouldn't try to interfere." More astute observers have said that Taylor's failure to regain his prewar popularity caused the breakdown of his relationship with Stanwyck.

During the summer of 1950, Barbara visited her husband on the set in Rome where he was making *Quo Vadis*, to be released in 1951. She seemed impatient with her enforced idleness and soon returned to Hollywood. After Stanwyck's departure, Taylor's name appeared in print with a variety of women. When he returned to Hollywood, Taylor asked Barbara for a divorce. Gossip columnist Louella Parsons wrote, "Of course, like everyone else on the inside, I had realized that things had not been all hearts and flowers between them for at least two years." Parsons added, "I had sincerely believed Bob and Barbara would see it through to steadier ground."

Apparently, Stanwyck had harbored similar hopes. She told the press, "We are deeply disappointed but we could not solve our problems. We really tried." When her eleven-year-old marriage ended on January 31, 1951, Stanwyck appeared depressed. To a reporter who asked her about future romance, Stanwyck replied, "I've had enough of that." To add to her despair, Stanwyck's growing alienation from Dion seemed complete.

During the 1950s, Stanwyck worked harder than she ever had, making film after film in quick succession. Some, of course, proved more artistically and financially successful than others. She also produced a spate of Westerns, which she admitted were her favorite type of film. Although she had made only five Westerns in the twenty-five years between her first film in 1927 and 1952, Stanwyck churned out an additional half-dozen between 1953 and 1957. From *The Moonlighter* (1953) to *Forty Guns* (1957), Stanwyck's western women rode and shot, wore trousers, bossed and loved men, and managed business enterprises of all sorts. Stanwyck, who had come into her own as an independent woman and a successful actress, seemed to revel in these multi-dimensional women's roles.

It is tempting to speculate that the postwar world readily accepted Stanwyck's interpretations of western women, but it would be inaccurate. Instead, Americans held mixed feelings regarding women's roles. During the mid-1950s, feminism had retreated to a subterranean level in American society. In 1956, *Life* magazine described the ideal American woman as a wife, hostess, volunteer, "home manager," and "conscientious mother." At the same time, however, women entered the workforce by the thousands. In 1950, women constituted 29 percent of paid workers in the United States; a decade later they accounted for nearly 35 percent. Apparently, women had reservations about the postwar "back-to-the-home" message.

As a result, women in Westerns often presented stereotypes suited to the age; glamour, glitz, and sex abounded. A good case was Stanwyck's idol, Annie Oakley. On the motion picture screen, Betty Hutton depicted Oakley as a local yokel turned shooting star, who dressed to the nines and was willing to lay down her gun to get her man. On Broadway, Ethel Merman's Annie Oakley sang and danced her way through a similar scenario.

At the same time, however, western women appeared as dynamic and effectual in other media. Again, Annie Oakley offers an example. During the mid-1950s, Gene Autry's Flying-A Productions, one of the most prolific creators of Westerns, began airing the series *Annie Oakley and Tagg* on CBS television, whereas Dell Publishing Company created "Annie Oakley" comic books. In both, Annie Oakley demonstrated significant characteristics of western women, including strong-mindedness, superior abilities to ride and shoot, and strong moral convictions. This Annie Oakley was no Betty Hutton or Ethel Merman.

How, then, were Stanwyck's western women received in such a contradictory era? In her 1953 film, *The Moonlighters*, Stanwyck constitutes a one-woman posse that brings her costar, Fred McMurray, to justice. At the same time, she falls for him and promises to wait while he serves his jail sentence. This reprise of the ending of her 1947 film, *California*, did not serve Stanwyck well. In addition, the film was shot in 3-D, which one scholar has described as "more exploitative than useful."

In 1954, Stanwyck did slightly better with *The Cattle Queen of Montana*. Costarring with Ronald Reagan, Stanwyck plays Sierra Nevada Jones, a hard-riding and hard-shooting woman set on filing on her father's land claim after seeing him killed by Indians in Montana. Although Reagan helps Stanwyck, she fights Indians and eventually shoots down the film's villain herself.

In her second Technicolor film and again wearing a wig, Stanwyck appeared slender, lovely, and powerful. This time more reviewers seemed to get her point. "Barbara Stanwyck registers impressively as a Western heroine," one wrote. Another critic concluded that "no one stands a chance of taking attention away from Barbara as the Lone Rangerette." Whether they realized it or not, Barbara Stanwyck scored not only for herself but for western women in general, who now demonstrated on-screen assertiveness without raising eyebrows.

Stanwyck followed this minor triumph with *The Violent Men* (1955). Appearing this time with Edward G. Robinson, Stanwyck is a pushy, acquisitive wife who is killed as she tries to kill her husband. Although it sounds like a poor story to promote strong-minded western women, Stanwyck portrayed it with malice of forethought. One observer called her "a sort of Lady Macbeth of the plains, who helps Robinson grab the land because she wants it for herself." Stanwyck played this bad woman role to the hilt, fully in command of her portrayal of a woman lusting after power. At last, Stanwyck had a Technicolor Western of which she could be proud—and a depiction of a western heroine that left no doubt that a woman can also be determined, even if she must pay for it in the end.

Stanwyck appeared to be on a roll. In 1956, she played a southern girl named Kit Banion opposite Barry Sullivan in *The Maverick Queen*. Like the ambitious young men of that time, Banion goes west to make her fortune. In operating a hotel–saloon known as the Maverick Queen, she gets involved with Butch Cassidy's Wild Bunch. She owns a good part of the Wyoming Territory town and wields immense power. She then falls for her faro dealer, who turns out to be a Pinkerton Agency detective on the trail of her outlaw friends. Kit chooses to break with the Wild Bunch and protect the man she loves, even though she says "there can be nothing between us," she being a bad woman who has operated a saloon and run with outlaws, whereas he is a good man who enforces the law. She shields him, shooting down a gang member who fatally wounds her in return.

An unremarked, yet important feature of this film was the inclusion of another strong woman character, Lucy Lea, played by Mary Murphy. Lucy is a good woman who takes over the family ranch after her father's murder. Lucy serves as her own trail boss, fighting men, wielding weapons, riding, and wearing trousers. She is the good woman opposite Stanwyck's "bad" woman. In combination, Lucy and Kit are equal players with men; they give orders, buy and sell, ride and shoot, and fight with men. The difference is that Lucy survives, whereas Kit dies, a necessary fate for a "bad" woman yet one that Stanwyck's character freely accepts.

The Maverick Queen did well at the box office even though critics were slightly skeptical. "Barbara Stanwyck must be saddle-sore after so many Westerns," one wrote. The review went on, "here she is again queening it on the ranch and giving both men and steers a run for their money." But the reviewer seemed to miss the message; this time Stanwyck chose everything, including her own death.

Trooper Hook (1957), which once again featured one of Stanwyck's costars, Joel McCrea, tackled the issues of miscegenation and mixed-heritage children, subjects usually undiscussed in public at the time. Stanwyck plays Cora Sutliff, a white captive of an Indian chief who, when "rescued," refuses to give up her son, Quito. As Trooper Hook, McCrea defends Cora's right to her son and eventually wins Stanwyck's hand. Stanwyck gives the role warmth, texture, and pathos. Although a hardened woman, she has a loving heart regarding her child—and eventually concerning McCrea as Hook.

That same year, Stanwyck played in another "issue" film, *Forty Guns,* this time opposite Barry Sullivan. Stanwyck portrays an Arizona rancher who controls the county through a bevy of forty hired gunslingers. According to the film's theme song, she is the "most dangerous women the West's ever seen!" After numerous plot twists and turns, Stanwyck's character reforms her hard ways and saves Sullivan from death. In the end, though, because she was a "bad" woman who lived outside the law, she fails to win the hero.

The film received mixed reviews. As one critic noted, Stanwyck looked "better on a horse than most lean and lanky heros." In addition, she continued to play western women with flair and enthusiasm. Nonetheless, the film attracted little attention, perhaps because it explored such topics as sex and violence in 1950s American society, an era that generally preferred to ignore such themes.

Stanwyck turned fifty shortly after she completed *Forty Guns*, which was her last film for four years and her final Western. But her career was not over. During the 1960s and 1970s, Stanwyck made six more films, including *Walk on the Wild Side* (1962) and *A Taste of Evil* (1971). Except for *Forty Guns*, which became something of a cult film during the turbulent 1970s, Stanwyck's 1950s Westerns became history. Of Stanwyck's four Academy Award nominations (the fourth for *Sorry, Wrong Number* in 1948) none was for a Western film. Yet, deeper analysis indicates that Stanwyck's Westerns were more significant than they may have appeared at the time.

First, Stanwyck's heroines exercised personal agency, even to the point of giving up a man or life itself. Stanwyck's women also controlled and directed others, even in romantic matters. Seldom was love easily given. Rather, a heroine had to be convinced, and on some levels compelled, to love. In such a setting, courtship sometimes became fierce. In *Forty Guns*, for example, Stanwyck tells a lover that she was bitten by a rattlesnake at the very place they stood. Aware of the danger involved in a relationship with her, he retorts, "I'll bet it died."

Second, Stanwyck's characters often experienced redemption, heretofore reserved for western heros. In *The Cattle Queen of Montana* and *Forty Guns* the heroine is saved from evil by the end of the film. Women are also seekers, as in *The Maverick Queen* where a female figure relocates in the West in search of a better life.

Third and last, Stanwyck's women always exhibited strength of mind, character, and will. Perhaps the best example was *Trooper Hook,* in which a western woman confronted social condemnation for the love of her mixed-heritage son.

During the late 1950s and 1960s, Stanwyck's personal life centered largely on her career. Certainly, Dion offered her little satisfaction. Although she said little to the press regarding her estrangement from her son, it is known that he married a Las Vegas showgirl in 1957 and was arrested in Los Angeles a few years later for selling pornography, actions that were unlikely to endear

Stanwyck in Trooper Hook *(1957), with Terry Lawrence. Courtesy of MGM CLIP & STILL.* Trooper Hook © *1957 Fielding Productions, Inc. All Rights Reserved.*

him to Stanwyck. In 1962, when his father, Frank Fay, died, Dion contested Fay's will, which excluded him. Eventually, he received approximately $100,000, which presumably took care of him, at least for a while.

Stanwyck herself was still beautiful, vital, and wealthy because of her investments in the stock markets. During the late 1950s, she credited her work as "responsible for all the good things that have come into my life." She added that, "I feel most completely alive when I'm starting a new picture."

Little wonder, then, that the medium of television attracted Barbara Stanwyck. Beginning in 1952, she lent her talents to a range of television productions. Starting with the *Jack Benny Show*, she also appeared on the *Loretta Young Show* and a variety of special programs, including *Zane Grey*

Theatre, Goodyear Theatre, and her own *Barbara Stanwyck Show* from September 19, 1960, to July 3, 1961. Whenever possible, Stanwyck filled the part of an independent, strong-minded western woman. She often declared, "I still love everything about the West—the people, the land, everything."

Eventually, Stanwyck conceived the idea of doing a dramatic Western television series of her own. After appearances on such shows as *Rawhide* and *Wagon Train,* Stanwyck proposed a series that would feature her as the iron-handed matriarch of a huge ranch set in California's San Joaquin Valley during the 1870s. As Victoria Barkley, Stanwyck would rule three sons and a daughter, keeping them unified against the frequent challenges to Barkley land and power.

Stanwyck had well-defined ideas about her portrayal of Victoria Barkley: "I want to play a real frontier woman, not one of those crinoline-covered things you see in most Westerns." She added that history showed women participating in everything from cattle drives to range wars. "Nuts to the kids and the cows," she said. At age fifty-eight, Stanwyck saw Victoria as "an old broad who combines elegance with guts," whose interest in romance was over.

Television producers were unconvinced. Why would viewers of the chaotic 1960s want to watch anything as tame as a woman and her children living on a ranch? Obviously, most had trouble imagining a woman character who could rival Ben Cartwright of *Bonanza.* Stanwyck commented that producers had the idea that women "don't do action," but maintained that she was the "best action actress in the world. I can do horse drags, jump off buildings, and I've got the scars to prove it."

Stanwyck argued for her series and showed her pilot program until ABC agreed to sponsor her idea. In September 1965, Stanwyck's show, *The Big Valley,* began a four-season run that encompassed 112 segments. All but seven included Stanwyck. In *The Big Valley,* Stanwyck successfully introduced a ranch woman into a male-dominated television West. She also confounded those producers who had doubted Stanwyck and the appeal of an independent, tough-minded heroine.

As Victoria Barkley, Stanwyck manifested the independent spirit and famous willfulness that she had spent nearly sixty years perfecting. Like women in her earlier roles, Stanwyck's character was far more than a wife, civilizer, schoolteacher, or "bad" woman. Victoria Barkley was a new archetype, even for Stanwyck. Barkley headed an enterprising, vital family unit that discussed, argued, and cried together. As she had promised, Stanwyck expanded her character to its fullest dimensions, seldom missing an opportunity to demonstrate that western women often combined guts and good sense.

Stanwyck's performances were so well received that she won an Emmy in 1966 and was awarded additional nominations in 1967 and 1968. Lesbian viewers especially loved Stanwyck as Barkley, admiring her ability to make decisions without a man. Certainly, Stanwyck's attitude suggested that she might lean toward the lesbian side, but when one gay journalist asked Stanwyck about her sexual proclivities he was shown out of her house. Although the topic of Stanwyck's supposed lesbianism comes up regularly, there is no basis for supposing that she was homosexual. Contemporary lesbian organizations simply regard Stanwyck as a strong model for some of their views regarding the ways women should behave; none claims that she was actually a lesbian.

Although *The Big Valley* achieved widespread popularity, ABC canceled the series in 1969, citing poor ratings and a declining interest in Westerns. *The Big Valley* lived on, however, in late night reruns and videocassettes. Although Stanwyck had appeared in her last *Big Valley* episode, her presence as a Western heroine endured.

In spite of her ability to play the consummate "tough broad" on movie or television screens, Stanwyck could not always maintain a similar facade in her personal life. Shortly after *The Big Valley* concluded its successful run, Robert Taylor died of lung cancer on June 8, 1969. According to one Hollywood columnist, Stanwyck was "devastated." When she attended Taylor's funeral, she offended some people with her open display of grief. Stanwyck had not forgotten the promise she had made years earlier to love Taylor forever.

Still, Stanwyck's great sorrow did not provide an opportunity for her to reconcile with her son, Dion. She had very little to say about him. In one interview Stanwyck described Dion as a "born outlaw," explaining that after "you do everything you can do for them and they remain bad . . . you try to see to it that they don't break your heart any longer." Dion's side of the story remains untold.

Typically, Stanwyck escaped her problems by throwing herself into work. She continued to accept television roles, ranging from *A Taste of Evil* (1971) to *The Thorn Birds* (1983). As always, Stanwyck's performances garnered awards. There was, for example, the 1973 Wrangler Award and induction into the Hall of Fame of Great Western Performers at the National Cowboy Hall of Fame in Oklahoma City. Two other accolades that meant a great deal to Stanwyck were a 1982 honorary Oscar from the Academy of Motion Picture Arts and Sciences and a 1987 Lifetime Achievement Award from the American Film Institute.

Stanwyck did not change perceptibly. As always, she was a tough-talking, hard-working, and hard-smoking woman. Although she suffered from emphysema and a bad back, she kept on horseback riding and doing many of her own stunts. In 1981, at age seventy-three her hair had turned completely white, yet she was still stunning. She told an interviewer that she lived "very quietly," enjoyed reading and traveling, and generally preferred solitude. "I don't even have many friends," she said. "Four, six maybe. I don't need any more. I'm entirely too old to futz around with all that crud."

Stanwyck lived nearly another decade in semi-retirement. On January 21, 1990, she died at age eighty-two of congestive heart failure complicated by emphysema. According to her wishes, no funeral was held, and she was buried in a private ceremony. Stanwyck's life had spanned most of the twentieth century, and her career lasted nearly as long.

Since her death, Stanwyck's reputation as a great actress has grown, but her contributions to Westerns are often overlooked or minimized. Clearly, she led the feminization of Hollywood Westerns. By standing in the center of western events, Stanwyck's heroines subtly subverted the customary western folklore that featured only men. Also, by creating "tough broads," Stanwyck made possible the intrepid western women played by such later film stars as Candace Bergen in *Soldier Blue* (1970), Jane Fonda in *Comes a Horseman* (1978), and Sharon Stone in *The Quick and the Dead* (1995).

Perhaps Stanwyck's greatest gift to the Western was the authenticity of her acting. She portrayed what she knew and felt. In 1981, she said, "I never had an acting lesson. Life was my only training." Moreover, Stanwyck exuded credibility because she did her own stunts, admitting "I'm a frustrated stunt-woman." Some observers viewed Stanwyck's penchant for stuntwork as professionalism, whereas others labeled it foolhardy. Regardless, Stanwyck sent the message that she believed women should be durable in truth as well in film. She believed in energetic women—and she was one.

Throughout her Western roles, Stanwyck consistently gained the admiration of her colleagues for her stuntwork. For instance, in *The Furies*, Walter Huston insisted on emulating Barbara by doing his own stunts. He declared that he did not intend to be outdone by a woman. Three years later in *The Moonlighter* Stanwyck rode across a ledge under a waterfall. The script called for her to fall, still on horseback, into the river below, churning up a landslide on the way down. Stanwyck emerged bruised yet uncomplaining. During the filming of *The Cattle Queen of Montana*, Stawyck performed her own bathing scene in one of Glacier National Park's lakes. Although Stanwyck "came out blue" she did not hesitate to do another take. Watching Stanwyck and admiring her, Indian actors in the film induted Stanwyck into their Brace Dog Society because of her "very hard work—rare for a white woman." In 1957, Stanwyck performed a stunt in which her foot gets caught in a stirrup and results in her mount dragging her across the range. After the third take, *Forty Guns* director Samuel Fuller was satisfied.

Clearly, Stanwyck loved Westerns. She explained, "I'm crazy about Westerns, that's why I've made so many of them." Her enthusiasm motivated Hollywood to accommodate her, and Westerns enlarged to meet her demands. Gradually, historical scholarship validated her, demonstrating that effective women flourished in the Old West.

Stanwyck was also prescient about Westerns. The accolade that most clearly identified Stanwyck's genius came from a former actor who had costarred with Stanwyck in *The Cattle Queen of Montana*. In 1981, President Ronald Reagan directed words of great praise to Stanwyck: "Long before it was fashionable, you were a paradigm of independence and self-direction for women all over the world."

Ultimately, Stanwyck was successful in enlarging Westerns, especially the roles of western women because she was smart. She could always see where Hollywood was going, or needed to go. Furthermore, she sensed what would work in televised Westerns. Stanwyck had a lifetime of experiences that gave her empathy and vision. Throughout her life she loved and lost. She dared to step onto the stage, and she won. She also asserted herself, often with mixed results. She understood the costs of independence and self-will, as well as the compensations that came with such risk taking. Like the western heroines she chose to portray, Barbara Stanwyck's life was dedicated to testing and breaking America's social and cultural boundaries.

◆ eight ◆

Katy Jurado
Mexico's Woman of the Western

CHERYL J. FOOTE

iery, sultry, tempestuous, Latin—so journalists described Katy (pronounced Caw-tee) Jurado during her Hollywood heyday in the 1950s. Film critics praised her performances as "compassionate and dignified." Jurado's talent in conveying a range of emotions and contrasting images made her a memorable presence on screen for more than half a century. Although her American debut was in *The Bullfighter and the Lady* (1951), it was not until Jurado's role as Helen Ramírez in *High Noon* a year later that provided a new direction for her career. During the next decade she became the primary Mexican actress to star in American Westerns, the most popular film genre of the era.

One of the most popular Westerns of the 1950s was *High Noon*, still regarded as a classic by movie critics and fans nearly half a century later. Katy Jurado had the good fortune to star in a very successful movie, which partially accounted for the subsequent expansion of her American film career. In addition, *High Noon* offered her the chance to display her great acting abilities. So strong was Jurado's performance as Helen Ramírez that she came to represent *the* Mexican woman in Hollywood Westerns.

In fact, Jurado's success in *High Noon* is paradoxical. Although it raised her to stardom and boosted her already established career, she never again enjoyed a role as rich and deserving of her talents as that of Helen Ramírez. Most of the other Westerns she made failed to achieve the status of *High Noon*, and few of the other U.S. movies in which she starred enjoyed great popularity. Still, even in minor movies or minor roles, Jurado gave fine performances embued with emotional complexity and passion in a career that has spanned more than fifty years.

By the time Jurado made her first American film, she had already spent eight years as an actress in Mexican cinema. As she moved into American movies, she was following in the footsteps of other Mexican actresses like

Dolores Del Rio and Lupe Vélez, who had risen to stardom in the United States in the 1920s and 1930s.

Since the early twentieth century, American audiences had become familiar with two basic screen images of the Mexican woman, images that had their counterparts in non-Mexican characters as well. One was the dark-haired, dark-skinned, passionately emotional and sexual creature, frequently a prostitute or "fallen woman." Often tempestuous and always alluring, these women violated traditional female norms in dress or in actions and paid the price as they were denied a happy ending with the hero and/or perished as retribution for their lascivious ways. This wanton but artless temptress, or "bad woman," was often portrayed as *la devoradora*, a wronged, predatory creature forced to support herself on the streets who not only seduces men but devours and destroys them as well. The alternative screen image was the lighter-skinned, lighter-haired, self-contained, aloof lady, whose sensuality, though suggested, was restrained. If she behaved properly (and she usually did), the lady could expect to win the hero, even if he was Anglo and she was not. This "good woman" might appear as a señorita, a virgin ready to fall into the arms of the hero at the end of the film, or as a señora, a patient yet long-suffering wife or mother ready to sacrifice everything in the interests of her family. The double standard regarding female sexuality and the acceptance — or expectation — of the viewing public of these characters perpetuated these roles in Mexico as much as, or more than, in the United States.

These two Mexicana characters — the bad woman and the good woman — have been variously labeled as "the whore and the Madonna," the "whore and the Virgin," or considered as two manifestations of the "dark lady," and appeared in countless incarnations in Westerns and other movies. Dolores Del Rio, whose acting career began in 1925, played both roles, but became better known as the purebred Spanish lady. On the other hand, Lupe Vélez, beginning in 1926, honed the role of the hot-tempered, sexually provocative Mexicana into "the Spitfire." She also used her zaniness and accented English as a source of comedy.

These stereotypical images of Mexicanas were variations on the good woman (blond) and the bad woman (dark) characters who appeared in American films that did not feature Mexicanas. Although these characterizations were at their worst demeaning and insulting, and at their best superficial and limited in scope, the movies provided a vehicle to stardom for Mexicanas Del Rio and Vélez in the United States.

In addition, these parts were generally far less degrading than roles for

Mexican men, who were often categorized as "the greaser and the bandido." Such negative portrayals of Mexicans had generated protests from the Mexican government to the U.S. film industry as early as 1924. When American filmmakers failed to respond, the Mexican government banned American movie imports for a time. However, although Mexico's film industry had shown promise during the first decade of the twentieth century, production had declined during and after the Mexican Revolution and World War I. By 1928, more than 90 percent of films shown in Mexico came from Hollywood.

A decade later, American producers began to pay greater attention to Mexican concerns as they recognized the importance of Mexico and Latin America as markets. The outbreak of civil war in Spain meant fewer Spanish-language films available in the western hemisphere, and the beginning of World War II cut off European markets for the American film industry. These economic concerns, coupled with a need for solidarity throughout the Americas, led Hollywood to produce more films with Latin American themes, improve characterizations of some Spanish-speaking characters, and import new talent, including Carmen Miranda from Brazil.

Meanwhile, the Mexican government under President Lázaro de Cárdenas used state support and financing to revitalize the Mexican film industry. By 1938, the golden age of Mexican cinema, which lasted until the early 1950s, was underway. The Mexican film industry expanded, and demand for talented actresses grew. Neither Lupe Vélez nor Dolores Del Rio had starred in Mexican films, but in 1943, Dolores Del Rio returned to her native country to make her first Mexican film. Her international career then continued until 1978. Vélez, despondent over a love affair gone wrong, committed suicide in 1944. However, new actresses began to appear in this period, among them María Félix, who made her first two films in 1942, and Katy Jurado, whose movie debut came in 1943.

María Cristina Estela Marcela Jurado García was likely born in Guadalajara, Mexico, on January 16, 1927. According to her "official" biography on file at the Academy of Motion Picture Arts and Sciences, and Jurado's recollections in interviews, she is descended from wealthy landowners of northern Mexico who lost their property during the Mexican Revolution of 1910. Her prosperous family saw that she was well educated and counted filmmakers and actors among their friends. In an interview soon after she began her acting career, Jurado related that director Mauricio de la Serna first tried to recruit her for the movies and that Emilio Fernández, soon to become one of Mexico's most famous directors and actors, encouraged her, but her parents refused. When she was sixteen, however, she defiantly married Victor Velázquez, another actor–director and immediately began work as an actress, making three movies in 1943.

When Katy Jurado launched her movie career in Mexico, four types of genres—the historical epic, the Cantínflas films, the *comedias rancheras*, and the melodramas—dominated the Mexican film industry. Jurado appeared primarily in melodramas that reinforced traditional roles for women as well as values of patriotism, home, and family. The social upheavals that occurred in the years following the Mexican Revolution of 1910 had raised questions about the proper place of women in Mexican society. By the 1940s, as machismo became a nationalizing theme for men, women were reminded that their primary role was in the home. In the movies women exemplified these values of the traditional good woman/bad woman split, which became popular with U.S. audiences and equally appealing to Mexican audiences.

Jurado's considerable acting talent as well as her dark beauty, large and expressive eyes, and "gypsy figure" gained her parts in more than a dozen films between 1943 and 1951. The most significant was a minor role in Ismael Rodríguez's *Nosotros los Pobres (We the Poor)*, the most popular movie in the history of Mexican film. Part musical comedy, part melodrama, *Nosotros los Pobres* is the tale of a poor but honorable man brought to ruin through the dishonesty of others, but redeemed through the love and devotion of family and friends. With its various plot twists and sympathetic characters, *Nosotros los Pobres* reinforced values of family devotion, honesty, and honor.

In the film, Jurado played an unsuccessful temptress of dubious virtue. Her career, like those of other actresses, grew based on such roles that were often sexist and judgmental of women's sexual behavior. Still, she sometimes secured other parts, and her versatility assured her success. She could portray the fiery-tempered hoyden, the voracious virago, or the selfless, controlled, and dignified lady.

In her private life Jurado had taken on yet another role, that of mother to two children, Victor and Sandra, born during her brief marriage to Victor Velázquez, whom she divorced in 1946. She also began to write a column about bullfighting for a Mexican newspaper, and it was in the bullring that she met John Wayne and Robert Stack, who were scouting out locations for *The Bullfighter and the Lady* (1951). Although she spoke little English, Jurado was recruited for a part in the film, which became her American debut.

In *The Bullfighter and the Lady* Jurado played Chelo, the wife of aging matador Manolo Estrada (Gilbert Roland). Leading man Robert Stack was an aspiring bullfighter seeking instruction from Estrada. As Chelo, Jurado portrayed a devoted, loving wife as well as a fiery defender of her husband's reputation in an admirable rendition of the "Spitfire" that Lupe Vélez had made popular. By the final scenes of the film, the Spitfire has vanished as Jurado, now widowed, displays deep suffering overlaid with dignity and self-control.

Jurado's performance in the film so impressed producer Stanley Kramer that he sought her for the role of Helen Ramírez in *High Noon,* despite his concern about her unfamiliarity with English. Jurado's English had improved during the production of *The Bullfighter and the Lady,* she later explained, because she enjoyed a brief affair with the film's director Budd Boetticher and "Love is the best method to learn another language." Still, she was not completely fluent and was grateful to writer Carl Foreman who revised her dialogue as necessary throughout the filming of *High Noon.*

High Noon marked a fork in the road for Jurado, as she embarked on an international career. Between 1952 and 1961, she starred in five films in Mexico, while making eight Westerns and three other movies in the United States. When Jurado began her work in Westerns, the genre was in the midst of its greatest popularity and its highest artistic achievement. The Western was also the main film genre to consistently include Mexican characters, since the American West historically had held the largest Mexican–Hispanic population in the United States. Although the Mexican–Hispanic characters often served only as background or adversaries easily overcome by superior Anglos, Westerns offered greater opportunities for a Mexican actress than any other types of American films. In addition, observers have commented that the screen depictions of Mexicanas improved somewhat during the 1950s and 1960s.

Still, the good woman/bad woman characters persisted. Some critics, directors, and scholars have argued that the Western itself is a masculine genre offering only stereotyped, peripheral roles for women of *any* ethnicity, and that these roles have changed little in their basic structure over time. Although numerous variations of these stereotypes occur, those writers who dismiss these images as stereotypical are virtually arguing that the roles of these women are not significant to plot development and serve only as a background or a spark to ignite the hero's actions.

To the contrary, other students of the Western have countered these arguments, agreeing with director Anthony Mann that women are essential to the Western. Although they concede that most women's roles fall within those

stereotypical categories discussed above, they argue that the Western itself
is full of stereotypes. As a popular art form, the Western includes stock
characters—the goodguy, the badguy, the sidekick—including the good
woman and the bad woman. What draws audiences to the basic formula
again and again with these routine characters is the possibility for variations
within the roles and storyline that are believable, compelling, and exciting.
Thus, these stereotyped female characters are often vital to plot development
and serve their own designated purpose within the genre. Women's presence
is required to create the tension between the untamed land and civilization, to
elevate conflicts to issues of morality, and to provide a counterpoint to masculine
values. When the heroine acts like a woman, the hero better understands
what he must do to be a man. Scholars in this camp also point out that strong
female roles appear in some Westerns within and outside of the stereotypical
conventions.

Those who argue that the Western has offered significant and interesting
roles for women, however, concede that women of color worked under a dual
handicap. Not only were limited roles available to them, but nearly always
their dark complexions confined them to the "bad woman" role. For Katy
Jurado, though, this truism did not always apply. She played a variety of
characters, and her first performance in a Western has been heralded as one
of the best female roles in the genre as well as the high point for Mexicanas in
American film.

As Helen Ramírez in *High Noon*, Jurado displayed her finest talents, and
it is fitting that a talented actress landed such a memorable role. Throughout
her performance, Jurado's Helen is in control, dignified, restrained, yet
passionate in her convictions. Helen Ramírez is unusual for numerous reasons.
She has had three lovers—Frank Miller (Ian MacDonald), the outlaw bent
on vengeance; Will Kane (Gary Cooper), the departing marshal; and Harvey
(Lloyd Bridges), the young deputy who hopes to take Kane's place. Because
she has known all three men intimately, Helen understands them in a way
that a good (nonsexual) woman cannot and evaluates them accordingly.
But despite her sexual history, Helen Ramírez is not relegated to a brothel;
instead, she occupies a well-appointed suite in the town's hotel, where
employees address her as Mrs. Ramírez. A skillful businesswoman, the owner
of a store and saloon, she is a respected, independent woman.

Jurado's flashing dark eyes, abundant black hair, and voluptuous figure
provide a striking contrast to Kane's prim, blonde Quaker bride Amy (Grace
Kelly), clad in virginal wedding white. This visual device suggests the familiar

struggle between the good woman and the bad woman. But Helen Ramírez is not a seductive whore destined for rejection and death. Instead, as several writers have noted, she is the moral center of the story. She understands Kane's devotion to duty and his refusal to leave town when Frank Miller returns to seek revenge. She is also contemptuous of Harvey when he refuses to stand with Kane against Miller and his friends. Harvey's insecurities about living up to Kane as a marshal are exceeded only by his worry about measuring up to Kane as Helen's lover. With devastating honesty, Helen addresses Harvey's worst fears. Although he has broad shoulders, she notes, it takes more than broad shoulders to make a man. According to her, Kane is a man — Harvey never will be.

Helen is equally direct with Amy Kane, who plans to leave town, forsaking her husband rather than her principles of nonviolence. She acts as a mentor to Amy, instructing her how to be a wife, to be worthy of the man she has married. In effect, there is no contest between Amy and Helen for Will Kane. Helen already has parted from Kane, and if he dies, she predicts, then the town will die too. Helen plans to leave town to start anew because she must provide for herself. Together, the two women set out for the depot and the noon train. As they pass Kane in the street, Amy faces straight ahead, perhaps to the future, while Helen turns to watch him fade from sight, bidding farewell to the past. And while Amy renounces her convictions and returns to shoot a man and save Kane's life, Helen follows through on her plan, leaving a town that she describes as "a difficult place to be a Mexican woman." Her courage and determination have brought her success in the face of the town's racism, although the town itself cannot overcome the collective cowardice of its population.

Gary Cooper won a best actor Oscar for *High Noon*. Despite her outstanding performance and favorable reviews, Jurado was not nominated for an Academy Award, apparently because producer Stanley Kramer erred in filling out the paperwork. Nonetheless, Jurado was honored for her work in *High Noon* with a Golden Globe award from the Hollywood Foreign Correspondents Association.

The same year she appeared in *High Noon* Katy Jurado starred in the grim and realistic Mexican production *El Bruto* (1952), with Pedro Armendáriz. Spanish-born Luis Buñuel, rapidly gaining recognition as an outstanding avant-garde director, cast Jurado as Paloma, a role that provides a fascinating contrast to Helen Ramírez. Paloma is *la devoradora*, the volatile, sexual devourer of men. The wife of a wealthy man, Paloma has everything she desires, but she is driven to seduce El Bruto, a poor and violent butcher who kills Paloma's husband. Soon, though, he tires of Paloma because he has fallen in love with the film's "good woman." Transformed from a seductress to vengeful virago, Paloma informs on El Bruto to the police and glories in his capture and death. In engineering his destruction, though, she brings about her own, losing everything she once possessed. For this performance, in 1954 the Academia Mexicana de Ciencias y Artes Cinematográficas honored Jurado with an Ariel (the Mexican equivalent of the Oscar) for best supporting actress.

However else they may have differed, Jurado's characters in *High Noon* and *El Bruto* were strong, determined women, and her performances garnered critical and popular acclaim. In most respects, these roles marked the high point of Jurado's career as a leading lady. In 1953, she starred in two Mexican films as well as two Hollywood Westerns, none of which provided her with memorable roles. She worked with Rod Cameron in the little-known *San Antone* (1953) and with Charlton Heston in the more popular *Arrowhead* (1953). It was in *Arrowhead* that Jurado first portrayed an Indian woman, since Mexicanas were often considered "all-purpose ethnic types." Jurado played Nita, an Apache mistress of civilian scout Ed Bannon (Charlton Heston). Press releases described her as "a sultry traitor" whose brother, Toriano (Jack Palance), returns to the reservation to lead an Apache uprising. Bannon suspects, correctly, that Nita will sneak off to aid her tribe. Captured and confronted, Nita is the Apache spitfire, declaring that although she loves Bannon, her loyalties lay with her people. To avoid imprisonment, she stabs herself in the heart as Bannon watches, unmoved in a performance worthy of a future president of the National Rifle Association. After her death, Bannon issues an order to a soldier: "There's a dead Apache in here; get it out." Although Jurado brought passion and energy to the role of Nita, it was the narrowest character she had yet played in American movies.

The strong anti-Indian sentiment of *Arrowhead* contrasted sharply with numerous other Westerns made in the early 1950s, such as *Broken Arrow* (1950), *White Feather* (1955), and *Broken Lance* (1954), which featured a much more complex and rewarding role for Jurado than that of Nita in *Arrowhead*. Director Edward Dmytryk intended to cast Dolores Del Rio as Señora Devereaux in her first Western. But fear of communists, particularly in the film community, gripped America in the early 1950s. Del Rio, who had been making films in Mexico for more than a decade, had befriended communists in the Mexican film industry, and the U.S. State Department thus delayed issuing her a visa. Instead, Jurado got the part, although she looked too young to play Robert

Wagner's mother. Skillful makeup aged her convincingly, and when asked whether she worried about playing an older woman Jurado responded, "All I ask is that a character show heart and this woman in the movie . . . does."

Broken Lance starred Spencer Tracy as cattleman Matt Devereaux, with Jurado as his Indian wife, and Wagner as their son, Joe. To disguise her Indian identity she is called "Señora," and the film makes clear the discrimination she and Joe have suffered because of their Indian blood. But Señora Devereaux is not interested in revenge; she wants family harmony and peace, and she urges her son to turn away from guns and seek alternative solutions to conflict. Her character—wife, mother, peacemaker—epitomizes the good woman, but Jurado's finely nuanced performance reveals the interior strength in the dignified, gracefully aging woman. The movie also features one of the most tender and poignant love scenes in the Western, between Tracy and Jurado as a couple growing old together. At the film's conclusion, Señora Devereaux's work is done, and she smiles a benediction on her departing son and his bride. But she is not alone; her husband lives on in spirit in the wolf that roams the nearby hills.

The role of Señora Devereaux was Jurado's favorite, and she received critical recognition as well, with an Oscar nomination for best supporting actress in 1954. She had strong backing from members of the press who thought she had been cheated out of a nomination for *High Noon,* and she was quoted as saying she was "happy for my country" that she was nominated. Although Jurado lost to Eva Marie Saint (*On the Waterfront*), she left her own impression on the ceremony's attending crowd:

> Best Supporting Actor nominee Rod Steiger dated Best Supporting Actress nominee Katy Jurado . . . in [what the *Los Angeles Mirror* described as] her "flame-colored gown which had at least four enormous red roses blooming across her shoulder." When the forecourt emcee complimented Jurado on the outfit, she elaborated, "It's a Dior and the bra and panties that came with it are flame-colored, too."

After *Broken Lance,* Jurado's career centered on Hollywood. Between 1954 and 1960, she made no movies in Mexico, probably because the Mexican cinema was in the doldrums from 1952 through 1964. Indeed, one writer has called the period from 1958 to 1964 "the dark days of Mexican cinema." Jurado also took a break from Westerns, playing instead supporting roles—not leading ladies—in *Trial* (1955) with Glenn Ford, *Racers* (1955) with Kirk Douglas, and *Trapeze* (1956) with Burt Lancaster and Tony Curtis.

Jurado's return to the Western and to a leading role came in *The Man from Del Rio* (1957). David Robles (Anthony Quinn) arrives in the town of Mesa seeking revenge on gunmen who terrorized him five years before in Del Rio. Then, he had no gun; now, he is a crack shot. Mesa has become a haven for gunslingers, and its sheriff is too frightened to stop them. Robles quickly outdraws his old enemy, although he is injured in the fray. At the doctor's office, he meets Estella (Jurado), a widow who works as the doctor's house-keeper and assistant. Her clothes, a high-necked white shirtwaist and a long skirt, confirm that she is not a prostitute; indeed, Estella has worked hard to carve out a position of respect and self-sufficiency, and she worries that Robles's attraction to her will undermine her position in the community.

She is also repelled by the violence of the gunslingers, who string up the sheriff to a high tree and begin to use him for target practice. Robles and the townspeople refuse to act until Estella rushes to cut down the sheriff, only to be captured and roughed up by the gunmen. Robles saves her, guns down the evildoers, and soon takes on the job of sheriff. Yet Estella, like Amy in *High Noon*, hates guns and urges Robles to seek a peaceful resolution to the conflicts brewing in Mesa.

At a town dance, another dimension is added to Robles's struggle. Even though Estella is, as a good Mexican woman, an acceptable partner for an Anglo man, Robles is snubbed and humiliated when he approaches an Anglo woman. As a showdown nears, Estella begs Robles to leave, arguing that the town despises him and is only using him. But Robles will not retreat. Although he has suffered a broken wrist and cannot handle his gun, he faces his challenger and bluffs him into surrender. At the end, Robles and Estella depart arm in arm.

The Man from Del Rio is an unusual Western in several respects. First, its hero is a Mexican who emerges as a strong and successful character; second, the hero wins, at the end, by his wits, not by his gun; and third, the film offers a worthwhile role for a Mexicana, although not as strong as those of Helen Ramírez or Señora Devereaux. Jurado's character is a capable, responsible, and moral Mexicana, although, like most women in Westerns, she is powerless to defend herself and to stop Robles from his intended purpose. Jurado's strengths in this performance are her dignity and her decisive action in defense of the sheriff and in her confrontations with Robles. When she turns to wheedling and begging, she begins to overplay the part a bit.

The Man from Del Rio directly addressed what it meant to be a Mexican in

Katy Jurado in The Man from Del Rio *(1957), with Anthony Quinn. Courtesy of MGM CLIP & STILL.* The Man from Del Rio *© 1958 United Artists Corporation. All Rights Reserved.*

the American West, although the answer the film provided was ambiguous. Robles and Estella are together, but exactly where they will spend their new life is not evident. What it meant to be a Mexicana in Hollywood in the 1950s is also unclear.

Jurado never considered American citizenship nor established a permanent residence in the United States, preferring instead to return to her home in Cuernavaca, Mexico, to visit her children, who were cared for by Jurado's parents. She expressed great pride in her nationality and homeland, saying, "It was very important for me to succeed there [the United States] as a Mexicana and yet continue being Mexican."

Still, judging from her interviews, Jurado enjoyed the time she spent working in the United States. For example, after *High Noon* was released *The New York Times* quoted her as saying, "I am very proud to make this picture because I look and act like a Mexican — not imitation. Some Mexicans go to Hollywood and lose career in Mexico . . . because they play imitation. I don't want this to happen to me." The following year she commented about her role in *Arrowhead:*

> It is wonderful to make pictures in Hollywood. Audience know it is just make-believe and they do not hate you in real life. In Mexico . . . if you play bad girl, they think you are bad girl yourself. . . . When I go on tour with picture (*High Noon*), I am respected. This make me glad because I am proud of my people, and it is good to play in American picture with pride and with dignity for my country. I wish to thank American people who are kind to me.

Was Jurado really content with the treatment she received in the United States, or did she feel demeaned because of her ethnicity and her nationality? In interviews she gave many years later, she continued to emphasize her positive experiences. For example, when Mexican journalist Juan Galindo spoke with her in 1969, he asked her if she felt that Hollywood owed her an Oscar, to which she responded, "No, good heavens. The day I would say something like that I would be the vainest woman on the earth."

In a U.S. interview in 1990, she recalled that "Gary Cooper was very nice to me . . . [he] was the most beautiful American—kind and relaxed," although she admitted that "Grace Kelly was cold. She knew what she wanted and acted like she was playing chess with people. We never had a friendship." Jurado also revealed that she enjoyed less than cordial relationships with other actresses, including María Félix and Gina Lollobrigida. In general, she noted, "I believe that men are capable of great friendships, but I don't have much confidence in friendships among women. Between them there is always a great deal of competition." Thus, she warmly praised Burt Lancaster, Spencer Tracy, Marlon Brando, Elvis Presley, and other actors as well as directors Fred Zinnemann and Eddie Dmytryk.

Perhaps Jurado's comments sincerely reflect her perception of her experiences as a Mexican actress in Hollywood. Or perhaps she was conscious of her image and cultivating her career, since the Mexican film industry was in crisis. An actress, after all, needs movies. Nevertheless, in the 1990s it is disturbing to read articles in American newspapers that label her "A torrid, glamourous tamale," call her native country "Tamaleland," and mimic Jurado's pronunciation of English as in a headline from the *Los Angeles Times* that read "Katy Hopes for Further Honors Now That She Speaks English." In addition, columnists seemed compelled to describe her as "fiery" or "colorful" and continually referred to her "Latin temperament." Still, Mexican journalists in the 1990s use similar terms, and even

Anthony Quinn, born in Mexico, described Katy during the 1950s in a similar view:

> She had everybody nuts with her eyes and that fiery-lady attitude. I was crazy about her. But she was so willful, so proud, so bellicose that nobody dared approach her. People expected her to be sweet like Dolores Del Rio or loony like Lupe Vélez. But Katy was different: she was temperamental.

Whatever way she found to be a Mexican woman in Hollywood, Jurado was foremost an actress and continued working in the United States, since so few movies were in production in Mexico. After *The Man from Del Rio* she landed a smaller role in *Massacre at Dragoon Wells* (1957) with Barry Sullivan. But by late 1956, Jurado had no further offers in Hollywood or in Mexico, so she went instead to New York to appear in a play entitled *The House of Naples*. To her great disappointment, the underfunded production folded after only three performances, and Jurado returned to Mexico, out of work for the first time in years. By early 1958, though, she was back in the United States to star in *The Badlanders*, a Western with Ernest Borgnine and Alan Ladd.

Jurado's role as Anita would be her last as a leading lady in an American film. In *Broken Lance* and *The Man from Del Rio*, Jurado had played the part of the good woman, but Anita (like Helen Ramírez) is nominally a bad woman. Still, the part offered a strong character and some interesting variations in the plot.

Costars Ernest Borgnine (McVane) and Alan Ladd (the Dutchman) are recently released from prison when they arrive in Prescott, Arizona, intent on recovering gold that rightfully belongs to them. As they arrive, the Dutchman calls attention to the exploitation of the Mexican miners who work for poor wages. Soon, McVane rescues Anita from a gang of Anglo thugs, and as a romance develops between them, Anita is forced to reveal that she is a prostitute (her low-cut blouse, short skirts, and rebozo have already alerted viewers). McVane assures her that he cares for her anyway, even referring to her as "my wife" in front of one of her former customers.

During the climactic gunfight, the Dutchman and McVane are pinned down, badly outnumbered by their enemies. But as the Cinco de Mayo celebration begins in the Mexican barrio (a cliche that proves useful to the plot), Anita rallies her people. While fireworks blaze in the plaza, Mexicano miners help defeat the bad guys, and Anita and McVane depart for their dream ranch in Mexico. A Mexican prostitute is redeemed and marries the hero (although it is the dark Borgnine, not the blonde Alan Ladd). Also, at the end, the film counters the image of Mexicans as indolent and passive.

Meanwhile, romance on-screen led to romance off-screen between Jurado and Borgnine. Although Jurado had dated a Hollywood producer as well as actor Hugh O'Brien, she had never remarried after her divorce from Victor Velázquez in 1946. Borgnine had separated from his wife, Rhoda, in April 1958, and she sued for divorce, which was granted in August. Immediately thereafter, Jurado and Borgnine began to appear together in public; in September, the couple traveled to Mexico so that he could meet her children. In March 1959, they announced plans to marry when Borgnine's divorce would be finalized in September. But on June 12, 1959, the *Los Angeles Mirror News*, in headlines several inches high, announced "Mrs. Borgnine Sues to Cancel Divorce — Katy Jurado Called Home Wrecker."

Alleging that Jurado had lured her husband away, Rhoda Borgnine tried to have the divorce set aside and now charged that Borgnine had frequently beaten her during their marriage. The resulting scandal kept columnists busy for some time, but the divorce was finalized, and on December 31, 1959, Borgnine and Jurado married in Cuernavaca, Mexico. Their struggles appeared to be over, but "happily ever after" would elude the pair in this marriage as it had in their earlier unions.

Before the wedding, Jurado had made a few television appearances and had finished filming *One-Eyed Jacks*, Marlon Brando's directorial debut (1961). Jurado played Maria, the Mexican wife of Dad Longworth (Karl Malden), once the partner of Johnny Rio (Brando). Maria has an illegitimate daughter who Longworth adopted when he married Maria, conveying respectability upon her much as he sought it for himself. To avenge himself on Longworth, Rio seduces his stepdaughter Louisa (Mexican actress Pina Pellicer), who becomes pregnant. Jurado's accomplished and well-drawn performance makes Maria believable as a compassionate mother who under-stands her daughter's disgrace. Her dignity also endures despite Longworth's insulting reminder that he has brought her out of a bean patch in Mexico. Maria's humiliation and suffering are redeemed when her daughter, another Mexicana, rides off into the sunset with the hero.

In 1960, the newly married Jurado returned to the Mexican screen for the first time since 1953, intending to resume her career in her homeland so that she would be closer to her children. But Borgnine was not content with the plan. Soon, the marital tension that had developed between these two strong personal-ities had erupted into violence at a party celebrating their first anniversary.

Witnesses noted that the couple's bickering escalated until Borgnine threw a glass of wine in Jurado's face, whereupon her son rose to defend his mother and Borgnine struck the teenaged boy. Two weeks later, Borgnine sued Jurado for divorce, alleging mental cruelty, and she responded with plans to countersue, charging him with "brutal and bestial conduct." Newspaper columnists licked their lips over "the hottest Hollywood divorce contest in years," while Borgnine departed for Italy to make a movie, and Jurado returned to Mexico.

Within a month, though, the couple reconciled after Jurado followed Borgnine to Rome. Their relationship was far from tranquil, and they soon furnished the press with new grist for the gossip mills. In mid-February, the couple argued loudly in a Rome restaurant, and later, while driving home, Jurado leapt from the car. Witnesses said that Borgnine followed her, slapped her, and knocked her to the curb, where she struck her head. Jurado and Borgnine denied those stories, explaining that she had slipped and that he had tried to help her up. Whatever the case, the two remained in Rome to work on *Barrabas* (1962), a biblical epic starring Anthony Quinn. Jurado played Sarah, a Jewish tavern keeper and occasional lover of Barrabas—a middle-eastern version of the bad woman—while Borgnine had a minor part in the film as well.

All appeared peaceful on the domestic front as the *L.A. Mirror* reported that "Ernie and Katy Purr Peacefully Like Cats (Not Tigers) in Rome," and the *Hollywood Citizen* agreed with a story entitled "Ernie, Katy Cooing Again." Soon after their return to the United States, however, the cooing and purring stopped. After acrimonious testimony, the couple agreed to a financial settlement and divorced on June 4, 1963.

During the divorce proceedings, Jurado returned to Mexico, where in 1962 she had a major role along with María Félix in *La Bandida*, the top-grossing Mexican film of the year. During the next several years Jurado made other movies in Mexico and starred in a German–Spanish film. She did not appear in another U.S. film until *Smoky* in 1966, which was filmed in Mexico.

In fact, Jurado's career as a leading lady in American films was over, for several reasons. First, the Western was in decline in the 1960s, and this genre provided most of the roles for Mexicanas. In Westerns Katy had enjoyed her greatest success because of her excellent acting skills and her undeniable beauty. Even so, Jurado never starred with John Wayne or James Stewart nor worked for John Ford, Howard Hawks, or Anthony Mann, among the greatest actors and directors of the Western, likely because most works of these artists did not feature many roles for

Mexicanas. When they did, as in *The Alamo* (1960) or *Cheyenne Autumn* (1964), Jurado faced competition for the parts from such actresses as Dolores Del Rio and Linda Cristal.

Other reasons why Katy no longer commanded leading roles included aging and changes in her appearance. By 1967, Jurado was forty, and for women in mid-life or older, any good roles were difficult to find. In the troubled years following her divorce from Borgnine she had gained weight, which caused her figure to look more bulky than voluptuous. Younger, more alluring actresses captured the few leading roles for Hispanas–Mexicans; for example, Linda Cristal starred in television's *The High Chaparral*. In addition, Jurado's English still had a strong accent, which limited her access to nonethnic characters. She had acknowledged this limitation when she was working on *The Badlanders* and admitted that it was still a problem when filming *Barrabas*, in which her voice was eventually dubbed.

Finally, Jurado's temperament—which she and others had described variously as fiery, volatile, tempestuous, Latin—also must have played a part in defining her career. She did not work for any American director more than once, and her temperament and reputation may have helped to assure this.

But careers are made of more than one or two great performances. Among Katy Jurado's most notable achievements is her refusal to allow personality, age, or weight to keep her from doing what she does well. In 1966, Jurado admitted that "I speak my mind so freely" and added, "Look at me. Me a grandmother and close to 40. Me, 25 pounds overweight and enjoying them." But, she went on, "Now, I ask: Am I going to be stopped from living a full life as woman, as actress? Never!"

Indeed, Jurado made an American comeback, playing the mother to George Maharis in *A Covenant with Death* (1967) and to Elvis Presley in *Stay Away Joe* (1968). Still, the transition from leading lady of the 1950s to peripheral character in the 1960s, from femme fatale to aging parent, must have been a difficult one. In addition, her children were now adults, living their own lives, and she had not found a man with whom to share hers.

Depressed and lonely, in February 1968, Katy Jurado attempted suicide in her Los Angeles apartment with an overdose of pills. But a friend found her in time, and after a short hospital stay she regained her health and a positive outlook on life. She resumed her career as an actress, and appeared briefly on American television and in two minor American films in 1970 and 1973.

She fared somewhat better in Mexico, where a part in the acclaimed, three-part Mexican production *Fe, Esperanza y Caridad* (1972) brought her renewed attention. In 1973, she finally returned to the setting of the American West when Sam Peckinpah cast her in his elegiac Western *Pat Garrett and Billy the Kid*.

In the film, which stars James Coburn as Pat Garrett and Kris Kristofferson as Billy the Kid, Slim Pickens plays the role of Sheriff Cullen Baker, and Jurado is his forceful partner. When Pat Garrett recruits Baker to capture outlaws, Mrs. Baker warns him, "I don't like this, Cullen. This town isn't worth it." Still, she is his partner in every respect—a Helen Ramírez grown older, with a chance to carry out what she promised in *High Noon*. In *Pat Garrett*, the sheriff *is* her man, and she fights courageously and skillfully at his side, killing men without a quiver.

But Baker is fatally wounded, and as he slowly walks toward the river to die, she watches from a distance, knowing that she cannot save him or share his death. A final glance between them conveys the love they have shared for a lifetime, and Jurado's face, never more expressive than here, is a moreeloquent portrayal of grief than all the screams and sobs of all other Western heroines combined.

After this outstanding performance, over the next twenty-five years Jurado made only brief appearances in two American films, *The Children of Sanchez* (1978) and *Under the Volcano* (1984), and acted on television in the miniseries *Evita* (1980) and in the short-lived series *AKA Pablo*. Her career in Mexico also slowed, in large part because Jurado had little interest in acting after the death of her son in a traffic accident in December 1981. Still, she remained connected to film; in 1985, she became film commissioner for the state of Morelos, arranging permits and accommodations for companies from the United States and Mexico that did business in her home state.

On both sides of the border, organizations began to recognize Jurado's lengthy career and recall her memorable performances. In 1981, for example, the Festival of New Directors and New Films in Santa Fe honored her career in Westerns, and NOSOTROS (an organization to promote Spanish-language actors in movies and on television) selected her for their Golden Eagle Award. In 1992, the Mexican Film Promotion Trust held a ceremony in her honor, and in an interview she remarked that "I am content with my work in the movies, and above all I feel satisfied that I was one of those actresses who opened up the possibilities for others [Mexicanas] in the United States." She also noted that she had yet to see anyone take advantage of that opportunity.

Within five years, though, Mexicana actress Salma Hayek had entered the world of Hollywood films. When interviewed about Hayek's prospects, Jurado predicted that Hayek had a bright future in Hollywood. She cautioned the younger actress to concentrate on her acting abilities rather than accept only roles as a sex symbol, because, Jurado warned, "beauty goes quickly." Hayek's career did expand, and in 1999 she appeared in the futuristic Western *The Wild Wild West*. Promotional photos showed her in a costume decidedly similar to that of Katy Jurado's in her role as Helen Ramírez. Hayek noted that her present recognition as an actress and producer "has been a quick journey, but we have to bear in mind that I've been working now for ten years." She failed to mention that the work of other Mexicanas might have paved the way for her success, but she acknowledged that "conquering the language has been my biggest hurdle," something with which Katy Jurado would sympathize.

If young Mexicana and Latina actresses have not recognized Jurado's impact on their careers, she has received acclaim from the Academia Mexicana de Ciencias y Artes Cinematográficas and her fans in Mexico. In 1997, the Academia awarded her a special golden Ariel—the equivalent of the U.S. Academy's lifetime achievement award. At the awards ceremony Katy Jurado also drew approval for a current performance. The Mexican newspaper *El Universal* reported that "The award winners were not permitted to speak. Until Katy Jurado put them in their place. 'We are not puppets, we are artists. Why can't we be allowed to say thank you? It is not right that we are treated this way!'"

Her defiant action delighted her fans, many of whom had come to recognize Jurado from her recent role in *Te Sigo Amando*, one of Mexico's most successful and popular *telenovelas*. They also eagerly awaited the opening of Jurado's new film, Arturo Ripstein's *El Evangelio de las Maravillas* (1997) in which she had the starring role as Mama Dorita.

Like most of Jurado's Mexican movies, *El Evangelio* is not available to American audiences, but in 1998 she made a cameo appearance in *The Hi-Lo Country*, her first Western since 1973 and her first U.S. film since 1984. In March 1999, she was the honoree at the Guadalajara Film Festival, where the first full-length examination of her career *El Cine de Katy Jurado* was released. Indeed, Katy Jurado's long and prolific love affair with the movies continues.

Although many of her roles in American films including Westerns were minor ones, they number among the best roles ever available to a woman from Mexico, and Jurado made the most of them. Devotees of the Western will recall her memorable performances as the calm and dignified Señora Devereaux in *Broken Lance*, and the courageous and sorrowing Mrs. Baker in *Pat Garrett and Billy the Kid*. Above all they will remember the lovely and passionate Helen Ramírez of *High Noon*. For them, Katy Jurado always will be Mexico's woman of the Western.

◆ nine ◆

Jay Silverheels, Iron Eyes Cody, and Chief Dan George

Native Americans and the Imagined West

GRETCHEN M. BATAILLE

Central to the vision of the Hollywood West is the Native American. Whether astride a pinto pony charging Custer's troops or a contemporary Spokane Indian, such as in Sherman Alexie's *Smoke Signals*, Native Americans are an integral part of America's cultural make-up, essential to the story of the American West. That story has been told on the screen from the beginning of the motion picture industry, and only as we begin a new century is this image changing. The stereotype of the Indian is as fixed in the public mind as is that of other ethnic groups. What is different for Native Americans is that from the early twentieth century until very recently, Native Americans in film rarely played themselves. The first portrayals of Native Americans on the screen evolved from the Wild West shows of the late 1800s and capitalized on the popularity of the Indian as entertainment.

From the very beginning of the motion picture industry, Thomas Edison commercialized Native traditions by using Native Americans in such early films as *The Sioux Ghost Dance* (1894) and *The Parade of Buffalo Bill's Wild West* (1898). Edward Curtis produced what some have called ethnographic films, and others have denigrated as "quasi-ethnographic" films. Still, early filmmakers, such as D. W. Griffith, Thomas Ince, Cecil B. DeMille, and William S. Hart, found that the public was more interested in Native Americans in general and less interested in the historical accuracy of how they were portrayed. These inaccurate images were formed early and remained fixed in films for half a century; it was an image rooted in the nineteenth-century destruction of Indian communities and lifeways.

Jay Silverheels as Tonto in The Lone Ranger and the Lost City of Gold *(1958).*
The Museum of Modern Art/Film Stills Archive.

The Native Americans we remember from such films were sometimes noted in the credits, unlike the many nameless extras who rode as thick as bison herds across movie screens. These Native Americans were ironically the "pioneers" in the industry, remembered sometimes for their negative portrayals and, now more frequently, for their efforts to change the stereotypes Hollywood sought to perpetuate.

The first Tonto, Victor Daniels/Chief Thundercloud, appeared in the 1938 Republic series of fifteen episodes of *The Lone Ranger* and again in 1939 in the sequel series *The Lone Ranger Rides Again.* Most Americans, though, remember the second actor who portrayed Tonto, Jay Silverheels. Silverheels was not the first Indian in the movies, of course, and he played roles other than that of Tonto, but for many he is the Indian we remember. His character was not a hero, but a foil for the hero, the Lone Ranger, and Tonto epitomized the Indian sidekick. Astride his tawny horse, Scout, and alongside or behind the masked man seated on his white horse, Silver, Tonto rode into American homes first on radio, then on television, and last in the movies for nearly twenty-five years. This image became firmly fixed in America's cultural consciousness. By the time filmmakers and the public—and Native Americans— began portraying a different view of Indians, the Lone Ranger and Tonto had disappeared from the airwaves and the screens, if not from our collective psyches.

Film images of Native Americans evolved from stereotypes that were created by frontier settlers, artists, and historians. These stereotypes were frequently contradictory, reflecting the ambivalence of Euro-Americans toward the peoples they attempted to annihilate. Tonto evolved from a tradition embodied in Wild West shows, dime novels, literary romances, and various artistic renderings. The story of white heros with Indian companions was told in James Fenimore Cooper's *The Last of the Mohicans* (Hawkeye and Chingachgook) and was featured in several films—*Broken Arrow* (1950), *The Outlaw Josey Wales* (1976), *Powwow Highway* (1989), and *Dances with Wolves* (1990).

Such mixed-race partnerships lasted longest, however, in the story of the Lone Ranger and Tonto, whose escapades took place in the popular time period for most Hollywood Westerns, from 1865 to 1890. The characters were created by Fran Striker, a freelance scriptwriter from Buffalo, New York, who had never been West. His radio scripts introduced the character of Tonto in the twelfth episode (February 25, 1933) of the radio series, which began in 1933. In the early episodes Tonto is referred to as a half-breed, and that label wasn't dropped until 1936. The Lone Ranger needed a companion, someone to talk to, and Striker created a character described as being from the

Potawatomi Tribe of Michigan. This probably worked well for the Detroit radio station that featured the series, but one wonders how an Indian from Michigan ended up in the West. The outdoor scenes for the television series were filmed in Utah and California, first for Hal Roach Studios and then for General Services Studios. The character Jay Silverheels played was loyal and subservient to his white partner, yet still possessed nearly supernatural powers of insight that embodied the contradictions and the ambivalence of America toward Indians on screen as well as in real life.

The unlikely pairing of an Indian whose tribe had been massacred and a member of the Texas Rangers who had been left for dead was believable by Hollywood standards. Bit-by-bit the story came out in the series and in the promotional Merita Bread giveaway printed in 1940 called *The Life of Tonto*. The story was that as a boy the Lone Ranger had saved Tonto's life, and now it was time for Tonto to pay back his friend by nursing him to health. Tonto similarly saves the Lone Ranger's horse, Silver, and together Tonto and the Lone Ranger set out to bring a new form of justice to the West, symbolized by silver bullets. The pair did not accept payment for their good deeds, apparently relying on the silver mine for both financial support and the famous silver bullets. Tonto's speaking parts were frequently limited to "kemo sabe" and "get-em up, Scout." Still Native and having only a rudimentary command of English, Tonto, nevertheless, was capable of great insights and wisdom that could "save" the West. Of course, he was helping save a world in which he and his descendents would not have a place. His simplistic use of language validated his secondary role to the white hero whose vocabulary marked him as superior. Tonto was repeatedly less able than the Lone Ranger except in the primitivistic ability to understand the natural world and the baser instincts of humans. Even today there are jokes about Tonto's abilities to hear better or see better, but it is usually the Indian who bears the brunt of the humor. What was clear to all viewers was that Tonto remained the loyal servant of the Lone Ranger, playing a character who critic Ralph Friar has described as an "Indian Stepin Fetchit."

Tonto became the prototype for other Indian sidekicks in the movies. During World War II nearly every war film included a loyal Indian buddy in the trenches, fighting for his country by using his "animal-like" powers to detect the enemy or to stand in for other persecuted minorities. Other "real" Indians appeared in the movies: Jim Thorpe, Chief Walachie, Red Wing, and Chief Thundercloud. But it is the character of Tonto that remains etched in the public mind, a character whose name has been translated into "fool" and who has spawned a series of even more foolish characters on television. In time, Indian characters became even more absurd as Chief Thunderthud and Princess Summer–Fall–Winter–Spring entertained children on *The Howdy Doody Show.*

Jay Silverheels was born May 26, 1919, as Harold J. Smith on Six Nations Reserve in Ontario, Canada. His exact birthdate has also been listed as June 26, 1919, and September 26, 1913. His screen credits sometimes identify him as either Harry S. Smith or Silverheels Smith, but those names did not gain him the fame of either Jay Silverheels or his most famous role. He finally legally changed his name to Jay Silverheels in 1971. Although his father, A.G.E. Smith, was a captain in the Canadian army, Silverheels was brought up in the traditions of his Mohawk family. Before he came to Hollywood in 1933, Silverheels was a lacrosse player. It was as a member of a touring lacrosse team that he first came to California. Before finding successful work as an actor, he was both an amateur and professional boxer.

Jay Silverheels's movie career began in the early 1940s, playing opposite such on-screen powerhouses as Tyrone Power, Elizabeth Taylor, and Errol Flynn. His first major role was with Tyrone Power in *Captain from Castille* (1947), and he gained notice as one of the Osceola brothers in *Key Largo* (1948). He married Mari DiRoma in 1946, and they had four children, Marilyn, Pamela, Karen, and Jay Anthony.

Throughout his career, Silverheels also played bit parts as a generic Indian. Reflecting Hollywood's preoccupation with Indians named after animals, Silverheels played Running Deer in *The Prairie* (1947), Little Crow in *Red Mountain* (1951), Spotted Bear in *The Nebraskan* (1953), Black Buffalo in *The Black Dakotas* (1954), Jimmy Wolf in *One Little Indian* (1973), and John Crow in *Santee* (1973). He also played the Apache chief Geronimo in three films: *Broken Arrow* (1950), *The Battle at Apache Pass* (1951), and *Walk the Proud Land* (1956). In *Brave Warrior* (1952), he portrayed Tecumseh, and in the screen version of Cooper's *Pathfinder* (1953), he played the noble Indian Chingachgook.

Although he had roles in more than sixty films and television shows from 1940 to 1973, Silverheels gained fame and popularity in his role as Tonto, the Lone Ranger's trusty sidekick, in 221 television episodes of *The Lone Ranger* from 1949 to 1957. His first role with Clayton Moore was in *The Cowboy and the Indians* (1949), and later that year he began his career as Tonto. The television series was based on a WXYZ Detroit radio show that played from 1933 and 1954 and had been created by George W. Trendle. Fran Striker

163

was the writer for the radio and television series, both of which were introduced by the classic music trademark, Gioacchino Rossini's "William Tell Overture."

The television Lone Ranger was played by John Hart (1951–1952) for fifty-two episodes during a period when Clayton Moore was demanding more money per show. But it is Clayton Moore who is most remembered for the role in the ABC television series *The Lone Ranger,* and Silverheels starred in every television episode. Ninety stations around the country carried the series. In the beginning critics panned the show for its weekly "cliff-hangers," but after only a year the show was reaching five million viewers a week and became ABC's highest-rated Western series ever. Moore was rehired for the 1954 season and remained for ninety-one episodes from 1954 to 1957. CBS and NBC continued to broadcast reruns through 1961. Silverheels also appeared as Tonto in two movies, *The Lone Ranger* (1956) and *The Lone Ranger and the Lost City of Gold* (1958), which were spin-offs from the television series. In *Alias Jesse James* (1959) he resurrected the character of Tonto, and in 1973, he again teamed up with John Hart—without the mask—in *Santee.*

The Lone Ranger received many awards beginning in 1938 with the Showmanship Award from *Variety* magazine. In 1940, the series was named the "Best Children's Program" by the Radio Guild, and three years later the Radio Editors selected it as the best program in the nation. Awards came to the program from the Federation of Women's Clubs, the *Radio–TV Mirror,* and the Academy of Television Arts and Sciences. The majority of the awards praised Clayton Moore's portrayal of the hero but failed to note the Indian companion played by Jay Silverheels. It was left to such groups as the Association on American Indian Affairs (AAIA) to bring attention to the inaccurate portrayals of Native peoples in the media. Although the AAIA expressed positive views of Tonto's character in 1960, according him "co-hero" status in the series, later evaluations of the role were more negative.

Conscious of the mounting criticisms during the Civil Rights era of the 1960s and his portrayal of the loyal Indian accompanying the masked white hero, Silverheels was a major force in forming the Indian Actors' Guild in Los Angeles in 1966. The guild sought to promote the employment of American Indian people in Native roles, to promote training Indians in horsemanship, and to promote the teaching of acting skills to Indians. In 1963, Silverheels helped establish the Indian Actors' Workshop at the Los Angeles Indian Center along with Buffy Sainte–Marie, Iron Eyes Cody, and Rodd Redwing. Some of those who were involved were Norman Allan Nathan, John Harjo, Paul Badhorse, Toni Lee Howard, Mahontah Jo Miller, Veronica D. Brooks,

Diana Dinah Martin, John R. "Jack" Thorpe, Candy "Ironcloud" Brown, Steve Shemayne, Jeri Silverton Wallace, Dianne Little Eagle, Herb Ricehill, June Crews, Margaret Cook, Preston Jefferson, Tony Manley, Foster Hood, Bill Blackmore, Red Skinadore, and Jeanne Freitag. Karl Roth was hired as a drama coach, and Chief George Pierre joined the workshop. In 1967, they put on the All-American Indian Expo, which included Jay Silverheels's Pageant at the Great Western Exhibit Center. Len Fairchuk, a Canadian Salteaux Indian, did the sound for the pageant, and dancers from several tribes participated, including Iron Eyes Cody, Victor Roebuck, and Hogan Red Cloud. Rod Redwing, Jeanne Freitag, and Ruby Laird contributed to the event as well. One white actor, Noble "Kid" Chissell, took the roles of Benjamin Franklin and General Howard. The American Indian Roughriders joined the acting class that used the Echo Park Methodist Church for their classes and rehearsals. Many of the actors who would appear in later movies started with this workshop, hoping to learn enough to become professional actors. In 1974, near the end of his acting career, Silverheels began a new career as a harness racing driver and raced competitively at such places as Vernon Downs Racing Track and Churchill Downs. In 1979, he became the first Indian to have a star on Hollywood Boulevard's Walk of Fame.

Silverheels's health rapidly declined after that, and he disappeared from public view. He died from either complications of pneumonia or a stroke at the Motion Picture and Television Country House in Woodland Hills, California, on March 5, 1980. A sports center in his honor was erected on his home reservation on ten acres of land donated by his mother. In recognition of Silverheels's support of Indian actors, the American Indian Registry for the Performing Arts in Los Angeles dedicated its 1984 American Indian Talent Directory to his memory. On May 21, 1998, Jay Silverheels was inducted into the Hall of Honor of the First Americans in the Arts for his contributions to Indians in films. At the ceremony, chair of the board of trustees Bob Hicks said, "Mr. Silverheels was not only a star in Hollywood, he was a hero to many in the Native American community. . . . He reached out to aspiring Native performers by creating the Indian Actors Workshop. His contributions, generosity and humor have left an indelible stamp on our community." In spite of frequent negative responses to his role as Tonto, Silverheels symbolized for many Indian actors the potential for employment in television and film, two areas that had long been dominated by white actors playing "Indian."

For over a half century, the face of Iron Eyes Cody was well known to American filmgoers. Unlike Silverheels's role as Tonto, Cody was never identified as closely to a single character. In this way, he more closely epitomizes the Plains Indian stereotype whose roles included everything from playing as unnamed Indian to playing chiefs. His face and the image he presented are important because Cody's image changed over time, from the frequently savage Indian depicted in the movies to the symbol of environmental consciousness spawned by an interest in the relationships between the natural world and Native Americans.

Known by some as the "crying Indian," because of his appearances in the "Keep America Beautiful" campaign that the Marsteller Advertisement Agency ran from 1971 into the early 1980s, Cody's image was an introduction to a new, albeit more benign, stereotype. The Public Service announcement, which was introduced on Earth Day in 1971, was listed by *Entertainment Weekly* as among the fifty best commercials of all time. Cody's caretaker, Belen Escarano, was quoted in *The New York Times* obituary as saying that Cody first resisted doing the commercial because "Indians don't cry." According to Ms. Escarano, Lady Bird Johnson persuaded him to do the commercial. In the end, he didn't have to cry because the tear was glycerin.

As a befeathered character in multiple films since the early days of film-making, Cody characterized the Indian stereotype. Some sources described him as Cree, Cherokee, or Cheyenne, whereas *The New Orleans Times-Picayune* and *Indian Country Today* identified him as an Italian with great compassion for Native Americans and a clear identification with the culture. Although there are several reports about his birth date, it is most likely April 3, 1907. Conflicting stories continue to circulate about Cody. In one version of his life, he was born as Espera DiCorti in 1904 in Gueydan, Louisiana, to Italians Antonio DiCorti (sometimes recorded as DeCorte) and Francesca Salpietra (sometimes spelled Salpit) and baptized at Holy Rosary Catholic Church in Kaplan, Louisiana. In another version, Cody was born in the Oklahoma Territory with the name Oscar Cody and started his show business career with his father Thomas Long Plume acting in Wild West shows. In his autobiography, Cody writes that his father's name was Thomas Longplume Codey and that he changed it to Cody when he toured with the other famous Cody—Buffalo Bill Cody. In yet other versions, Cody was born on his family ranch in Texas, where he was home-schooled and learned Indian skills from his father.

Still, some sources indicate he was given the name Little Eagle as a child, but when he arrived in Hollywood was given the more adult and historical name Iron Eyes by an Arapaho family friend named Chief White Horse. According to his account in *Indian Talk,* Cody was taught sign language by Two Gun White Calf, a Blackfoot Indian, and Buffalo Man, a Cheyenne Indian, both friends of his father. Cody also credits the Arapaho Chief White Horse and Colonel Tim McCoy with helping him to learn his sign language skills. In some sources, McCoy denounces Cody as "a complete fraud." The descriptions of the relationship between the two men embrace the contradictions that marked Cody's life history. He danced before the King and Queen of England and toured Australia with the Sydney Royal Agricultural Show, competing in archery while he was there and winning the 40-yard trophy from both the Melbourne Centenary Archery Association and the Coogee Archery Association.

Cody's first major role was in Cecil B. DeMille's 1947 motion picture *Unconquered.* He served as both actor and technical advisor throughout his career. An expert in sign language and Native cultures, Cody was committed to accuracy in the movies, although his advice was not always taken. In addition to appearing in nearly one hundred motion pictures, Cody also appeared in the television series *Bonanza, Gunsmoke, Zane Grey Theater, Rawhide,* and *Adventures of Wild Bill Hickok.* He was a collector of authentic Native American arts and memorabilia, an author, and a supporter of his community. He worked with the Boy Scouts of America to direct their craft programs and to help dancers and artists understand Indian crafts. He served on the advisory board for the Southwest Museum where his wife worked for many years and had her own career as an archaeologist. For more than thirty years, he was a regular in the annual New Year's Day Rose Parade in Pasadena, California. Cody continued to live in the Silver Lake district of Los Angeles where he created the Moosehead Museum, a repository for the Indian regalia he had collected over the years. For twenty years, he conducted powwows at the Eagle Rock recreation center near his home.

His books include his autobiography *My Life as a Hollywood Indian, Indian Talk: Hand Signals of the North American Indians,* and *How Indian Sign Talk in Pictures,* which includes photographs of 246 words, phrases, and counting methods in sign language. Critics continue to question the version of his life records in *My Life as a Hollywood Indian,* arguing that the account is fiction. In this book recorded by Collin Perry, Cody's Hollywood story begins when he goes to Hollywood as a twelve-year-old with his father. There he has one of his first encounters with a Hollywood "star," working as a technical advisor in 1925 when he was eighteen years old.

Much of the autobiography elaborates on the scant accounts elsewhere about Cody's life. He writes that his great-great-grandfather was among the Cherokees on the Trail of Tears, supporting the version of his life that says he was born in Oklahoma to a Cree mother and Cherokee father. He brags about his movie experiences on and off the set with Clark Gable, Cary Grant, Buster Crabbe, John Wayne, and Johnny Weissmuller. Although the details of Cody's life recounted in his book are probably debatable, what he presents is a lively account of the movie business from its very beginnings through the 1980s. When he wasn't working on movies, Cody toured with the Buck Jones Wild West Show, the Ringling Brothers, Barnum and Bailey Circus, and what he called "circus tours." During his lifetime, he met Presidents Jimmy Carter and Ronald Reagan, William Randolph Hearst, and the Pope.

He worked as a technical advisor for Cecil B. DeMille and Walt Disney, pointing out that as a Hollywood Indian he also became a "Hollywood actor," playing the roles defined for him by America's attitude toward Native Americans. As time went on, Cody demanded more and more authenticity in the medium and, like Jay Silverheels, took an interest in the portrayals, working to change the stereotypes that had existed for so long. Perhaps the image of Cody as the spokesperson for the environment is the most lasting image of the actor. He had already appeared in *A Man Called Horse* (1970) as the medicine man who inserts the bones into the hero Morgan's chest and as the Apache Santana in *El Condor* (1970) when the Marsteller Agency came to him with the offer to participate in the environmental movement by appearing in the television ad shot by Columbia studios. Ironically, after a lifetime of acting the part of the Hollywood Indian with all its contradictions, it was this image of the environmentalist that would be the best remembered role of Iron Eyes Cody.

Cody was honored by the Los Angeles City Council on March 21, 1969, for his accomplishments on behalf of American Indians. He served as a board member of both the Los Angeles Indian Center and the Friends of the Los Angeles Library Association. He was also vice president of the Little Big Horn American Indian Club, a board member and photographer for the Los Angeles Corral of the Westerners, and remained active in the Boy Scouts of America as a Life Member of Verdugo Council. He also was a Vigil Member of the Spe–Le–Yai Lodge 249 of the Order of the Arrow in Glendale, California. Cody was a member of the Screen Actors Guild and AFTRA. In 1983, he was honored with a star on Hollywood's Walk of Fame and a year later was named Indian of the Year.

Iron Eyes Cody in El Condor *(1970). The Museum of Modern Art/Film Stills Archive.*

Cody's was married to Yeawas, Bertha "Birdie" Parker, listed in some sources as the daughter of the Seneca anthropologist Arthur C. Parker and related to General Ely S. Parker, the first Indian to become commissioner of Indian Affairs. Most sources indicate Cody and his wife had two sons, Robert and Arthur, although some sources suggest the sons were adopted. His son, Arthur, died in 1996, and his son, Robert Tree, lives in Phoenix, Arizona. In Cody's autobiography, Birdie's last name is given as Dark Cloud. Birdie died in 1978.

Cody died of natural causes at his home in Los Angeles on January 4, 1999. Cody's life and identity remain contradictory, and he characterized the conflicting stereotypes of the media's view of Native Americans—from savage threats to expansion and development to guardians of the earth and its sacred spirit. What Cody brought to the environmental movement was not only sympathy for the land and its destruction but a sense of guilt over what America had done to the Indians, evoking sympathy and even pity about the past. To clean up the streams and rivers would symbolize America's compensation for past mistreatment of the people who had always cared for the land. In spite of the confusion about his identity, his life, and his credentials, Cody remains an icon of the Hollywood Indian and the environmental movement. Although he was criticized for playing demeaning roles, and his ethnic identity will probably always be questioned, Cody opened many doors for Indian actors.

Together, Silverheels and Cody made it possible for other Native American actors to enter the movie business and to do so on their own terms. Among the first Native American actors performing independently from either a white hero or ethnic misidentification was Chief Dan George. He was born July 24, 1899, as Teswano, great-grandson of Tslaholt, son of Watsuki in North Vancouver, British Columbia, and later christened as Dan George. Before he became an actor, Dan George was a chief of the Salish Band in Burrard Inlet. He learned to log from his father and grandfather and spent twenty-six years as a longshoreman until injury forced him to give up his occupation. Returning to his tribe in 1947, Dan George spent twelve years as the elected chief of his tribe and was made honorary chief of both the Squamish and Shuswap bands. Chief Dan George and his wife, Amy, who died in 1971, had six children — Marie, Ann, Irene, Rose, Leonard, and Robert.

He began his acting career with a role in a television series produced by the Canadian Broadcasting Company, *Cariboo Country*. His first role in a feature film was as Chief Joseph in *Smith!* (1959). After not acting for several years, he jumped at the chance of a speaking role in *Little Big Man* (1970). In his first major film role as Old Lodge Skins he adopts and teaches Dustin Hoffman in Arthur Penn's revisionist view of the West. Although film critics and scholars hail *Little Big Man* as marking a change in the image of Native Americans and how they are portrayed on screen, the character has been criticized for his too-easy acceptance of the inevitability of white domination. Just as *Broken Arrow* had introduced a certain humanity into Native American characters in 1950, twenty years later *Little Big Man* told the story of the West by witnessing the destruction of Indian villages from the Native's point of view. As Old Lodge Skins, Chief Dan George demonstrated that Indians had feelings as well as a sense of humor. The image of the stoic Native, almost always portrayed without wife or family and at one with a horse carrying him across the Plains, suddenly took on a transformation in that film and paved the way for new actors to further challenge the old Hollywood stereotypes.

Along with Navajo actor Geraldine Keams as Little Moonlight and Will Sampson playing Ten Bears, Chief Dan George played Lone Watie, traveling with Clint Eastwood in *The Outlaw Josey Wales* (1976). In this post–Civil War

drama, the quartet of three Indians and an outlaw are still together at the
end of the film. Chief Dan George played the Old Sioux in the television
miniseries *Centennial* (1978) and performed in several Canadian films. He
wrote *My Heart Soars, My Spirit Soars,* and *You Call Me Chief: Impressions of the
Life of Chief Dan George.* Two of his books—*My Heart Soars* and *My Spirit
Soars*—appear to be children's books; however, the messages contained in
them are clearly also directed to adults. He ends *My Heart Soars* by saying, "I
am a chief, but my power to make war is gone, and the only weapon left to
me is speech. It is only with tongue and speech that I can fight my people's
war." These illustrated books convey the spirit of Indian life as well as the
words of the wise chief who found new mediums to convey his commitment
to his culture.

Chief Dan George received a best supporting actor nomination for both
an Oscar and a Golden Globe Award for his role in *Little Big Man* and won
the National Society of Film Critics and New York Film Critics Award for
that part. Chief Dan George's fame came to him late in life, but after his role
as Old Lodge Skins he was sought after for performances and appearances,

Chief Dan George as Old Lodge Skins in Little Big Man *(1970). The Museum of
Modern Art/Film Stills Archive.*

including a state dinner on the yacht *Britannia* with Queen Elizabeth in 1971. An Honorary Con for Life award was given to him by the inmates of the British Columbia Penitentiary in honor of the many performances he had provided to that prison and others. In 1971, he received the Human Relations award from the Canadian Council of Christians and Jews.

When he was in his seventies, he sang with a rock group named Fireweed, received an Honorary Doctor of Laws from Simon Fraser University, and continued to act in everything from commercials to comedies to serious theater. He was in *Cancel My Reservation* (1972) with Bob Hope, and, in an ironic twist of characters and names, he played Sam Two Feathers in the 1974 movie *Harry and Tonto.* In 1973, he performed as Rita Joe's father in the play *Rita Joe* at the Washington Theatre Club in Washington, D.C.

Chief Dan George's fame and powerful presence drew the attention of young militants during the protests of the 1970s, but he refused to be identified with the confrontations. In spite of his success on the screen, he was called an "Uncle Tom" and an "apple" by the activists who were angry that he didn't capitalize on his fame by joining their movements in both the United States and Canada.

Chief Dan George died in his sleep on September 23, 1981, at Lions Gate Hospital in Vancouver, British Columbia. At the end of *Little Big Man,* Chief Dan George, in his role as Old Lodge Skins, is surprised to find out that rather than having died, he is still alive—"sometimes the magic works; sometimes it doesn't." In the novel version, this character dies, no longer a part of the new world in which the Indian will have a diminished role. That he lives in the movie version may be Arthur Penn's way of saying that the Native American character will survive in the movies and will venture into the changed, modern world.

All three actors—Jay Silverheels, Iron Eyes Cody, and Chief Dan George—depict an on-screen tradition of representation that is consistently linked to the American past and is predominantly male. What has remained constant has been the dominance of male roles for Native Americans in the movies. American views of the West have focused on the impediments to development, which almost always have been portrayed as male warriors. Indian women were rarely considered anything more than "squaws" who remained back in camp tanning buffalo hides or digging for roots. That the main Native American actors until recently were also male has defined the image of the Hollywood West. Female Native American characters in the movies generally have had positive roles only if they were loyal to the white soldiers or trappers, and in most of the films, any romantic relationship was temporary, reflecting a national bias against miscegenation. Just as Sonseeahray had to die in *Broken Arrow* rather than marry the white hero, and Nophaie had to die rather than marry the white school teacher in *The Vanishing American*, the heroine Stands with a Fist who falls in love with John Dunbar in *Dances with Wolves* turns out to be a white woman raised by the Indians.

But the times—and the movies—are indeed changing. The first dramatic shift came on the heels of the Vietnam War. Filmmakers, eager to capitalize on images of genocide abroad, used American history to demonstrate the domestic genocide of the United States. *Little Big Man* (1970), *A Man Called Horse* (1970), and *Ulzana's Raid* (1972) were revisionist Westerns attacking American values and simple definitions of good and bad. In 1981, Michael Horse played Tonto in *The Legend of the Lone Ranger,* and his character spoke better English than the Jay Silverheels character ever did and, unlike the Tonto of the past, he was willing to argue for Indian rights. It has taken many years for the images to change, for the introduction of positive Native American characters, and for both male and female Native actors playing nonstereotypical parts. Only in the 1990s have such actors as Wes Studi, Gary Farmer, Irene Bedard, Lois Red Elk, and Floyd Red Crow Westerman received serious screen roles. Even so, the box-office stand-out of the 1990s, *Dances with Wolves,* has been both criticized as yet another formula, white hero-driven Western and praised for its use of Native actors and languages.

Wesley Studi follows in the paths of Jay Silverheels, Iron Eyes Cody, and Chief Dan George, but it is clear that the parts he plays and the views of Native Americans on the screen have undergone major changes. From his performance as an unnamed (and, according to most, viciously stereotypical) Pawnee in *Dances with Wolves* (1990) to Magua in *The Last of the Mohicans* (1992), Geronimo in *Geronimo: An American Legend* (1993), and Hanover in *Deep Rising* (1998), his roles reflect Hollywood's new acceptance of Native actors and its willingness to portray the past in different ways.

Cherokee actor Wesley Studie was born December 17, 1947, in NoFire Hollow, Oklahoma. He attended Chilocco Indian School in Oklahoma, served in Vietnam, and started acting in his thirties. Before reaching Hollywood, Studi (he shortened the spelling of his name) had written two children's books—*The Adventures of Billy Bean* and *More Adventures of Billy Bean.* Once he was established in Hollywood, he sought out film roles that would bring dignity to Native Americans. Studi has been recognized repeatedly by the First Americans in the Arts for his performances beginning with *Powwow Highway* (1989) to his nontraditional roles such as Hanover in *Deep Rising* (1998).

Actors such as Gary Farmer (Mohawk), Kateri Walker (Chippewa), Lois Red Elk (Dakota/Lakota), Matthew Montoya (Taos Pueblo), Floyd Red Crow Westerman (Dakota), Graham Greene (Oneida), Rodney Grant (Winnebago), and Evan Adams (Coast Salish) have established careers in roles as Native Americans who do not always play Native American parts. Perhaps most significant in the changing Hollywood West is the emergence of writers such as Gerald Vizenor (Ojibwa) and Sherman J. Alexie (Spokane/Coeur d'Alene). Professor, author, and filmmaker Vizenor wrote *Harold of Orange* (1984), the satiric story of Harold Sinseer (played by Charlie Hill) and the merry trickster warriors who come up with outlandish schemes to bilk money out of foundations. Sherman Alexie's movie *Smoke Signals* (1998) evolved from his own powerful writing and his novel *The Lone Ranger and Tonto Fistfight in Heaven*. In order to introduce a new vision of the present, he went back to those icons of the past. His novel *Indian Killer* (1998) will appear on screen as well. Tribal governments have financed such films as *Running Brave* (1983), which was funded by the Canadian Ermineskin tribe and portrays the life of 1964 Olympic gold medalist Billy Mills, a Sioux Indian who succeeded against all odds. That white actor Robbie Benson played the role of Mills and that several of the Indian characters were stereotypical detracted from the film and, for many, was a reminder that change comes slowly.

The faces of Jay Silverheels, Iron Eyes Cody, and Chief Dan George dominate America's vision of Native Americans on the screen. They do so because they fulfill both the stereotypes of the past and the hopes of the American Dream. They are instantly recognizable as Indians and so the viewing public thinks it knows and understands them. At the same time, all of them are somewhat benign, not likely to attack unless provoked, keepers of both history and the environment, and viewed as existing more in the past than in the present. That these three characters epitomize Hollywood's image of Native Americans suggests that we may be more rooted in the imagined West than we want to believe.

ten

Clint Eastwood

A New Type of Hero

JIM HOY

As an actor with a reputation for being able to communicate more effectively with a squint and a stare than with words, it is ironic that Clint Eastwood has coined some of the most memorable catch phrases of late-twentieth century American culture. Many of these mots have been delivered from the mouth of Dirty Harry Callahan, the San Francisco detective whose tough-guy attitude toward law enforcement seems more appropriate to frontier justice than to a contemporary big-city police force: "Do you feel lucky, punk? Well, do you?" (from *Dirty Harry*); "A man's got to know his limitations" (from *Magnum Force*); and, most famous of all, "Go ahead, make my day" (from *Sudden Impact*). Eastwood's Westerns have also produced their share of quotable lines: "Where life had no value, death sometimes had its price" (from *For a Few Dollars More*); "Dying ain't much of a living, boy" (from *The Outlaw Josey Wales*); and "We've all got it coming, Kid" (from *Unforgiven*).

Yet, of all the many memorable phrases from Eastwood's films, probably the most personally relevant is a line from *Bronco Billy*. In response to an incredulous query from Sondra Locke's spoiled rich girl character, who simply cannot comprehend or credit the straightforward actions and expectations of the ingenuous hero, Billy tells her "I am who I want to be." If Clint Eastwood is not who he wants to be, it is not for lack of will, effort, and intention. The determination and self-awareness with which Eastwood has shaped his career are in many ways reflected in the persona he has projected on screen.

Eastwood did not set out to become an actor, certainly not a major movie star. Once involved in the business, though, he soon discovered that filmmaking offered a way to gain a measure of control over his own life as well as provided him an outlet for his creativity. Calculating is perhaps too pejorative a term to describe his actions, but there is no doubt that Clint Eastwood thinks well beyond his next project. His artistic talent is balanced with a shrewdness and a toughness that continue to make him one of the world's most popular stars, and, in the opinion of Orson Welles, one of its most talented directors as well.

Throughout his career, Clint Eastwood has appeared in, produced, or directed some sixty films, ranging from uncredited bit parts in forgettable genre movies to Academy Award–winning films. He first achieved popularity as Rowdy Yates in the long-running television series *Rawhide* (1959–1966). His movie stardom began as The Man with No Name in the Spaghetti Westerns of Sergio Leone and was secured as Dirty Harry Callahan, the establishment-defying San Francisco detective. In addition to Westerns and detective films, Eastwood has also made action/adventure and war movies, comedies, dramas, a romance, and a musical.

Eastwood has always been popular with general audiences, appearing twenty-one times on the annual Quigley Publications poll of top box-office stars (only John Wayne has had more appearances) and topping that list four times. He was named the top box-office star of the 1970s, and a 1985 Roper Poll found him to be the person most admired by young Americans, finishing ahead of, among others, Mother Teresa.

On the other hand, critical appreciation of Clint Eastwood's abilities as an actor and as a filmmaker developed much more slowly, with critics generally dismissing his early work and greeting his later efforts much more favorably. Undoubtedly, the fact that he came out of television, combined with the perceived nihilism of the Spaghetti Westerns, colored his reception among early critics. His proclivity to underplay his roles and understate his characters led many critics to the assessment that, in Eastwood's case, less was less. Moreover, critics tended to see Dirty Harry as a reactionary conservative, with the most implacable of Eastwood's critics, Pauline Kael, famously labeling his films "fascist."

Eastwood was a dozen years into his career as a movie star before critics began to appreciate the subtlety of his characterizations. By the 1980s, critics were beginning to consider his films as a complete body of work, according him auteur status, an artist possessed of a vision, not just an actor whose most effective expression was a squint. Jack Kroll, in *Newsweek*, noted that Eastwood "gets better as he gets older . . . creating new nuances beneath his stony exterior."

In 1992, popular and critical opinion of Eastwood's work reached a high point with the reception of *Unforgiven*, a huge box-office hit and winner of four Academy Awards—for editing (Joel Cox), supporting actor (Gene Hackman), director (Eastwood), and best picture. The film also won four

Eastwood in Unforgiven *(1992). Courtesy, Diane Sponsler, Warner Brothers.*

Golden Globe Awards, three Los Angeles Film Critics Awards, and the Directors Guild of America Award for best director. Two years later Eastwood received the Irving G. Thalberg Memorial Award for lifetime achievement in film. Without question Clint Eastwood ranks among the most popular film stars of all time and one of America's most honored filmmakers.

When looking back to Eastwood's early years, however, such future success in the motion picture industry was certainly not apparent. His childhood, although apparently a happy one, was not particularly settled, with the Eastwood family moving several times to various cities up and down the West Coast during the Depression-era of the 1930s as his father, Clinton Sr., scrambled to find work. At the time the elder Eastwood married Margaret Ruth Runner in 1928, he was a bond salesman living in Oakland. Clinton, Jr., their first child of two (a daughter, Jeanne, would follow), was born on May 31, 1930. At eleven pounds, six ounces, Clinton Jr.'s entry into the world seemed to suggest a future that would in some way transcend the ordinary. Shortly after Clint's birth, the family moved to Spokane, Washington, for a year, then south to the Los Angeles area, where Clinton Sr. worked in a filling station. From there he got a job at a bank in Redding in northern California, then as a bond salesman in Sacramento. Finally, in 1940, he landed a good position with a large jewelry firm in San Francisco, settling his family in Piedmont where they would live for eight years. Shortly after moving, Eastwood got a job as a shipbuilder so that he could stay with his family during the war. One of the major influences on young Clint during these formative early years was his maternal grandmother, Virginia Runner, with whom he and Jeanne actually lived for a year during the 1930s.

As a student at Piedmont High School, young Clint was unexceptional. His size (always tall for his age) augmented his natural shyness, and, although athletic, he tended toward individual activities, not team sports. Nor was he inclined to seek entry into the socially "in" groups. Music (particularly jazz) and cars were important to him, not high school sociability. As a result, he transferred from upscale Piedmont to Oakland Technical High School where he felt more comfortable with a working-class student body.

Ultimately, school had two notable effects on Eastwood, one of which was ironic in the extreme. First, the constant moving occasioned by his father's search for jobs often put Clint, in the early grades, in the uncomfortable position of being the new face on the block, having to face a roomful of kids who had long ago formed their alliances. He was, in other words, like many of the characters he would later portray in his Westerns, a stranger in a strange town, reliant only on his own physical and mental resources for survival. Perhaps the inscrutable cool stare that preceded so many cinematic confrontations had its origin in the aloofness of a boy too big for others to pick on, but too shy himself to seek out new friends. Later, while in the middle of the eight-year stretch of job stability for his father, young Clint formed many lasting friendships, some of which eventually spilled over into his professional career.

When Clint was in the eighth grade, a second formative school event took place: he had his first introduction to acting. It was an experience he did not enjoy. His English teacher, Gertrude Falk, had decided that the shy, gangly boy in her class would be perfect to play the lead role in a one-act play to be performed at an all-school assembly, a skit about a shy, backward boy. So without tryouts, without even his assent, Eastwood found himself thrust on stage. He and a friend, who was cast as the father, considered skipping the day of the performance, but they screwed up their courage and carried through. The result, to Eastwood's surprise, was positive, with some of the high school boys even complimenting him. Although he liked the attention he received, he still found the overall situation very uncomfortable. Ironically, considering his later choice of careers, his comment summarizing the experience was "I don't ever want to do that again, ever in my life."

During and after high school, Eastwood held a number of jobs, which later allowed him to colorfully describe himself as being at one time a bum and a drifter, the latter term holding at least a modicum of truth. Before settling on a career in acting, Eastwood had earned money from a paper route, sacking groceries, caddying, baling hay, fighting fires and cutting trails for the California State Forest Department, and logging in Oregon. He also worked as a laborer in a pulp mill, in a steel mill, at Boeing, and at a sugar refinery, as well as a bartender and a bouncer. Like his father, he also pumped gas for a time, then managed some apartments. This succession of jobs, most of them held before he was twenty-one, convinced Eastwood that he did not want to spend the rest of his life doing manual labor. However, just as he determined to go to college (to study music at Seattle University), he received a draft notice and was inducted into the army in 1951, taking his basic training at Fort Ord.

As is true for many young men, Eastwood found the army a valuable formative experience, directly and indirectly. On one level, the bureaucratic tangles of military life reinforced Eastwood's proclivity toward individualism, an anti-establishment frustration that would be expressed fully later on by Harry Callahan. On another level, Eastwood met a number of young actors who also had been drafted, among them Richard Long, David Janssen, and Martin Milner. Better known at the time, although not later, was Norman Barthold, who had a role in the Virginia Mayo film *She's Working Her Way Through College* (1952). Talking with Barthold undoubtedly encouraged Eastwood's ultimate interest in acting. Part of his duties included making repeated screenings of John Huston's army training film *The Battle of San Pietro*. Later, Eastwood would make the film *White Hunter, Black Heart* (1990), which was about Huston.

Except for the boredom of routine, Eastwood's army career was generally a pleasant experience. He spent his hitch at Fort Ord, California, serving most of the time as a lifeguard and swimming instructor at the base swimming pool. It was during this time he experienced a brush with mortality that ranks as one of the key moments in his life.

Eastwood and a buddy, on weekend passes, hitched a ride on a military reconnaissance plane to Seattle, where Clint's parents were living at the time. The weekend itself was uneventful, but getting back to Fort Ord proved nearly fatal. No planes were headed to San Francisco, and the pair of young soldiers faced the prospect of being AWOL. Finally, they found two Navy torpedo bombers headed that way. These planes were small, with room for only the pilot in the cockpit, but with a small radar compartment in the rear. The compartment was not meant for a passenger, but the pilot agreed to take Eastwood if he could squeeze in.

With much effort, he did manage to squeeze in, but the door would not close and he had to fasten it with a cable. The intercom did not work, so Eastwood was not able to tell the pilot that the oxygen mask was not working, either. As the plane gained altitude, Eastwood blacked out, regaining consciousness only when the pilot flew lower because his own oxygen supply had run out. Because of a heavy fog the pilot was unable to land and was forced to ditch the plane at sea. When the plane hit the ocean, both the pilot and Eastwood jumped into the water and started swimming. Although they soon became separated in the heavy sea, both reached shore safely.

This close call had a profound effect on Eastwood's psyche and made explicit to him the relative insignificance of the individual in the overall scheme of nature and the world. Somewhat akin to the heroic ideal of classical times, the individual must survive by his wits and strength and not expect anyone else to come to his assistance. This credo of self-reliance and responsibility can be seen as pivotal to the characterizations of many of Eastwood's film personae from The Man with No Name to Dirty Harry to William Munney.

As he neared the end of his two-year stint in the army, Eastwood had a blind date with a girl named Maggie Johnson. They would marry in December 1953. At the same time he had enrolled at Los Angeles City College on the G.I. Bill. His original intention was to earn a degree in business administration, but somewhere along the way he grew more interested in acting and began taking some acting classes and frequenting the Universal–International (UI) lot. Following a screen test Eastwood signed on with Universal, becoming one of dozens of aspiring young actors and actresses drawing $75 a month and hoping for the big break that would propel them to stardom.

For most it was a vain hope. Other than providing him with some training and an inside view of the movie business, Eastwood got little from the experience other than the small stipend bit roles in some eight UI films. He was a Saxon warrior, a ranch hand, twice a lab technician, a pilot, a sailor, and once appeared with the popular talking mule in the film Francis in the Navy (1955). In September 1955, not quite a year after signing him, and despite some positive comments from its drama coaches on Eastwood's developing abilities, Universal dropped Eastwood from its payroll. Most likely he was cut because he did not fit the standard then current for bland, handsome, nonthreatening male leads (of the Rock Hudson/Tab Hunter mold). Eastwood himself realized that he probably would not have much opportunity to make a mark until he was more mature. This realization can be see as evidence of his ability to take the long view, a trait that has always marked his career.

Over the next few years Eastwood picked up a couple of other bit movie roles. He played in an RKO comedy (where was he cast as a hunk, the object of Carol Channing's ogling), a Warner Brothers war movie, and a Twentieth Century-Fox Western in which he played an embittered ex-Confederate soldier, a role Eastwood hoped would serve as a springboard into more and better work. Unfortunately, the movie was a bomb. Eastwood did pick up a few scattered jobs in television and a couple of commercials, but at one stretch he went nearly a year without an acting job. During this time he found work where he could, including digging swimming pools.

An anecdote from this period illustrates his sense of loyalty. When a fellow pool digger got fired for standing up to a foreman who was giving him a hard time, Eastwood also headed off the job, with this laconic response to the boss's question as to why he was leaving: "Well, I got to drive him home, so I guess I'll have to be fired, too."

From this low point Eastwood's professional fortunes made a permanent swing upward in the summer of 1958 when he landed the role of Rowdy Yates on the long-running CBS television series *Rawhide*. While walking down a hall at CBS Television City with a friend, Sonia Chernus (who would later become story editor at Malpaso Productions), Eastwood ran into Robert Sparks, a CBS executive, who invited the young actor to meet with him and Charles Marquis Warren. Warren, who had written and directed both feature Westerns and a number of episodes of *Gunsmoke*, was currently developing a cattle-drive Western series for CBS and was looking for someone to play the ramrod, the second-in-command to Eric Fleming's trail boss. After a less-than-auspicious screen test, in which he displayed much energy but failed to remember all the words of a lengthy speech, Eastwood found himself with a steady paycheck of $700 per episode, not to mention the huge exposure that a series on a major network gave him. The one possible negative aspect of the situation was that the series might not make it to the air. At this time nearly 25 percent of evening television was taken up by Westerns, with Matt Dillon,

Paladin, and Bart Maverick making household words of the actors who portrayed them. After having nine episodes in the can, production halted, leaving Eastwood with money in his pocket but anxiety in his mind. On January 9, 1959, however, the first of *Rawhide*'s 217 episodes was aired. Eastwood would eventually appear in all but a handful.

The premise of the show was that Gil Favor and Rowdy Yates, in charge of a trail crew and a herd of longhorn steers, were on their way from Texas to Sedalia, Missouri. Each episode was framed by regular cast members at work on the routine tasks of droving, who were invariably interrupted by some incident that involved guest stars, thus giving Eastwood the opportunity to work with many well-known actors as well as with rising newcomers. An added benefit of the show's format was that Eastwood got to experience many different directorial styles, which helped him in developing his own directorial style in later years.

Despite the professional experience he was accumulating and the relative financial security offered by a hit series, Eastwood soon tired of the routine and the limitations of his character, "Rowdy Yates, Idiot of the Plains," as he termed him. He chafed from his inability to "grow" the character, as well as from the strictures placed on his professional exposure by CBS. At first the network declined to allow him to take employment in the off-season or to guest on other programs, options he was finally granted after threatening to leave the show.

The series became one of the longest running in television history. Later, when Eric Fleming left the show, Eastwood took over as trail boss, his salary rising commensurately to around $100,000 per season. In another example of his tendency to take the long view, Eastwood wisely chose to have some of this compensation deferred, which gave him a measure of economic freedom when the show ended, thus allowing him to be selective in future roles instead of having to grab whatever work he could. *Rawhide* ended its long run in January 1966.

By that time, Eastwood had already made the most fateful decision of his life. Two years earlier, in April 1964, he traveled to Italy—in no small part, he has stated, because he had never been to Europe before—to take the lead role as Texas Joe in the low-budget Western *The Magnificent Stranger*. It was not exactly an enviable role—James Coburn, Charles Bronson, and Rory Calhoun had already turned it down—and the pay, $15,000, was not all that great, especially considering the rigors and hardships of the location shooting in Spain. Eastwood's initial reaction was also to reject the role, thinking that a

European Western must be some kind of joke (not knowing of the great popularity of the American West in Europe, as epitomized in the work of German novelist Karl May). When he read the script sent to him by his agent, he changed his mind. He immediately recognized that the Italian movie was in essence a remake of Akira Kurosawa's samurai film *Yojimbo* (1961), a film he had seen and liked. The film that emerged from this venture, the aptly renamed *A Fistful of Dollars* (1964), along with its two sequels (of sorts), *For a Few Dollars More* (1965) and *The Good, the Bad, and the Ugly* (1967), created a huge worldwide market for a new genre, the Spaghetti Western. Many other American stars, including Bronson, cashed in on this new craze, but none of the knock-offs ever matched the original trilogy in their impact.

Sergio Leone was the creative genius behind the trilogy, although Eastwood did contribute significantly, particularly by insisting that the explanatory exposition about his character be dropped. The son of an Italian director and of an actress, Leone, nine years Eastwood's senior, had grown up in and around the film industry, serving a long and varied apprenticeship before eventually getting his opportunity to direct in the early 1960s. He had viewed hundreds of films and read much, including James Fenimore Cooper (the creator of the original western hero in American popular culture), coming to believe that many American genre films had become moribund.

The Spaghetti Westerns have been called postmodern and nihilistic, largely because they seem to lack any message and seem to be amoral. The hero is defined more by style than by a sense of right. At the beginning of *A Fistful of Dollars,* for instance, The Stranger rides into San Miguel, ignoring the obvious plight of a small boy being abused by ruffians as he is trying to reach his mother, who is a prisoner behind a barred window. Moreover, The Stranger is riding a mule, hardly the mount of a typical western hero. His first action is to order three coffins from the only business that seems to be thriving in this desolate town. Then, in comic book superhero fashion, he kills four members of the Baxter Gang, led by a matriarch dressed in black. As he walks back past the coffin maker, he offers a humorous apology: "My mistake, four."

The motivation of The Stranger is financial: "There's money to be made in this town," he tells the saloon keeper who befriends him. He gets his money by selling his services, first to one of the two warring factions, the Rojos, and then to their enemies, the Baxters. At only one point, when he helps the imprisoned woman, Marisol, escape to her husband and son, does The Stranger seem to be doing a chivalrous deed but only after he first accidently knocks her out. The film is filled with violence—gunfire, beatings, drunkenness, and improbabilities such as two dead soldiers propped up by The Stranger in a moonlit cemetery in order to precipitate a gun battle between the Rojos and the Baxters. The film is also replete with religious imagery, as are all three films in the trilogy. Churches, crosses, priests, churchyards pervade. Critics have noted that the films have a ritualistic quality reminiscent of passion plays, and in fact, although they lack the obvious moral preaching of a standard Western, the Leone films do reflect the religious rituals of his southern Italian upbringing. They also reflect the comic violence of Italian puppet shows, as well as a belief that survival, in this world, is more important than mere honor. As critic Pauline Kael has noted, no one in *A Fistful of Dollars* operates out of principle. The weak are weak and the strong oppress them. The hero is left with the option of style, not of honor.

In truth, the hero also has the option of guile. The Stranger, after being savagely beaten and left for dead by the Rojos, escapes by hiding in a coffin while the Baxters are being wiped out by bullets and fire. In a scene obviously meant to parallel resurrection and transcendence, The Stranger is hidden in a cave and nursed back to health by his bartender friend. While there, recalling the boast of Ramon Rojo (played by Gian Maria Volonte) that a rifle is superior to a pistol and that one must always shoot the heart, he fashions himself a breastplate of steel. When he comes back into San Miguel for his final confrontation with the Rojos, they believe, with reason, that they are seeing a ghost. Well-placed bullets from Ramon's rifle might knock him down, but they fail to stop his implacable progress. After this final dispatching of his enemies, The Stranger once more mounts his mule and rides out of the still desolate town. Any promise of a brighter future for San Miguel is dim at best.

A Fistful of Dollars was a surprise hit. Yet Eastwood, in the midst of another season of *Rawhide* and unaware that the film's original title had been changed, didn't know of that success for some time. Leone himself came to California to enlist Eastwood to play another serape-wearing, cheroot-chewing stranger, this time called Monco, in a sequel entitled *For a Few Dollars More*. The budget had more than doubled to $750,000, while Eastwood's salary more than tripled to $50,000. The second film in the trilogy, considered by some critics to be the best of the lot, is about two competing bounty hunters, Monco and Mortimer, played by Lee Van Cleef.

The film opens with set pieces displaying the lethal abilities of each character before settling into the main plot, the pursuit of master bandit El Indio (again played by Volonte) and his gang. At first rivals who each attempt, in a masterful comic scene, to drive the other out of town, they eventually join in an uneasy alliance to collect the bounty on El Indio. The outlaw has determined, as evidence of his invincibility, to rob a supposedly impregnable bank. Again, amid much mayhem the two bounty hunters eventually dispatch the entire gang, at which point we learn that although Monco's motive has been entirely monetary, Mortimer's is more profound. El Indio, we learn, has raped Mortimer's sister on her wedding night, a powerful scene made even more shocking by her suicide with Indio's gun during the very act of violation.

With the greater financial success of the sequel, Leone commanded an imposing budget of $1.5 million for the third in the series, with Eastwood's salary rising to more than $250,000. Unfortunately, as the budget increased, so did Leone's aspirations in terms of length of film and elaborateness of sets. No longer did he work in the quick, efficient fashion that Eastwood preferred. Also, with the addition of a third major role (Eli Wallach joined Eastwood and Van Cleef in the cast), Eastwood found his own role less important than in the previous films.

Set in Texas during the Civil War, *The Good, the Bad, and the Ugly* is epic in length and episodic in structure. Eastwood's character Blondie (the Good) and Wallach's outlaw Tuco (the Ugly) make a living through a precarious partnership, Blondie turning Tuco in for the reward, then shooting the hangman's rope and rescuing him before he is executed. Each double-crosses the other, however, and Blondie undoubtedly would have died in the desert if he had not managed to learn the site of buried Confederate gold, a grave in a military cemetery. Reconciled in an uneasy truce, the two find themselves on the wrong side of the war, having mistaken dust-covered Union uniforms for the gray of the Confederacy. Angel Eyes (Van Cleef's character, the Bad), a sadistic warden at the prison, is also after the gold.

After a lengthy Sisyphean scene in which Union and Confederate forces pointlessly take and retake a bridge, at great expense of life and limb on both sides, Blondie and Tuco blow up the bridge, to the great satisfaction of the dying Union commander. "I've never seen so many men wasted so badly," the Captain says, in an obvious topical reference to the slaughter in Vietnam. Critics have pointed out that the relatively few bodies left in the wake of the three main characters' quest for the buried gold pale in comparison to the hundreds of thousands lost as nations pursue goals no less mercenary, though more thickly cloaked in pieties and patriotism.

At the film's climax the three opponents meet in an arena-like circle in the midst of the graveyard where the gold is hidden in one of the thousands of graves. In the ensuing shootout, Blondie, who alone knows the location of the gold, kills Angel Eyes, Tuco having been armed with an unloaded gun (thanks to an earlier ploy by Blondie). Blondie makes Tuco dig up the treasure, then leaves him there with half the gold, hands tied behind his back, a noose around his neck, and precariously perched on a wooden cross grave marker. Just before he rides out of sight, Blondie once more shoots the rope, freeing Tuco.

The three Sergio Leone films were released to great commercial success in Europe in 1964, 1965, and 1966, respectively; they were all released within eleven months of one another in the United States, from February 1967 to January 1968. Fans and reviewers both raved, but in opposite directions. Ignoring the complaints of critics, who deplored the violence and nihilism while bemoaning the betrayal of the Western form, moviegoers turned out by the millions, giving Clint Eastwood, already topping the box offices in Europe, a major boost toward stardom in America. More important, the success of these films gave Eastwood status as an innovator, one who had given a new direction to, and thus helped to rejuvenate, a genre grown moribund and stale. During the 1960s and 1970s, as Western film stars (Wayne, Stewart, Scott, McCrea) had grown older, so too had the film scripts moved in time from the post–Civil War frontier era to the early twentieth century. At the same time, social unrest and dissatisfaction with government—the civil rights movement, contemporary feminism, Native American protests, the Vietnam conflict—had pierced forever the bubble of naive optimism and invincibility that had previously characterized our culture. The Spaghetti Westerns captured the Zeitgeist, and Eastwood epitomized the new cultural hero, one marked by style and cool, unburdened by either the moral ambiguity of a Gary Cooper film or the moral certitude of John Wayne.

Eastwood's first two American films, released in 1968, were both Westerns—one set in the nineteenth century, the other set in contemporary times. *Hang 'em High* (1968) is the story of Jed Cooper, a young rancher in Oklahoma Territory falsely accused of stealing cattle, then lynched and left for dead by a powerful rancher and his crew. Rescued by a marshal bringing in a wagon load of accused criminals to be tried at the court of a hanging judge, Cooper is sworn in as another of the judge's marshals, on the condition that he brings in his would-be lynchers for trial rather than executing on them the summary judgment they had attempted to accord him. The film is notable for several reasons, not least among them that it is essentially a Western in the classic, not the Spaghetti, mode. Rather than an invincible hero characterized by his ability to mete out stylish deaths by the score, Jed

Cooper is instead a vulnerable man, torn by ambiguity and by his inability to make the world correspond with his sense of what is right. A telling moment in the film, which occurs just before he is ambushed and nearly killed by some of his previous attackers, concerns the impotence he experiences with a prostitute, mirroring the failure of his plea for mercy for two youths who had risked their own lives to help him bring in a murderer. Shot at almost exactly the same time that the boys are hanged, he is nursed back to health by a young woman, Rachel, who has been raped and her husband killed. She too is seeking retribution, carefully looking over each tumbleweed wagon of fugitives as it is brought into town, hoping to find her tormentors. Played by Inger Stevens, Rachel provides an Eastwood character his first cinematic love scene.

The film ends with Cooper riding out to search for the two remaining men who had lynched him, having successfully, for the first time, pleaded for Judge Fenton (played by Pat Hingle) to spare the life of one of the lynch mob, an old man who had spoken out for Cooper at the time of the hanging. His successful plea, however, is accomplished only by threatening to quit, by throwing down his badge and accusing the judge of conducting legalized lynchings. *Hang 'em High* presents a serious message, a consideration of the ambiguous line between law and criminality, of police power unchecked in a society that could easily descend into anarchy without that power. Which is worse? How does a territory, far removed from the checks and balances that control our nation's system of government, protect itself? Eastwood's early exploration of this theme suggests that the answer must be found within individuals, who must control their desires for revenge and seek instead to temper justice with mercy. *Hang 'em High* is the first (of more than three dozen) films to be coproduced by Malpaso, the production company Eastwood founded to help him gain better artistic and financial control of his own career.

Coogan's Bluff (1968), a contemporary Western/detective story, was a less successful, although still popular, film, and became the progenitor of Dennis Weaver's long-running television series *McCloud*. It also foreshadows Dirty Harry in the character of Coogan, an Arizona marshal long on violence and sex drive but short on concern for the niceties of the legal system. Sent to New York City to retrieve a man wanted in Arizona, Coogan's story is primarily a sixties vehicle of drugs, dance clubs, and darkness. By showing Eastwood in a modern setting dealing with contemporary issues, the film suggested to critics that he could play something other than a western hero.

Eastwood's next two films were action/adventure war movies — *Where Eagles Dare* (1968) and *Kelly's Heroes* (1970). In 1969, he costarred in *Paint*

Your Wagon, with Lee Marvin and Jean Seberg, in the most unlikely film of his career, a Lerner and Loewe musical set in a western gold rush town and featuring a woman married simultaneously to two men. Suffice it to say that one of the best things about the film is Eastwood's singing.

Two Mules for Sister Sara (1970) was probably the least successful of Eastwood's Westerns. Set in Mexico during a time of revolution, with Eastwood's character Hogan dressed in a poncho and chewing a cheroot, the film has the appearance of a Spaghetti Western, but without the saving grace of Leone's nihilism. It also lacks realism, with Hogan being cool beyond rationality, particularly in defusing a stick of dynamite he has tossed at a villain just before shooting him. A large part, although not all, of the film's shortcomings can be attributed to Shirley MacLaine playing a prostitute who pretends, quite unconvincingly, to be a nun. Although succeeding in its obvious intent as a crowd-pleasing comedy with plenty of gratuitous violence and an incredible plot, this film has none of the freshness and elan of the Italian trilogy, nor any of the serious underpinnings of his mythic Westerns.

Following the psychological thrillers *The Beguiled* (1971) and *Play Misty for Me* (1971), along with *Dirty Harry* (1971), Eastwood starred in his most mundane Western yet, *Joe Kidd* (1972). As usual, the Eastwood hero is unbeatable. Set in high country where the original Spanish settlers are being deprived of their land by legalities and hired killers, Joe Kidd, like the Man with No Name, appears to care for nothing but money, which he takes to lead Robert Duvall as the land baron Frank Harlan on a supposed hunting trip for big game. (As the film opens, Kidd is in jail for having poached deer out of season.) When the game turns out to be John Saxon, playing Luis Chama, the leader of the Hispanic resistance to Duvall's land grab, and when Kidd himself is imprisoned in a church with the townspeople, his sympathies merge with those of the oppressed. Literally sitting in the seat of judgment in a corrupt judge's courtroom, Kidd, as have so many other Western heros, dispenses his own form of violent justice.

So, too, does the lead character in *High Plains Drifter* (1973), literally a man with no name, dispense his own justice. He does, however, have a cause—to wreak revenge on the citizens of Lago, who killed their sheriff in order to protect the secret that the mine that provides the town's prosperity actually lies on government   land. This dark, compelling film's hero, known only as the Stranger, rapes prostitutes, seduces wives, terrorizes, and browbeats the citizens, forcing them to paint all the buildings in the town red and rename it Hell, then abandoning them to the ex-convicts who are returning to wreak vengeance on Lago. Unlike the towns in classic Westerns, where civilization is equated with progress, Lago is ramshackle, even before the arrival of the Stranger, a symbol of impermanence and exploitation. Who is this mysterious stranger who brings pain and destruction, not comfort and salvation, whose very identity is ambiguous? Is he the revengeful brother of the slain sheriff? Or is he an agent of the supernatural, the ghost of the dead sheriff, an avenging angel? This ambiguity surrounding the nature—material or ethereal— of the agent of vengeance in Eastwood's films, first encountered in *A Fistful of Dollars* and explored further in *Hang 'em High*, reappears full blown in *Pale Rider* (1985).

Of the sixteen films Eastwood made in the intervening years, only two were Westerns, one classic and one modern, both excellent in their own ways. *The Outlaw Josey Wales* (1976), considered by many to be one of Eastwood's best films, is the story of a Missouri farmer, whose family is murdered by Kansas irregulars during the Civil War, and who joins the fight against them. When the war ends, he heads to Texas rather than surrender. There, pursued by Terrill, leader of the Kansas Redlegs, he is joined by a motley group of hangers-on: an old Cherokee who has also fought for the Confederacy, an Indian woman he rescues from unwilling prostitution, an old lady from Kansas who is seeking the asylum of her son's ranch in Texas, and the old lady's somewhat simple daughter, both of whom Wales rescues from a band of Comancheros intent on robbery and rapine.

Although Wales is essentially a loner, he finds himself the de facto head of this community of multicultural misfits. At the ranch they prepare to fight off Chief Ten Bears and his Comanche warriors, but Wales, in what is perhaps the most prolix speech to come from an Eastwood character, forges a peace with the Indians. Their preparations for defense prove useful, however, when Terrill attacks the ranch. He is beaten off, and Wales pursues him into the nearby town, where the Redleg is impaled on his own sword in the climactic fight.

Although the film is epic in length, action, geographic scope, and concept, there is an intense bitterness displayed by Wales and the other characters that is tempered through the need for community. Even the old woman, whose son has been killed by Confederates, comes to Wales's aid, thus showing that friendship triumphs over politics. Unlike other Eastwood Westerns, this film provides the main character with plausible and sympathetic motivation for his killing. It also provides healing and redemption, expressed in human terms. Reconciliation, in fact, seems a major theme in the film, appropriate for the aftermath of the Vietnam War. In critic Richard Schickel's view, the film forges a new myth for the Western, one that offers a "middle ground between western revisionism and western traditionalism," between the sentimental conservatism of the John Ford/John Wayne Westerns and the nihilistic brutality of the Leone films. There is an underlying tenderness in this tough film.

Eastwood's next Western, *Bronco Billy* (1980), is the story of a modern-day shoe salesman from New Jersey whose longing for the moral certitudes of a bygone era finds expression in such strange ways as an attempted robbery, from horseback, of a diesel streamliner. *Bronco Billy* concerns an endearing but inept Wild West show barnstorming in Idaho. Led by Eastwood's Billy, the troupe includes an Indian snake dancer (always being bitten by his rattlesnakes) and his pregnant wife, a young rope-trick artist who (unknown to Billy) has deserted from the army, a longtime friend who has lost his hand in a gun trick, a black ringmaster, and a spoiled rich girl who is taken into the group, at first against her wishes and later willingly. The little world of the Bronco Billy show is as diverse as that which assembles itself around Josey Wales, both groups seeking a figure of strength to offer them refuge from the dangers of the larger worlds that surround them.

Billy has an abiding faith in human goodness and truly believes the precepts he ladles out to the "little cowboys and cowgirls" in his audience. His naivete, however, becomes evident when, while chastising these children for not being in school, they inform him that it is a Saturday. Billy is about as far from the Man with No Name or Dirty Harry as he could possibly be. When the smarmy, sadistic sheriff forces Billy to grovel in order to keep Lasso Leonard (Sam Bottoms) out of jail, despite Billy's disapproval of his desertion, there is the expectation that the sheriff will somehow pay before the movie is over. But he does not. In this world, the good do not always win, and the powerful often exercise their power capriciously. At the end, however, having survived a fire that has destroyed their old tent, the troupe carries on under their new big top, which has been stitched together from thousands of American flags by the patients of a mental hospital where Billy plays every year as a benefit. The values and precepts of the old Westerns might seem corny in this contemporary world, but to Billy and his followers they are still valid, as essential to our national character as the symbolic star-spangled "big tent" in which they perform.

Released the same year as *Bronco Billy* was a film that at the time was thought to have driven the ultimate stake through the heart of the Western—*Heaven's Gate* (1980). The genre, however, has gone through as many lives and manifestations as Count Dracula himself, and five years later Clint Eastwood helped to rejuvenate the Western with the tale of a resurrected hero in *Pale Rider* (1985). In a story owing an obvious debt to what many consider the classic telling of the cowboy-hero story, *Shane*, Eastwood's character Preacher rides into a community of gold-panners, struggling to collect enough dust to keep food on the table and to protect their claims from the clutches of a corporate mining venture that literally destroys the earth in its quest for gold. Scenes paralleling those of *Shane* include Preacher and Hull Barrett (leader of the miners, played by Michael Moriarity) together sledge-hammering a boulder (as Shane and Joe had attacked a tree stump), and trips into town by various miners in which they are bullied by the hired thugs of the evil mining mogul, Coy LaHood (Richard Dysart). The violence in *Pale Rider* is more pervasive and more brutal than in *Shane*, undoubtedly reflecting a cultural change in the taste of moviegoers that Eastwood himself had helped to instill.

One difference between the two films is that the implied love triangle in *Shane* is made explicit in *Pale Rider* when Preacher spends the night with Hull's intended wife, Sarah (Carrie Snodgrass). Also, the hero worship of Joey for Shane is given an added uncomfortable twist in Eastwood's film when Sarah's teenage daughter, Megan (Sydney Penny), feeling her first stirrings of womanhood, also vies for the physical affections of the Preacher.

In *Shane* the landscape is pristine, reflecting a nearly Edenic world that Joe and his fellow farmers are attempting to turn into farms for their families. Their struggle is symbolized by the scene in which Joe and Shane take axes to the tree stump, the removal of which opens up a field for planting. In *Pale Rider* that scene is replicated by Preacher and Hull wielding sledge hammers against a huge boulder in a stream, which just happens to be covering a vein of ore. But the pristine environment in this film is being threatened not by the panners, but by the dynamite and huge hydraulic machinery of LaHood's mining syndicate. The explosives and machines are literally blasting and washing mountains away. Thus Preacher could be interpreted as an ecological hero who uses the tools of the bad guys (dynamite and bullets) to protect underdogs, both human and natural.

Perhaps the major difference between the two films, however, is in the essential nature of their respective heroes: Shane is mortal; Preacher is ethereal. Shane's savior figure comes into the valley seeking escape from his past; he leaves redeemed by sacrifice, but wounded. Preacher, on the other hand, comes into the valley seeking retribution for past wrongs done to himself, with deep scars of old bullet wounds marking his back. He is, in the sense of a Christ-figure, the returned Christ, while Shane's Christ makes his (symbolic) mortal sacrifice during the course of the film. In this respect, *Pale Rider* carries on a theme suggested in *For a Fistful of Dollars* and manifested in *Hang 'em High* —a hero who is not of the ordinary world. Although satisfying on a mythic level, such a mystic hero cannot be identified with on a realistic level, nor can he serve as a reflection of vulnerability in the rest of us. Thus he lacks an essential facet of humanity. It is the mortal heros of *The Iliad,* no matter how superior their skills to ours, that we find most interesting, not the immortal gods and goddesses who insert themselves into that conflict. We can aspire to match the deeds of a Hector or an Achilles, but we can never become immortal in this world.

Eastwood finally confronts mortality in his best and most mature film, and what may well be his final Western, *Unforgiven* (1992), which he starred in and directed. Briefly, the plot is of a widowed former killer (William Munny), at least partially redeemed by love, who, in 1880, is struggling to raise his two children on a small Kansas hog farm. Partly motivated by a sense of injustice, partly by the reward money, he joins with a young would-be gunfighter (Jaimz Woolvett as the Schofield Kid) and an old companion (Morgan Freeman as Ned Logan) to avenge the mutilation of a prostitute in the town of Big Whiskey, Wyoming. There is no comic-book violence in this film; the two cowboys responsible for cutting the prostitute are killed by Munny and his companions in realistically gruesome fashion. The sadistic sheriff (Gene Hackman, in an Oscar-winning role as Little Bill Daggett) savagely beats three men: Munny, English Bob (Richard Harris as a pretentious but cowardly British gunfighter), and Ned Logan (who dies as a result).

In the climactic scene, Munny comes into the saloon where the original violence against the prostitute occurred and where Little Bill is organizing a posse to search for Munny and the Schofield Kid. Armed with a shotgun and two pistols, Munny first kills the saloon keeper who has displayed (at the behest of the sheriff) Logan's body, then shoots at Little Bill, the second barrel of the shotgun misfiring. The resultant battle, in which Munny kills three or four deputies as well as Little Bill, has been denigrated by critics for seeming to fall back on the typical Eastwoodian invincible hero, but Munny's success has been realistically foreshadowed. Not only are the deputies shown to be fearful of facing an armed and dangerous foe, but Munny also tells the inquiring journalist, who marvels at his feat and asks Munny how he knew which deputy to shoot first, that he "was lucky in the order."

This dark, moving film is fraught with the ambiguity, indecision, and insecurities of real people confronting real life scenarios. It also confronts one of the key contradictions of the American experience. As Americans we hold to a strong belief in the rule of law, yet at the same time we hold an equally strong belief in the rightness of individuals to take action outside the law if in the cause of justice. In his previous Western roles, Eastwood had, to one extent or another, portrayed a manifestation of James Fenimore Cooper's *Leatherstocking* hero: the man who stands outside civilization and fights the agents of savagery with a force akin to, but, because of his innate morality, superior to those very forces employed by the savages.

In almost all cases (Jed Cooper is an exception), Eastwood's hero has shown little, if any, compunction about the morality of his actions or about taking responsibility for them. Thus Eastwood's cowboy hero, from The Stranger to the Preacher, has used violence to end violence, has broken the law to enforce the law, has used might to make right. The Spaghetti Westerns are, indeed, nihilistic, presenting an essentially immature view of human nature where style and might are all that matter. Films, such as *High Plains Drifter* and *Pale Rider*, attempt to resolve the dilemma by suggesting that the agent of vengeance is otherworldly, an entity impervious to death himself but who brings justice in the form of death to the wicked. Only in *Hang 'em High* is the hero caught between the desire for revenge and the need for the objectivity of law, a moral ambiguity that Eastwood fully explores in *Unforgiven*.

In *Unforgiven* Eastwood confronts this basic contradiction in his most mature and realistic mode. Both the characters of Little Bill, the serenity-loving sheriff whose violent outbursts make explicit the dangers of unchecked authority, and of William Munny, whose lawless past haunts his troubled conscience, show the need for a humane reconciliation between the strict rule of law and the moral rights and responsibilities of the individual.

In summary, Clint Eastwood occupies an important position in the history of the Hollywood West. Audiences, both European and American, responded enthusiastically to the Man with No Name, a new type of hero whose skills in administering death and violence answered to no authority higher than himself. Moreover, this hero was young, his freshness a bright contrast to the aging generation of Western stars — Wayne, Cooper, Scott, Fonda, Stewart, McCrea — whose movies in the 1960s and 1970s tended to depict an aging West running headfirst into a mechanistic and uncaring twentieth century. Whether nostalgic or elegiac, these films suggested a culture that had taken a wrong turn, whose technical advances had come at too real a price. Eastwood's hero showed none of the angst, none of the despair of the earlier generation. His anger was directed at a tangible foe, not at a changing world.

Certainly one of Eastwood's greatest contributions to the Western was keeping it alive and re-establishing its viability as an artistic genre. *Pale Rider* was the most important and, along with *Silverado*, the first successful Western to be made after *Heaven's Gate*. *Unforgiven*, with eight Academy Award nominations and four Oscars, is one of the most aesthetically and intellectually successful Westerns ever made.

One hopes that *Unforgiven* will be Eastwood's last Western. It is difficult to imagine a film that more perfectly epitomizes his own Western screen career. His transformation over the years from a cynical youthful killer with indomitable skills, to an ethereal agent of justice with powers that transcend the mortal, to a doubting, rueful, erring, aging human has shown that Eastwood's western hero is, finally, just a man.

Contributors

GRETCHEN M. BATAILLE is the senior vice president and vice president for academic affairs for the University of North Carolina system in Chapel Hill, North Carolina. She is known for her work on media images, including *The Pretend Indians: Images of Native Americans in the Movies*, with Charles L.P. Silet (1980). She is the author or editor of several books on Native Americans in film and on Native American women, including *Images of American Indians on Film: An Annotated Bibliography*, with Charles L.P. Silet (1985); *American Indian Women Telling Their Lives*, with Kathleen M. Sands (1984); *American Indian Women: A Guide to Research*, with Kathleen M. Sands (1991); and *Native American Women: A Biographical Dictionary* (1993).

RONALD L. DAVIS is professor of history at Southern Methodist University in Dallas, where he teaches courses in American cultural history, the American West, and American society through film. He is the author of *The Glamour Factory: Inside Hollywood's Big Studio System* (1993); *Celluloid Mirrors: Hollywood and American Society Since 1945* (1998); *Hollywood Beauty: Linda Darnell and the American Dream* (1991); and *Duke: The Life and Image of John Wayne* (1998). He is currently working on a biography of silent movie star William S. Hart and is the editor of a series of film biographies for the University Press of Mississippi.

RICHARD W. ETULAIN is professor of history and director of the Center for the American West at the University of New Mexico in Albuquerque. Among his recent books are *Re-imagining the Modern American West: A Century of Fiction, History, and Art* (1996); *By Grit & Grace: Eleven Women Who Shaped the American West* (1997, coedited with Glenda Riley); *With Badges & Bullets: Lawmen &*

Outlaws in the Old West (1999, coedited with Glenda Riley); and *Telling Western Stories: From Buffalo Bill to Larry McMurtry* (1999). Past president of the Western Literature Association and the Western History Association, he is also the editor or coeditor of eight book series.

CHERYL J. FOOTE received her Ph.D. in history from the University of New Mexico and teaches history at Albuquerque Technical Vocational Institute. She is the author of *Women of the New Mexico Frontier, 1846–1912* (1990), which the Historical Society of New Mexico voted outstanding publication on New Mexico history in 1991.

JIM HOY, a professor of English at Emporia State University, studies and writes about the folklife of ranching. He is the author of *Cowboys and Kansas: Stories from the Tallgrass Prairie* (1995) and coauthor of *Herders of North America: Vaqueros, Cowboys, and Buckaroos* (forthcoming from the University of Texas Press).

JOHN H. LENIHAN is associate professor of history at Texas A&M University. A specialist in U.S. cultural history and film, he is the author of *Showdown: Confronting Modern America in the Western Film* (1985) as well as various articles and essays on film genres, including Westerns, comedies, and period costumers.

RAY MERLOCK is professor of communications–journalism at the University of South Carolina–Spartanburg, where he teaches courses in mass media, video production, and film studies. He has been a radio, television, and film critic in Oklahoma and South Carolina and has written a number of articles on B Westerns. He regularly attends Western film festivals and is an enthusiastic collector of Western memorabilia.

JACK NACHBAR is professor emeritus of popular culture at Bowling Green State University in Ohio. For twenty-five years he coedited the *Journal of Popular Film and Television*. He has written or edited three books and more than a dozen articles on Westerns.

GLENDA RILEY is Alexander M. Bracken Professor of History at Ball State University and past president of the Western History Association. She has received numerous awards for her books and articles on women in the

196

American West. In addition she has held two Fulbright awards, one to Dublin, Ireland, in 1986–1987 and the other to Nairobi, Kenya, in 1998. Her most recent book is *Women and Nature: Saving the "Wild" West* (1999).

LOUIS TANNER is an independent historian who specializes in intellectual and literary history. He has written extensively about the political opinions of novelists and journalists with special attention to the western writer Owen Wister. Currently he is examining Cold War imagery in children's books of the 1950s and 1960s.

RAYMOND E. WHITE is professor emeritus of history at Ball State University in Muncie, Indiana. He has authored a number of articles and papers dealing with the American West and Western movies. White's most recent work is *Roy Rogers and Dale Evans: King and Queen of the West*, forthcoming from Popular Press.

Sources and Further Reading

CHAPTER 1: BRONCHO BILLY, WILLIAM S. HART, AND TOM MIX
Scholars, general readers, and film viewers lack a recent, full history of the
Hollywood West. There are, however, several reference volumes and partial
overviews that, if used together, provide the necessary information for an
understanding of the historical development of the Western film during the
twentieth century. More than a quarter century ago, George N. Fenin and
William K. Everson produced the only full-scale history in English, *The
Western: From Silents to the Seventies* (New York: Penguin, 1973), with particular
emphasis on silent and B Westerns. Jon Tuska also produced an early
overview, which contains much useful information, often in the form of chatty
interviews and memories, in his *The Filming of the West* (Garden City, N.Y.:
Doubleday, 1976). Two other volumes that offer alphabetically or chronologically
organized summaries of the Western are Brian Garfield's *Western Films* (New
York: Rawson Associates, 1982) and Phil Hardy's *The Western* (New York:
William Morrow, 1983).

The best reference guide to the Hollywood Western is Edward
Buscombe's, ed., indispensable *The BFI Guide to the Western* (New York:
Atheneum, 1988). It contains a short history of the Western, discussions of
western cultural history, and wonderfully useful guides to major stars and
films. Meanwhile, Jack Nachbar furnished helpful annotated guides to schol-
arship on the Western in his two books: *Western Films: An Annotated Critical
Bibliography* (New York: Garland, 1975), and with Jackie R. Donath and
Chris Foran, *Western Films 2: An Annotated Critical Bibliography from 1974 to 1987*
(New York: Garland, 1988). Briefer bibliographical listings of the Hollywood
Western are available in Richard W. Etulain's, ed., *Western Films: A Brief
History* (Manhattan, KS: Sunflower University Press, 1983), and Etulain's

"Recent Interpretations of Western Films: A Bibliographical Essay," *Journal of the West* 22 (October 1983): 72–81.

For those wishing to learn more about the Western in the larger context of Hollywood and the American film industry, several important volumes are available. The best one-volume survey of American movies is Robert Sklar's *Movie-Made America: A Cultural History of American Movies*, rev. and updated (New York: Vintage Books, 1994). Also useful, especially for the silent era, are William K. Everson's *American Silent Film* (New York: Oxford University Press, 1978) and three thorough volumes in the *History of American Cinema* series: Charles Musser's *The Emergence of Cinema: The American Screen to 1907* (1990; Berkeley: University of California Press, 1994), Eileen Bowser's *The Transformation of Cinema, 1907–1915* (New York: Charles Scribner's Sons, 1990), and Richard Koszarski's *An Evening's Entertainment: The Age of the Silent Feature Picture, 1915–1928* (1990; Berkeley: University of California Press, 1994). For superb photographs of the early silents, one must also consult two marvelous books by Englishman Kevin Brownlow: *Hollywood: The Pioneers* (New York: Knopf, 1979), and his even more impressive *The War, The West, and The Wilderness* (New York: Knopf, 1979).

Several historians, literary critics, and film specialists have also produced interpretive/analytical studies of the Hollywood Western. One might begin with the brief critical overview in Philip French's *Westerns*, rev. ed. (London: Secker and Warburg, 1977), or the provocative comments about the Western and American popular culture in John Carwelti's *Six-Gun Mystique*, 2d ed. (Bowling Green, OH: Bowling Green University Popular Press, 1984), and *Adventure, Mystery, and Romance* (Chicago: University of Chicago Press, 1976). Sociologist Will Wright rides his interpretive horse hard—but provocatively—in his *Six Guns and Society: A Structural Study of the Western* (Berkeley: University of California Press, 1975). Cultural historian John H. Lenihan deals with post–World War II Westerns as cultural artifacts in his model study *Showdown: Confronting Modern America in the Western Film* (Urbana: University of Illinois Press, 1980). Meanwhile, Jane Tompkins's *West of Everything: The Inner Life of Westerns* (New York: Oxford University Press, 1992) and Lee Clark Mitchell's *Westerns: Making the Man in Fiction and Film* (Chicago: University of Chicago Press, 1996) deal with matters of gender in literature and films about the West.

Unfortunately, we lack book-length, well-researched, interpretive studies of the three Western stars discussed here. On Broncho Billy Anderson, there are a handful of useful book sections and essays. In addition to the brief comments in Fenin and Everson's *The Western*, Brownlow's *The War*, and Everson's *American Silent Film*, one should consult several essays. Donald Parkhurst deals with

Broncho Billy's years in the Bay area in "Broncho Billy and Niles, California: A Romance of Early Movies," *Pacific Historian* 26 (Winter 1982): 1–22, whereas Glenn Shirley, a historian of the outlaw West, essays a brief summary in "Broncho Billy," *True West* 32 (No. 8, 1985): 10–15. The most recent summary, with references to several older magazine essays, is Lane Roth and Tom W. Hoffer's "G. M. 'Broncho Billy' Anderson: The First Movie Cowboy Hero," in Gary A. Yoggy, ed., *Back in the Saddle: Essays on Western Film and Television Actors* (Jefferson, NC: McFarland, 1998), 11–24. An interview with Gilbert M. ("Broncho Billy") Anderson is on file in the Oral History Collection at Columbia University. A few of Broncho Billy's short films are available from Blackhawk Films, Davenport, Iowa, and in *Films of G. M. Anderson*, Vol. 1 (Phoenix, AZ: Grapevine Video, 1970, 1995).

There is much more research on William S. Hart, but we still lack a full-length study of this important figure in the development of the Western. Anyone interested in Hart should begin with his autobiography *My Life East and West* (Boston: Houghton Mifflin Co., 1929). The 350-page volume must be used with caution, however, since Hart reveals so little about himself and is much more willing to see others, rather than himself, as the cause of his problems. For a brief biographical essay on Hart and a thorough summary of all of Hart's films, one should consult Diane Kaiser Koszarski's *The Complete Films of William S. Hart* (New York: Dover Publications, 1980).

Nearly every study of the Western includes at least an abbreviated section on Hart, but only a few of these deserve special mention. Fenin and Everson give Hart perhaps too much credit in their salute to his "realism" in *The Western*, but their discussion is a helpful introduction to Hart's Westerns. Also of note is Michael K. Schoenecke's "William S. Hart: Authenticity and the West," in Archie P. McDonald, ed., *Shooting Stars: Heroes and Heroines of Western Film* (Bloomington: Indiana University Press, 1987), 1–19.

For those wishing to view Hart's Westerns, *Hell's Hinges* (1916), *The Toll Gate* (1920), and *Tumbleweeds* (1925) are widely available. For scenes from several of Hart's films, plus additional comments on his career, see *The Saga of William S. Hart* (Davenport, Iowa: Blackhawk Films, 1979).

More has been published on Tom Mix than on Broncho Billy Anderson and William S. Hart. Unfortunately, much of the material is uncritical. The most useful studies are Paul E. Mix's *The Life and Legend of Tom Mix* (South Brunswick and New York: A. S. Barnes and Co., 1972), as well as his later *Tom Mix: A Heavily Illustrated Biography of the Western Star . . .* (Jefferson, NC: McFarland, 1995). For a brief, helpful summary, see William E. Tydeman

III's "Tom Mix: King of the Hollywood Cowboys," in Gary A. Yoggy's *Back in the Saddle*, 25–42. The volumes by Fenin and Everson, Brownlow, and Everson also contain useful comments on Mix.

Several other books, of varying merits, have been published on Mix. They include Robert S. Birchard's *King Cowboy: Tom Mix and the Movies* (Burbank, CA: Riverwood Press, 1993); Richard Seiverling's *Tom Mix: Portrait of a Superstar . . .* (Hershey, PA: Keystone Enterprises, 1991); M. G. Norris's *The Tom Mix Book* (Waynesville, NC: World of Yesterday, 1989); John H. Nicholas's *Tom Mix, Riding Up to Glory* (Oklahoma City, OK: National Cowboy Hall of Fame, 1980). One should also consult a brief work by Mix's third wife, Olive Stokes Mix, *The Fabulous Tom Mix* (Englewood Cliffs, NJ: Prentice-Hall, 1957).

This essay on Broncho Billy Anderson, William S. Hart, and Tom Mix draws upon, without merely repeating, earlier information published in Richard W. Etulain's "Changing Images: The Cowboy in Western Films," *Colorado Heritage* 1 (1981): 37–55, and Etulain's *Telling Western Stories: From Buffalo Bill to Larry McMurtry* (Albuquerque: University of New Mexico Press, 1999).

CHAPTER 2: ROY ROGERS AND DALE EVANS

This essay draws largely from two of my previous research efforts on Roy Rogers and Dale Evans: a biographical reference work, *Roy Rogers and Dale Evans: King and Queen of the West* (Bowling Green, OH: The Popular Press, forthcoming), and the chapter "Roy Rogers: An American Icon," in Gary Yoggy, ed., *Back in the Saddle: Essays on Western Film and Television Actors* (Jefferson, NC: McFarland, 1998), 77–95. The reference work includes a biographical chapter plus four chapters analyzing Rogers and Evans's work in regard to radio, recordings, television, and comic books. A final chapter examines the couple's use of Christianity in their public performances. Reference materials complement each chapter and include filmographies, discographies, radio and television logs, a comicography, and an annotated list of Evans's twenty-eight inspirational books.

Although the personal and professional papers of Roy Rogers and Dale Evans are not available, the couple reveals much about their careers in two published autobiographies, *Happy Trails: The Story of Roy Rogers and Dale Evans*, with Carlton Stowers (Waco, TX: Word Books, 1979), and *Happy Trails: Our Life Story*, with Jane and Michael Stern (New York: Simon & Schuster,

1994). Both works provide a general outline of the stars' careers and personal lives. Dale Evans in her twenty-eight published books combines autobiographical information with her spiritual beliefs. One of the best, *The Woman at the Well* (Old Tappan, NJ: Fleming H. Revell, 1970), is rich in autobiographical detail. Another book of hers, *Dale: My Personal Picture Album* (Old Tappan, NJ: Fleming H. Revell, 1971), contains interesting and rare photographs of Evans, her career, and the Rogers family. Roy Rogers, Jr.'s book, *Growing Up with Roy and Dale*, with Karen Ann Wojahn (Ventura, CA: Regal Books, 1986), details the Rogers family from the perspective of their son.

Interviews of the two stars are numerous and provide all kinds of information on their careers and personal lives. Rogers and Evans talk about their lives in Georgia Morris and Mark Pollard's *Roy Rogers: King of the Cowboys* (San Francisco: Collins Publishers, 1994), which also includes dozens of beautifully reproduced photographs of the two western stars. David Rothel, an important authority on Roy Rogers, included interviews in his two books, *The Singing Cowboys* (New York: A. S. Barnes, 1978), and *The Roy Rogers Book* (Madison, NC: Empire Publishing, 1987). Other published interviews include James Morgan's "Conversations with the Cowboy King," *TWA Ambassador* (October 1976): 16; Joan Winmill Brown's "Roy Rogers and Dale Evans: A Marriage Made in Heaven," *Saturday Evening Post* 252 (April 1980): 50–53; "Roy Rogers: King of the Cowboys," *Hollywood Studio Magazine* 10 (May 1981): 8–13; Neil Pond's "Roy Rogers, King of the Cowboys," *Country America* 3 (February 1992): 34–38.

The published secondary material relating to Roy Rogers and Dale Evans is voluminous and varies greatly in quality. Biographies have been written for both adult and juvenile audiences. The most comprehensive book is Robert W. Phillips's *Roy Rogers* (Jefferson, NC: McFarland, 1995), an encyclopedic work that covers every aspect of Rogers's career with the strongest chapters discussing Rogers's comic books, commercial art, and collectibles. Rather than supplying a narrative or interpretive biography of Rogers, Phillips furnishes an interesting two-chapter chronology that includes unpublished information. Also important is Elise Miller Davis's *The Answer Is God: The Inspiring Personal Story of Dale Evans & Roy Rogers* (New York: McGraw–Hill, 1955). Davis spent several months with the Rogers and did extensive interviews with family members and Rogers's agent, Art Rush. She provides a personal and revealing account of the couple at the height of their careers in the 1950s. Two juvenile biographies are Frank Rasky's *Roy Rogers: King of the Cowboys* (New York: Julian Messner, 1955) and William L. Roper's *Roy Rogers: King of the Cowboys*

(Minneapolis, MN: Denison, 1971). Chockful of information is the memorial on the western star in *Western Clippings*, Boyd Magers, ed., No. 25 (September/October 1998).

A number of works document Rogers and Evans's film careers. Especially important is Bob Carman and Dan Scapperotti's *Roy Rogers, King of the Cowboys: A Film Guide* (privately published, Robert Carman, 1979). Richard Maurice Hurst's *Republic Studios: Between Poverty Row and the Majors* (Metuchen, NJ: Scarecrow Press, 1979) sets Rogers's career at Republic in context of the studio's larger history. William Witney directed twenty-six of Rogers's Republic features. His autobiography, *In a Door, Into a Fight, Out a Door, Into a Chase* (Jefferson, NC: McFarland, 1996), provides important and interesting information on Rogers' films, as does his *Trigger Remembered* (Toney, AL: Earl Blair Enterprises, 1989). Two books that discuss Rogers and the low-budget Western are Don Miller's *Hollywood Corral* (New York: Popular Library, 1976) and Jon Tuska's *The Filming of the West* (Garden City, NY: Doubleday, 1976).

In 1951, Roy Rogers and Dale Evans moved directly from film into television to make thirty-minute Westerns. For a general view of Rogers's television series, *The Roy Rogers Show*, see Gary Yoggy's exhaustive *Riding the Video Range: The Rise and Fall of the Western on Television* (Jefferson, NC: McFarland, 1995).

Roy Rogers's career as a singing cowboy starts with his early days in radio and his effort to organize the Sons of the Pioneers in 1933. For a history of the Pioneers, see Ken Griffis's *Hear My Song: The Story of the Celebrated Sons of the Pioneers*, JEMF Special Series No. 5 (Los Angeles: John Edwards Memorial Foundation, 1974). Bill C. Malone's *Country Music U.S.A.*, rev. ed. (Austin: University of Texas Press, 1985) provides information on Rogers and the Sons of the Pioneers. Also see Douglas B. Green's "The Singing Cowboy: An American Dream," *Journal of Country Music* 7 (May 1978): 4–61. David Rothel's *The Singing Cowboys* (New York: A. S. Barnes, 1978) devotes considerable attention to Rogers, comparing him with other B Western warblers.

For the best understanding of Roy Rogers and Dale Evans's recording and singing careers, one must hear their music. Several recent reissues of their recordings make this possible. One of the most important is *Sons of the Pioneers: The Standard Transcriptions, Part I, 1934–1935* (Bear Family Records BCD 15710 EI, 1998), an excellent five-CD set that showcases vintage Leonard Slye (Roy Rogers) and the Sons of the Pioneers in their early years. Equally interesting is *Happy Trails: The Roy Rogers Collection, 1937–1990* (Rhino R2 75722, 1999), a three-CD box set that includes a wide-range selection of Rogers and Evans's recordings, spanning seven decades, as well as a booklet with a brief but penetrating biography of Roy Rogers by Larry Zwisohn. *The First Classic Recordings of Roy Rogers* (Cattle Records CCD209, 1998) includes Decca material that Rogers recorded between 1938 and 1942. *Peace in the Valley* (Pair Records PDC-2-1352, 1996) and *Roy Rogers and Dale Evans* (The Beautiful Music Company DMC1-16547, 1997) include some of Rogers and Evans's RCA recordings made in the 1940s and 1950s. A superb collection of their Little Golden songs can be found on *Roy Rogers and Dale Evans: 16 Great Songs of the Old West* (Drive Records, DE2-47007, 1998). Reissue of a number of Rogers's Capitol recordings made in the 1960s and 1970s can be found on *Roy Rogers: A Musical Anthology* (A & E Biography 72434-97851-2-0, 1998).

If listening to Rogers and Evans's recordings is fun, watching their Westerns mixes nostalgia with excitement. Videos of their Western features and television shows are available from several commercial distributors. One can purchase individual videos or a box set of features. In the mid-1990s, Republic Pictures Home Video issued *The Roy Rogers Collection,* an eight-feature set of Rogers and Evans's B Westerns that also includes a 60-minute biography entitled *Roy Rogers: King of the Cowboys* (1992). Madacy Music Group produced a ten-feature box set entitled *Roy Rogers: Collectors Edition* (n.d.), which includes Rogers's Westerns from the 1930s and 1940s. Paramount Home Video, Shokus Video, and Moviecraft distribute selected episodes of *The Roy Rogers Show.*

CHAPTER 3: GENE AUTRY

A reliable biography of Gene Autry does not yet exist. For those who want to read in more detail about the life and career of Gene Autry, a number of useful sources are available, but many details of Autry's life remain hazy. Autry's autobiography *Back in the Saddle Again,* cowritten by Mickey Herkowitz (Garden City, NY: Doubleday & Co., 1978), is folksy and self-serving but is an invaluable source for determining the public image that Autry himself wanted to endure. Two fan-oriented books by David Rothel, which are perhaps too lavish in their praise of Autry and his Westerns but which contain much useful information, are *The Singing Cowboys* (South Brunswick, ME: A. S. Barnes and Co., 1978), a survey of the entire singing cowboy genre, and *The Gene Autry Book* (Waynesville, NC: World of Yesterday, 1986). Jon Tuska's two books, *The Vanishing Legion: A History of Mascot Pictures 1927–1935* (Jefferson, NC: McFarland & Co., 1982) and *The Filming of the West* (Garden City, NY: Doubleday & Co., 1976), present a more skeptical view of what Tuska terms "the Autry fantasy."

For information about Autry at Republic Pictures, see Richard Maurice Hearst's *Republic Studios: Between Poverty Row and the Majors* (Metuchen, NJ: Scarecrow Press, 1979). For some valuable insights into Autry as a recording artist, consult Douglas Green's excellent history, *Country Roots: The Origins of Country Music* (New York: Hawthorne Books, 1976), and Green's biographical booklet in *Gene Autry, Sing, Cowboy, Sing: The Gene Autry Collection* (Rhino Compact Disc Set, R272630, 1997). Jon Guyot Smith's track-by-track notes in this set are also excellent.

Much more work needs to be done in locating Autry and his Westerns within their cultural context. Two articles have begun this process. Jack Nachbar's "Horses, Harmony, Hope, and Hormones: Western Movies, 1930–1946," *Journal of the West* 4 (October 1983): 24–33, examines the renewal of interest and creativity in the Hollywood Western during the Depression. Autry and other singing cowboys are seen as reflections of a renewed confidence in traditional American values. Ray Merlock, in "Gene Autry and the Coming of Civilization," *Shooting Stars: Heroes and Heroines of Western Film*, Archie P. McDonald, ed. (Bloomington: Indiana University Press, 1987), 87–108, examines contemporary settings and the uses of technology in Autry's films.

Those who wish to gain a better understanding of Autry's importance in the broader scope of Westerns and American films in general may find three books especially useful. Andrew Bergman's *We're in the Money: Depression America and Its Films* (New York: Harcourt Brace Jovanovich, 1976) explores how the movies made during the Depression reflected national attitudes both before and after FDR took office. Phil Hardy's *The Encyclopedia of Western Movies* (Minneapolis, MN: Woodbury Press, 1984) briefly describes most of the Westerns made between 1929 and 1983. The book is organized on a year-by-year basis, making it easy to see what other Westerns were being released at the same time as Autry's. Don Miller, in *Hollywood Corral* (New York: Popular Library, 1976), presents movie-by-movie career overviews of most of the popular B Western stars.

A quick look at the above sources suggests how little has been written about Autry and the other singing cowboys. Most of these sources are more than fifteen years old. It is high time for scholars of American movies and the Hollywood Western to examine Autry as a monumental figure in movie history and in American popular culture.

CHAPTER 4: JOHN FORD

This essay is drawn largely from my biography *John Ford: Hollywood's Old Master* (Norman: University of Oklahoma Press, 1995), in which I make extensive use of the Ford papers in the Lilly Library at Indiana University in Bloomington, as well as a vast collection of oral histories I conducted, now housed in the DeGolyer Library on the Southern Methodist University campus in Dallas. These interviews and other oral histories consulted are listed in my book.

Earlier biographies of the director include his grandson Dan Ford's *Pappy: The Life of John Ford* (Englewood Cliffs, N.J: Prentice-Hall, 1979), which was reprinted by DaCapo Press in 1998, and Andrew Sinclair's *John Ford* (New York: Dial, 1979). More recent is Scott Eyman's *Print the Legend: The Life and Times of John Ford* (New York: Simon and Schuster, 1999). Other major studies of Ford are headed by Lindsay Anderson's *About John Ford* (New York: McGraw-Hill, 1981); John Baxter's *The Cinema of John Ford* (New York: A. S. Barnes, 1971); Tag Gallagher's *John Ford: The Man and His Films* (Berkeley: University of California Press, 1986); Joseph McBride and Michael Wilmington's *John Ford* (New York: DaCapo, 1975); J. A. Place's *The Western Films of John Ford* (Secaucus, NJ: Citadel, 1974); Andrew Sarris's *The John Ford Movie Mystery* (Bloomington: Indiana University Press, 1975); and Peter Stowell's *John Ford* (Boston, MA: Twayne, 1986). Joseph W. Reed's *Three American Originals* (Middletown, CT: Wesleyan University Press, 1984) is an interesting comparison of John Ford, Charles Ives, and William Faulkner.

The longest published interview with the director is Peter Bogdanovich's *John Ford* (Berkeley: University of California Press, 1978). A shorter one is contained in Walter Wagner's *You Must Remember This* (New York: Putnam's, 1975), 55–65. Comments from Ford may be found in Jay Leyda, ed., *Voices of Film Experience* (New York: Macmillan, 1977), and Andrew Sarris, *Interviews with Film Directors* (Indianapolis, IN: Bobbs-Merrill, 1967).

Articles of importance are "John Ford Gives Us Another Great Example of Screen Art," *Film Spectator* 9 (February 15, 1930): 5–6; "John Ford: The Quiet Man from Portland," *Maine Life* (July 1976): 56–59; Richard A. Blake, "John Ford: A Sense of Worth," *America* 129 (October 6, 1973): 243–44; Peter Bogdanovich, "The Autumn of John Ford," *Esquire* 61 (April 1964): 102–7, 144–45; Ron Chernow, "John Ford: The Last Frontiersman," *Ramparts* 12 (April 1974): 45–48; David Coursen, "John Ford: Assessing the Reassessment," *Film Quarterly* 29 (Spring 1976): 58–60; Kirk Ellis, "On the Warpath: John Ford and the Indians," *Journal of Popular Film and Television* 8 (No. 2, 34–41); Peter Ericsson, "John Ford," *Sequence* (Winter 1947): 18–25; William K. Everson,

"Forgotten Ford," *Focus on Film* (Spring 1971): 13–19; Michael Goodwin, "John Ford: A Poet Who Shot Great Movies," *Moving Image* 1 (December 1981): 59–63; Grady Johnson, "John Ford: Maker of Hollywood Stars," *Coronet* 35 (December 1953): 133–40; Stanley Kauffmann, "The Unquiet Man," *The New Republic*, 195 (August 11, 1986): 24–28; Douglas McVay, "The Five Worlds of John Ford," *Films and Filming* 8 (June 1962): 14–17, 53; Frank S. Nugent, "Hollywood's Favorite Rebel," *Reader's Digest* 55 (October 1949): 53–57; Jeffrey Richards, "Ford's Lost World," *Focus on Film* (Spring 1971): 20–30; Charles Silver, "The Apprenticeship of John Ford," *American Film* 1 (May 1976): 62–67; H. Peter Stowell, "John Ford's Literary Sources: From Realism to Romance," *Literature/Film Quarterly* 5 (Spring 1977): 164–73; and Robin Wood, "Shall We Gather at the River?: The Late Films of John Ford," *Film Comment* 7 (Fall 1971): 8–17.

Doctoral dissertations worth consulting include Michael N. Budd's "A Critical Analysis of Western Films Directed by John Ford from *Stagecoach* to *Cheyenne Autumn*" (Iowa City: University of Iowa, 1975); William C. Howze's "The Influence of Western Painting and Genre Painting on the Films of John Ford" (University of Texas at Austin, 1986); and Peter Robert Lehman's "John Ford and the Auteur Theory" (Madison: University of Wisconsin, 1978).

On Monument Valley and Gouldings' trading post, see Richard E. Klinck's *Land of Room Enough and Time Enough* (Salt Lake City, UT: Peregrine Smith, 1984); Frank McNitt's *The Indian Traders* (Norman: University of Oklahoma Press, 1962); and Samuel Moon's *Tall Sheep: Harry Goulding, Monument Valley Trader* (Norman: University of Oklahoma Press, 1992). Three of the better articles on those subjects are Neil M. Clark, "Desert Trader," *Saturday Evening Post* 209 (March 29, 1947): 36–37; Todd McCarthy, "John Ford and Monument Valley," *American Film* 3 (May 1978): 10–16; and Allen C. Reed, "John Ford Makes Another Movie Classic in Monument Valley," *Arizona Highways* 32 (April 1956): 4–11.

CHAPTER 5: JOHN WAYNE

The most extensive biography of John Wayne is Randy Roberts and James S. Olson's *John Wayne: American* (New York: Free Press, 1995). Reflective of the lingering controversy surrounding Wayne is the review essay of this book by historian Jackson Lears, "Screw Ambiguity," *New Republic* (April 22, 1996): 38–41. A more brief but elegant and incisive biography that draws heavily from the author's extensive interviews of those associated with the actor is Ronald L.

Davis's *Duke: The Life and Image of John Wayne* (Norman: University of Oklahoma Press, 1998). Both biographies provide bibliographies, with Davis offering a particularly useful and complete annotated listing of sources. Complementing these biographical accounts is Garry Wills's study of Wayne's political imagery in *John Wayne's America* (New York: Simon and Schuster, 1997). Parts of Wills's book appeared earlier in "American Chronicles: John Wayne's Body," *New Yorker* (August 19, 1996): 39–49, and in "American Adam," *New York Review of Books* (March 6, 1997): 30–33.

Earlier assessments of Wayne's career and screen image are Emmanuel Levy's *John Wayne: Prophet of the American Way of Life* (Metuchen, NJ: Scarecrow Press, 1988) and Richard D. McGhee's *John Wayne: Actor, Artist, Hero* (Jefferson, NC: McFarland, 1990).

For a brief glance at Wayne's life and career, see Archie P. McDonald's "John Wayne: Hero of the Western," *Journal of the West* 22 (October 1983): 53–63. A slight variation under the same title appears in *Shooting Stars: Heroes and Heroines of Western Film* McDonald, ed. (Bloomington: Indiana University Press, 1987), 108–25. Even more condensed is my entry on Wayne in *American National Biography*, John A. Garraty, ed., and Mark C. Carnes (New York: Oxford University Press, 1999), 22: 829–31.

For many years, the standard book on the star's life was Maurice Zolotow's *Shooting Star: A Biography of John Wayne* (New York: Simon and Schuster, 1974). A more interesting portrait drawing on recollections by one of Wayne's make-up artists is Donald Shepherd and Robert Slatzer's *Duke: The Life and Times of John Wayne*, with Dave Grayson (Garden City, NY: Doubleday, 1985). The most sensible of the several recollections by personal intimates is Pilar Wayne's *John Wayne: My Life with the Duke* (New York: McGraw-Hill, 1987).

A handy reference to Wayne's films, complete with credits and plot synopses, is Steve Zmijewsky, Boris Zmijewsky, and Mark Ricci's *The Complete Films of John Wayne* (Secaucus, NJ: Citadel, 1983). Allen Eyles provides a more elaborate account of Wayne's films in *John Wayne* (South Brunswick, NJ: A. S. Barnes and Co., 1979). For an "everything you wanted to know" compendium on Wayne and his films, see Charles John Kieskalt's *The Official John Wayne Reference Book* (Secaucus, NJ: Citadel, 1985).

Other books on Wayne are mentioned in the Roberts–Olson and Davis biographies. Davis also lists numerous articles and journalistic reports that span Wayne's career. Some are insightful and many are little more than anecdotal tributes, although even these can be revealing of how Wayne was perceived through the years. Both biographies also list the considerable literature on those who worked with Wayne and include published studies and interviews of these associates as well as their memoirs. An earlier and still useful bibliographical guide is Judith M. Riggin's *John Wayne: A Bio-Bibliography* (New York: Greenwood Press, 1992).

An obstacle to pursuing biographical work on Wayne is the lack of access to primary materials held by the Wayne family. Still, as is evident in the bibliographies of Roberts–Olson and Davis, a wealth of sources exists on Wayne's film career, including studio production files at the University of Southern California, collected papers of associates (particularly valuable are those of Wayne's agent Charles K. Feldman at the American Film Institute and those of director John Ford at Indiana University), oral history collections (notably in the Southern Methodist University Oral History Program that biographer Ronald Davis directs), and clippings files on Wayne's early life housed in the public libraries of Winterset, Iowa, and Glendale, California.

CHAPTER 6: GARY COOPER

Cooper never wrote a full-length autobiography, but he published (with others) several autobiographical magazine articles that can be used carefully as primary sources. The longest and most complete is Gary Cooper (as told to George Scullin), "Well, It Was This Way," *Saturday Evening Post* 228 (February 18, 25; March 3, 10, 17, 24, 31; April 7, 1956). Also useful is Gary Cooper (as told to Leonard Slater), "I Took a Good Look at Myself and This Is What I Saw," *McCall's* 88 (January 1961): 62, 138–42. There were also several shorter, less formal pieces published over the years in movie magazines such as *Motion Picture*, *Hollywood Reporter*, and *New Movie Magazine*. One of the best of these, covering Cooper's cowboy years in Montana, is Gary Cooper (as told to Dorothy Spensley), "The Big Boy Tells His Story," *Photoplay* 35 (April 1929): 64–65, 133–35; and *Photoplay* 35 (May 1929): 70–71, 84, 110.

Several full-length biographies are currently available. The most recent and comprehensive is Jeffrey Meyers's *Gary Cooper: American Hero* (New York: William Morrow and Co., 1998). Meyers interviewed Cooper's wife (now Veronica Cooper Converse), his daughter, Maria Cooper Janis, and close friends and associates such as Fred Zinnemann, Patricia Neal, and Fay Wray. Meyers also viewed Cooper archival materials at the Warner Brothers Archive, Doheny Library, University of Southern California; and at the Paramount Archive at the Margaret Herrick Library of the Academy of

Motion Picture Arts and Sciences. Meyers footnotes his sources (which sets him apart from other Cooper biographers), provides a good bibliography, and brings his usual perspicacity to bear. Three other useful overviews are Stuart M. Kaminsky's *Coop: The Life and Legend of Gary Cooper* (New York: St. Martin's Press, 1980); Larry Swindell's *The Last Hero: A Biography of Gary Cooper* (Garden City, NY: Doubleday & Co., 1980); and Hector Arce's *Gary Cooper: An Intimate Biography* (New York: William Morrow and Co., 1979). For those who want all the juicy, X-rated gossip (the sources generally anonymous) on Cooper's frantic love life, there is Jane Ellen Wayne's *Cooper's Women* (New York: Prentice-Hall Press, 1988), which is always entertaining. Also entertaining in its use of fictional narrative techniques and undocumented interior monologues is George Carpozi, Jr.'s *The Gary Cooper Story* (New Rochelle, NY: Arlington House, 1970). Carpozi, trying to let Cooper tell his own story, squeezes as much as he can out of the published autobiographical writings. The result, anecdotal in the extreme, is fun but of limited use to historians. The two best-illustrated indexes of Cooper movies are René Jordan's *Gary Cooper: A Pyramid Illustrated History of the Movies* (New York: Pyramid Publications, 1974) and Homer Dickens's *The Complete Films of Gary Cooper* (New York: Citadel Press, 1970). These two have only black-and-white pictures, most of which are studio stills or promotional shots.

High Noon has received more press than Cooper's other movies. Rudy Behlmer provides a good, basic background in "Do Not Forsake Me, Oh My Darlin': *High Noon*," *America's Favorite Movies: Behind the Scenes* (New York: Frederick Ungar Publishing Co., 1982), 269–88. Behlmer follows the filmmakers' writing, casting, and production decisions and gives details on the film's reediting. Carl Foreman discusses *High Noon* in "Dialogue on Film: Carl Foreman," *American Film* 4 (April 1979): 35–46. Here Foreman explains that in his rewritten script he intended the frightened townsfolk to represent certain timid Hollywood figures, including producer Stanley Kramer, who had deserted him after the HUAC subpoena. Director Fred Zinnemann's contributions to the final product are discussed in Louis Giannetti's "Fred Zinnemann's *High Noon*," *Film Criticism* 1 (Winter 1976–77): 2–12. John H. Lenihan's *Showdown: Confronting Modern America in the Western Film* (Urbana: University of Illinois Press, 1980) compares *High Noon* to other Cold War Westerns and helps establish its historical context. Will Wright's *Six Guns and Society: A Structural Study of the Western* (Berkeley: University of California Press, 1975) examines *High Noon* in theoretical ("structural") terms and concludes that it represents a transition between the earlier "classical" Westerns and the later "professional" ones, the three categories being distinguished by how the hero relates to society. Wright wants to systematize our thinking about western mythology, an admirable goal, but he is too academic for the average Western fan. Stephen Tatum offers a good, accessible analysis of *High Noon* and Cooper's other important Westerns in "The Classic Westerner: Gary Cooper," in Archie P. McDonald, ed., *Shooting Stars: Heroes and Heroines of Western Film* (Bloomington: Indiana University Press, 1987), 60–86. A good handbook that summarizes much of the scholarship on this film and provides an extensive bibliography is Phillip Drummond's *High Noon* (London: British Film Institute, 1997).

CHAPTER 7: BARBARA STANWYCK

The best source for understanding Barbarba Stanwyck's Westerns is the films themselves. Readily available in videocassette are *Annie Oakley* (1935), *The Union Pacific* (1939), *The Great Man's Lady* (1942), and *The Maverick Queen* (1956). In addition, detailed and extremely useful accounts of Stanwyck's films and television appearances, including casts, synopses, some reviews, and revealing photographs, can be found in Homer Dickens's *The Films of Barbara Stanwyck* (Secaucus, NJ: Citadel Press, 1984).

Some of Stanwyck's most memorable words are found in Bernard Drew's "Stanwyck Speaks," *American Film* 17 (No. 2, 1981): 43–46; Robert Blees' "Interview with Barbara Stanwyck," *American Film* 12 (No. 6, 1987): 39–43; and "The Fifteenth Annual Film Institute Life Achievement Awards, April 9, 1987," American Film Institute.

In addition to Stanwyck's work and words, book-length treatments on her include Ella Smith's *Starring Miss Barbara Stanwyck* (New York: Crown Publishers, 1974); Jerry Vermilye's *Barbara Stanwyck: A Pyramid Illustrated History of the Movies* (New York: Pyramid Publications, 1975); Al DiOrio's *Barbara Stanwyck* (New York: Coward-McCann, 1983); Jane Ellen Wayne's *Stanwyck* (New York: Arbor House, 1985); and Axel Madsen's *Stanwyck* (New York: HarperCollins, 1994). The Smith and Vermilye books emphasize Stanwyck's films more than the actress herself. Those by DiOrio, Wayne, and Madsen are neither scholarly, analytical, nor confidence-inspiring in their reliability.

Only a few scholars have studied Stanwyck. The most useful essays are Sandra Schackel's "Women in Western Films: The Civilizer, the Saloon Singer, and Their Modern Sister," in Archie P. McDonald, ed., *Shooting Stars: Heroes and Heroines of Western Film* (Bloomington: Indiana University Press, 1987), 196–217, and "Barbara Stanwyck: Uncommon Heroine," *California History* 72 (Spring

1993): 40–55. Stanwyck is recognized as the best example of strong women in Westerns in Cheryl J. Foote's essay, "Changing Images of Women in the Western Film," *Journal of the West* 22 (October 1983): 64–71.

Other articles and books that include mention of Stanwyck are James Robert Parish and Don E. Stanke's *The Leading Ladies* (New Rochelle, NY: Arlington House, 1977), 423–93, whose chapter on Stanwyck contains detailed biographical information; Gerald Peary's "Barbara Stanwyck: Even When She Was Bad She Was Good," *American Film* 14 (July–August, 1989): 60–64; Kathleen Murphy's "Farewell My Lovelies," *Film Comment* 26 (No. 4, 1990): 33–38; Buck Rainey with "Foreword" by Barbara Stanwyck, *Sweethearts of the Sage* (Jefferson, NC: McFarland, 1992); and Ian Cameron and Doughlas Pye's, eds., *The Book of Westerns* (New York: Continuum, 1996).

Several general treatments are helpful for understanding the changes in characterizations of western women in films. These discussions include Molly Haskell's *From Reverence to Rape: The Treatment of Women in the Movies* (New York: Holt, Rinehart and Winston, 1973); Ralph Brauer with Donna Brauer's *The Horse, The Gun and The Piece of Property: Changing Images of the TV Western* (Bowling Green, OH: Popular Press, 1975); Jeanine Basinger's *A Woman's View: How Hollywood Spoke to Women, 1930–1960* (New York: Alfred A. Knopf, 1993); and Ruth Vasey's *The World According to Hollywood, 1918–1939* (Madison: University of Wisconsin Press, 1997), which discusses how production codes shaped film images and stereotypes.

CHAPTER 8: KATY JURADO

Foremost, I wish to thank Sandy Ferguson, Julianne Burton–Carvajal, and Patricia Torres for their invaluable assistance in obtaining information for this essay. All translations of material in this essay that originally appeared in Spanish are my own. Biographical dictionaries and encyclopedias offer the general information with which to begin a study like this one. Although entries for Katy Jurado appear in many such works, the most informative are Luis Reyes and Peter Rubie's *Hispanics in Hollywood: An Encyclopedia of Film and Television* (New York: Garland, 1994), which also contains a very useful introduction; Nicholas E. Meyer's *The Biographical Dictionary of Hispanic Americans* (New York: Facts on File, 1997); and Gary D. Keller's *A Biographical Handbook of Hispanics and United States Film* (Tempe, AZ: Bilingual Press, 1997). Buck Rainey's *Sweethearts of the Sage: Biographies and Filmographies of 258 Actresses Appearing in Western Movies* (Jefferson, NC: McFarland & Co., 1992) is an invaluable compilation and includes information about many lesser-known actresses. Although suggested readings and a useful bibliography are included, readers should exercise caution, since some of the information is in error, and Rainey does not include footnotes.

The most comprehensive survey of the way Mexicans appear in American literature and film is Arthur Pettit's *Images of the Mexican American in Fiction and Film,* Dennis E. Showalter, ed. (College Station: Texas A&M University Press, 1980). Two works by Gary D. Keller that concentrate on film are essential: *Chicano Cinema, Research, Reviews, and Resources,* edited by Keller (Tempe, AZ: Bilingual Review/Press, 1985), and *Hispanics and United States Film: An Overview and Handbook* (Tempe, AZ: Bilingual Review/Press, 1994). George Hadley-Garcia's *Hollywood Hispano: Los Latinos en el Mundo del Cine* (New York: Citadel Press, 1991) offers additional information in a more popular format. Readers may also wish to consult Juan R. Garcia's excellent article "Hollywood and the West: Mexican Images in American Films," in *Old Southwest, New Southwest: Essays on a Region and Its Literature,* Judy Nolte Lensink, ed., (Tucson: Tucson Public Library, 1987). Finally, John C. Coatsworth and Carlos Rico's, eds., *Images of Mexico in the United States* (San Diego, CA: Center for U.S.–Mexican Studies, 1989), offers additional relevant information.

In addition to the works mentioned above, two articles merit special attention: Sylvia Morales's "Chicano-Produced Celluloid Mujeres," and Carlos E. Córtes's "Chicanas in Film: History of an Image" in Keller, *Chicano Cinema.*

The best source for information about Mexican movies and the Mexican movie industry is the Emilio García–Riera's multivolume work *Historia documental del cine mexicano* (Mexico: Ediciones Era, 1992–1997). Information about specific Mexican films was taken from this source for the essay in this book. A very useful overview, and one more accessible to the majority of American readers, is Carlos Mora's *Mexican Cinema: Reflections of a Society, 1896–1968* (Berkeley: University of California Press, 1982). Joanne Hershfield's *Mexican Cinema/Mexican Women, 1940–1960* (Tucson: University of Arizona Press, 1997) examines the place of women in Mexican society and Mexican film.

Secondary information about Katy Jurado is limited in English and in Spanish. Emilio García Riera and Javier González Rubio's *El Cine de Katy Jurado,* (Guadalajara, Mexico: Universidad de Guadalajara y Instituto Mexicano de Cinematografía, 1999) is richly supplemented with photographs and includes a short biographical chapter based on interviews with Jurado, followed by summaries of the major films in which she appeared. Most of the biographical entries in other published sources appear to come from the "official" biography in the Katy Jurado file at the Margaret Herrick Library, Academy of Motion Picture Arts and Sciences in Los Angeles, California. Most of the English-language newspaper articles mentioned below are in the Jurado clippings file, also at the Herrick Library. Jurado's date of birth and place of birth cannot be determined precisely. Birth dates include 1924, 1925, and 1927, and sources disagree about her place of birth, some arguing Guadalajara, whereas others say Mexico City. I have chosen to follow the path with the most evidence. Articles based on interviews with Jurado (in the United States and Mexico) provide additional biographical information and are cited below.

An error that occurs in most sources is the claim that Jurado received two Academy Award nominations. Her only Oscar nomination came for *Broken Lance*.

Sources about Western films are voluminous. Jon Tuska, *The American West in Film: Critical Approaches to the Western* (Westport, CT: Greenwood Press, 1985), offers a negative appraisal of women's roles in Westerns. Among the most useful works for information about specific films is Phil Hardy's *The Western: The Complete Film Sourcebook* (New York: William Morrow and Co., 1983). Also helpful was *Microsoft Cinemania 1994* (Microsoft Corp. CD-rom, 1993). A recent work that examines the Western as a masculine genre is Lee Clark Mitchell's *Westerns: Making the Man in Fiction and Film* (Chicago: University of Chicago Press, 1996). An invaluable collection of essays is Jim Kitses and Gregg Rickman's, eds., *The Western Reader* (New York: Limelight Editions, 1998). Part three of this volume includes eleven articles about women and minority groups in the Western. Of particular interest for this article are Pam Cook's "Women and the Western" and Blake Lucas's "Saloon Girls and Ranchers' Daughters: The Woman in the Western." John Lenihan's *Showdown: Confronting Modern America in the Western Film* (Urbana: University of Illinois Press, 1980) examines the period in which Jurado made most of her Westerns and places these films in the context of the times.

Newsweek labeled Jurado "compassionate and dignified" in a review of *The Bullfighter and the Lady*, May 14, 1951. For Jurado's recollections of beginning her career in the movies, see Martha Elba's "Katy Jurado: Una de las mejores promesas de 1944" in *Cinema Reporter* 282, 10 de diciembre, Mexico, 1943, cited in Fernando Muñoz Castillo, "Katy Jurado: El Temperamento Latino," *Uno Mas Uno*, 18 de abril 1998, courtesy of La biblioteca del Cineteca, Mexico. For the types of movies made in Mexico in the 1940s, see Mora,

Mexican Cinema, 56. For Jurado's introduction to American films, see John Cavallo's "The Career of Katy Jurado," *Classic Images* 184 (December 1990): 18; also see García-Riera and González Rubio's *El Cine de Katy Jurado*, 22, for Jurado's recollections about her methods to improve her English.

Discussions of Jurado's role as Helen Ramírez appear in Pettit's *Images of the Mexican–American*, 204–5; in Córtes's "Chicanas in Film," 94, 101–2; and in Reyes and Rubie's *Hispanics in Hollywood*, 125. For information about the Academy Awards, see Mason Wiley and Damien Bona's *Inside Oscar: The Unofficial History of the Academy Awards*, ed. by Gail MacColl (New York: Ballantine Books, 1986), 225. Mention of Jurado's Golden Globe Award appears in the *Los Angeles Times*, April 5, 1953. The Ariel is mentioned in Garcia-Riera's *Historia Documental*, vol. 3.

"A sultry traitor" is cited in Lenihan's *Showdown*, 40–41. The delay in issuing a visa to Dolores Del Rio is described in Reyes and Rubie's *Hispanics in Hollywood*, 393. Jurado's "character with heart" comes from "I'm All the Time in Love," says Katy Jurado in *Los Angeles Examiner*, May 9, 1954; she identified the role as her favorite in Cavallo's "The Career of Katy Jurado," 18. Jurado was quoted as "happy for my country" in Wiley and Bona, *Inside Oscar*, 248; for the description of her Dior dress, see Wiley and Bona's *Inside Oscar*, 250.

"The dark days of Mexican cinema" is from Mora's *Mexican Cinema*, 56. Jurado's remarks about returning frequently to Mexico and her desire to achieve success in the United States are in García-Riera and González Rubio's *El Cine de Katy Jurado*, 19. Jurado also said she was proud to be a Mexican in an interview in *The New York Times* (no title), July 20, 1952. Her comments after *Arrowhead* can be found in *The Hollywood Citizen News*, February 15, 1953. For her comments to Juan Galindo, see Muñoz Castillo's "Katy Jurado: El Temperamento Latino" 18 abril 1998. Her recollections of Hollywood actors and directors are found in Cavallo, "The Career of Katy Jurado," 18, and her comments about the differences between men and women appear in García- Riera and González Rubio's *El Cine de Katy Jurado*, 30.

The "tamale" quote appears in the *Los Angeles Daily News*, November 17, 1951. The article from the *Los Angeles Times* appeared April 5, 1953. Anthony Quinn was quoted in Meyer's *Biographical Dictionary*, 122. Mention of her performance in "House of Naples" occurs in "Katy is Expressive and Volatile," *Los Angeles Mirror*, April 1, 1958.

For a discussion of Borgnine's divorce and the couple's plans, see *Los Angeles Mirror News*, June 12, 1959. For the Jurado–Borgnine marriage, see *Hollywood Citizen Reporter*, January 1, 1960. On Jurado's television appearances, see Harris M. Lentz III's *Western and Frontier Film and Television Credits 1903–1995,* vol. 1 (Jefferson, NC: McFarland and Co., 1996).

For discussions of the Borgnine–Jurado separation and plans to divorce, see "Borgnine 'Brutal,' Katy to Charge," *Los Angeles Examiner,* January 16, 1961. For a summary of the incident in Rome, see "Helping, Not Beating Katy, Borgnine States," *Los Angeles Mirror,* February 20, 1961. "Purr Peacefully" appeared in the *Los Angeles Mirror,* August 16, 1961, and "Cooing" in the *Hollywood Citizen* on August 15, 1961.

Articles about the divorce include "Katy Jurado Loses Plaint for Alimony," *Los Angeles Citizen News,* October 2, 1962, and "Borgnine Divorced by Tearful Katy Jurado," *Los Angeles Times,* June 4, 1963.

About Jurado's problems with English, see *Los Angeles Times,* August 10, 1958; " 'We Were Framed' Say Katy and Ernie," *Los Angeles Mirror,* June 14, 1961. For Jurado's comments about her weight and her age, see "Katy Jurado Tells Why She's Misunderstood," *Los Angeles Times Calendar,* July 24, 1966. Her suicide attempt is covered in "Katy Jurado Found in 'Pill Coma,'" *Los Angeles Herald Examiner,* February 15, 1968.

For *AKA Pablo,* see Reyes and Rubie's *Hispanics in Hollywood,* 269. For her awards, see "Jurado to receive award at Santa Fe western festival," *Hollywood Reporter,* June 28, 1981, and no title, September 1, 1992; for Jurado's comments about her role in opening opportunities for other actresses in the United States, see Muñoz Castillo's "Katy Jurado: El Temperamento Latino II."

The interview in which Jurado discusses Salma Hayek is "Katy Jurado: La belleza acaba," *El Universal, el gran diario de Mexico,* 30 de junio, 1997. Hayek's interview appears in Carmen Teresa Roíz's "The Wild, Wild Salma Hayek," *Vista: The Magazine of All Hispanics, Albuquerque Tribune,* July 1999, 6–8.

For information about the Ariel award and speech, see "'Cilantro y Parsley' flavor Ariel awards," *Variety,* December 8, 1997, and "Desangelada entrega de los Arieles," *El Universal,* 5 de diciembre, 1997. For *Te Sigo Amando,* see Maricarmen Barragan's "CRONICAS: Adicciones de Nuestro Tiempo," *El Sol de Texas,* 11 de septiembre 1997, and for *El Evangelio de las Maravillas,* see Katy Jurado's fact sheet at the Biblioteca de la Cineteca, Mexico.

CHAPTER 9: JAY SILVERHEELS, IRON EYES CODY,
AND CHIEF DAN GEORGE

Several books tell the story of Native Americans in Western movies, although specific information on individual actors remains sparse. Of particular interest are the following books: Gretchen M. Bataille and Charles L. P. Silet's *Images of American Indian on Film: An Annotated Bibliography* (New York: Garland, 1985) and *The Pretend Indians: Images of Native Americans in the Movies* (Ames: Iowa State University Press, 1980); S. Elizabeth Bird's *Dressing in Feathers: The Construction of the Indian in American Popular Culture* (Boulder, CO: Westview Press, 1996); Ward Churchill's *Fantasies of the Master Race: Literature, Cinema, and the Colonization of American Indians* (Monroe, ME: Common Courage Press, 1992); Philip Joseph Deloria's *Playing Indian* (New Haven: Yale University Press, 1998); Ralph E. and Natasha A. Friar's *The Only Good Indian: The Hollywood Gospel* (New York: Drama Book Specialists, 1972); Michael Hilger's *From Savage to Nobleman: Images of Native Americans in Film* (Lanham, MD: Scarecrow Press, 1995) and *The American Indian in Film* (Metuchen, NJ: Scarecrow Press, 1986); Jacquelyn Kilpatrick's *Celluloid Indians: Native Americans and Film* (Lincoln: University of Nebraska Press, 1999); John E. O'Connor's *The Hollywood Indian: Stereotypes of Native Americans in Films* (Trenton: New Jersey State Museum, 1980); Louis Owens's *Mixedblood Messages: Literature, Film, Family, Place* (Norman: University of and Oklahoma Press, 1998); and Peter C. Rollins and John E. O'Connor's *Hollywood's Indian: The Portrayal of the Native American in Film* (Lexington: University Press of Kentucky, 1998).

Information on Jay Silverheels is sparse and is limited to short pieces in Marion E. Gridley's *Indians of Today*, 4th Ed. (Indianapolis, IN: ICFP, 1971), 126; David Ragan's *Who's Who in Hollywood 1900–1976* (New Rochelle, NY: Arlington House, 1976), 430; Ephraim Katz's *The Film Encyclopedia* (New York: Thomas Y. Crowell, 1979), 1,058; and Roland Turner's *The Annual Obituary, 1980* (New York: St. Martin's Press, 1981), 156–57. Brief obituaries appear in *Newsweek* 95 (March 17, 1980): 86; *Time* 115 (March 17, 1980): 65; and *The New York Times* (March 6, 1980): D-19. A longer obituary appears in *The New York Times Biographical Service* (March 6, 1980): 448. Silverheels discussed the role of Native American actors in an interview with Will Tusher in *The Hollywood Reporter* (March 23, 1972). *Who Was That Masked Man: The Story of the Lone Ranger* by David Rothel (New York: A. S. Barnes, 1976) tells the story of the Lone Ranger and Tonto.

When Iron Eyes Cody died on January 2, 1999, almost every newspaper published an obituary of him. His passing was particularly noted in Native papers such as one published in Glendora, California, *OCB Tracker* 6 (December 1998/January 1999): 1, 4. Obituaries also appeared in *The Boston Globe* (January 5, 1999): A13, and *The New York Times* (January 5, 1999): A15. Iron Eyes Cody was the author of

Iron Eyes: My Life as a Hollywood Indian, as told to Collin Perry (New York: Everest House, 1982); *Indian Talk: Hand Signals of the North American Indians* (Happy Camp, CA: Naturegraph Publishers, 1970, 1998); and *How Indian Sign Talk in Pictures* (Los Angeles: Homer H. Boelter Lithography, 1952).

Although not as well known as either Jay Silverheels or Iron Eyes Cody, by the time of his death, major newspapers carried Chief Dan George's obituary — *The New York Times* (September 24, 1981): D27, and the *San Francisco Chronicle* (September 24, 1981): 36. Chief Dan George also wrote two children's books with Helmut Hirnschall, *My Heart Soars* (Saanichton, BC: Hancock House, 1974) and *My Spirit Soars* (Surrey, BC: Hancock House, 1982). He wrote *You Call Me Chief: Impressions of the Life of Chief Dan George* with Hilda Mortimer (Toronto: Doubleday Canada Limited, 1981).

There are sound recordings featuring Chief Dan George: *Proud Earth* (released in 1990 by Salt City), and *The Ecstasy of Rita Joe* (released in 1980 by Jabula Records). King Broadcasting Company has produced the video *Out Totem Is the Raven* (1971, 1992), featuring Chief Dan George.

CHAPTER 10: CLINT EASTWOOD

Popular literature on Clint Eastwood is extensive. Hundreds of reviews, profiles, interviews, and promotional articles have appeared in newspapers and magazines from early in his career through the present. Major American papers giving Eastwood coverage have included *The New York Times, The Village Voice, The Washington Post, Chicago Tribune,* and *Los Angeles Times.* Major articles on Eastwood have also appeared in *The London Times,* the *Guardian,* and *Paris–Match.* Periodicals, from weekly news magazines to monthly "slicks" and journals of opinion (such as *Esquire, The Atlantic Monthly,* and *The New Yorker*), have run major pieces on Eastwood.

The more significant of these journalistic pieces include the following: Eastwood's first major cover story, which appeared on the July 23, 1971, issue of *Life*; a cover story (with Burt Reynolds) on the January 9, 1978, issue of *Time*; a *Playboy* interview in the February 1978 issue; and a *Rolling Stone* interview in the July 4, 1985, issue. One of the first critical articles to consider Eastwood as a serious artist, and not just as a popular phenomenon, is found in Robert Mazzocco's "The Supply-Side Star," *The New York Review of Books,* April 1, 1982. The high European regard for Eastwood's work is well set forth in John Vinocur's "Clint Eastwood, Seriously," *The New York Times Magazine,* February 24, 1985.

As is true of many popular culture figures, Eastwood has been the subject of many books that track his life and work. The best of these is Richard Schickel's intelligent biography, *Clint Eastwood* (New York: Knopf, 1996; issued in paperback by Vintage a year later). In addition to its thorough (more than 500 pages) account of Eastwood's life and work, the book also includes an extensive bibliography and a filmography complete through 1996. The filmography in Christopher Frayling's biography, *Clint Eastwood* (London: Virgin Publishing, 1992), is complete through 1990 and contains more detail, including a complete listing of *Rawhide* episodes.

Other biographies, most of them published in England, include Patrick Agan's *Clint Eastwood* (London: Coronet Books, 1975); Minty Clinch's *Clint Eastwood* (London: Coronet Books, 1995); Gerold Cole and Peter Williams's *Clint Eastwood* (London: W. H. Allen, 1983); David Downing and Gary Herman's *Clint Eastwood: All-American Anti-Hero* (London: Omnibus Press, 1977); Edward Gallafent's *Clint Eastwood: Actor and Director* (London: Studio Vista Books, 1994); Iain Johnstone's *Clint Eastwood: The Man with No Name* (New York: Quill/Morrow, 1988); Stuart Kaminsky's *Clint Eastwood* (New York: New American Library, 1974); Michael Munn's *Clint Eastwood: Hollywood's Loner* (London: Robson Books, 1992); and Douglas Thompson's *Clint Eastwood Riding High* (London: Smith Gryphon, 1992). Eastwood was the subject of a *Barbara Walters Special* ABC television interview on June 15, 1982.

Scholarly studies of Eastwood's Westerns are sparse. Philip French's *Westerns: Aspects of a Movie Genre* (New York: Oxford University Press, 1977) analyzes *Coogan's Bluff* as an example of a "post-Western." Christopher Frayling's *Spaghetti Westerns* (London: Routledge & Kegan Paul, 1981) is an insightful study that thoroughly examines Eastwood's role in the genre that started his rise to stardom. More recently, Michael Coyne's *The Crowded Prairie: American National Identity in the Hollywood Western* (London: I. B. Tauris Publishers, 1999) discusses *The Outlaw Josey Wales* in a chapter entitled "Legends Revisited, Legends Revised."

Eastwood is well represented on the Internet, both in websites dedicated to him and his career and in websites dealing with various aspects of films and celebrities in general. Particularly useful are the "Complete Clint Eastwood Homepage" (www.cadvision.com/eastwood/) and the "Clint Eastwood World Wide Web Page" (www.man-with-no-name.com). Both contain such materials as photographs, video clips, biographical material, and up-to-date filmographies. Also useful is the Yahoo! GeoCities site (www.geocities.com), which provides links to many Eastwood and related (e.g., Spaghetti Westerns) sites.

Index

(Note: Italic page numbers indicate photographs. In foreign titles, initial articles [El, La)]
are not considered in alphabetizing; in American titles foreign articles [El, La] are.)

COLLECT THE ENTIRE

Notable
WESTERNERS
Series

BY GRIT & GRACE
Eleven Women Who Shaped the American West

Edited by Glenda Riley &
Richard W. Etulain

From "Wild West" performer Annie Oakley to entrepreneur Mary Ellen Pleasant to reformer Abigail Scott Dunway, these women of the hardscrabble nineteenth-century West played prominent and influential roles.

WITH BADGES & BULLETS
Lawmen & Outlaws in the Old West

Edited by Richard W. Etulain & Glenda Riley

By turns notorious, praised, and damned, those profiled here—from Wyatt Earp and Billy the Kid to Belle Starr and Doc Holliday—remain larger than life.

$17.95 PB · 6 x 9 · 240 pages
37 B/W photographs, illustrations
ISBN 1-55591-259-1

WITH BADGES & BULLETS
LAWMEN & OUTLAWS
IN THE OLD WEST

EDITED BY
RICHARD W. ETULAIN &
GLENDA RILEY

$17.95 PB · 6 x 9 · 240 pages
30 B/W photographs, illustrations
ISBN 1-55591-433-0

AND ARRIVING FALL 2002 . . .

WILD WOMEN OF THE OLD WEST
Edited by Glenda Riley & Richard W. Etulain

Portraits of some of the wildest, most notorious, freedom-seeking women of the Old West are gathered in **WILD WOMEN OF THE OLD WEST**. The rousing stories of madams, faith healers, outlaws, cross-dressing ranchers, and more bring to life such real-West figures as Calamity Jane and Madame Moustache.

256 pages · PB · ISBN 1-55591-295-8

MORE BOOKS FROM THE WEST . . . BOOKS FOR THE WORLD

DESERT HONKYTONK
The Story of Tombstone's Bird Cage Theatre

by Roger A. Bruns

Called the "wickedest night spot between Basin Street and the Barbary Coast," the Bird Cage Theatre was the most infamous variety house of the nineteenth-century Southwest, and helped Tombstone, Arizona, make its mark on the map.

AMIDST THE GOLD DUST
Women Who Forged the West

by Julie Danneberg

A colorful collection of individual biographies about five women who braved the western frontier in the mid- to late 1800s.

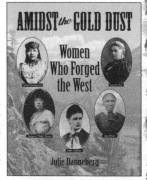

$17.95 PB · 6 x 9 · 240 pages
28 B/W photographs
ISBN 1-55591-416-0

$12.95 PB · 7 x 9 · 96 pages
20 B/W photographs, sidebars
ISBN 1-55591-997-9
Ages 8–12

Available at your local bookstore or through

FULCRUM PUBLISHING

16100 TABLE MOUNTAIN PARKWAY • SUITE 300 • GOLDEN, CO 80403
800-992-2908 • FAX 800-726-7112 • WWW.FULCRUM-BOOKS.COM